ASIAN AMERICAN LITERATURE

READERS' GUIDES TO ESSENTIAL CRITICISM

CONSULTANT EDITOR: NICOLAS TREDELL

Published

ASIAN AMERICAN LITERATURE

Jinqi Ling

BLOOMSBURY ACADEMIC
LONDON • NEW YORK • OXFORD • NEW DELHI • SYDNEY

BLOOMSBURY ACADEMIC
Bloomsbury Publishing Plc
50 Bedford Square, London, WC1B 3DP, UK
1385 Broadway, New York, NY 10018, USA
29 Earlsfort Terrace, Dublin 2, Ireland

BLOOMSBURY, BLOOMSBURY ACADEMIC and the Diana logo are trademarks of
Bloomsbury Publishing Plc

First published in Great Britain 2023

Copyright © Jinqi Ling, 2023

Jinqi Ling has asserted his right under the Copyright, Designs and Patents Act,
1988, to be identified as Author of this work.

For legal purposes the Acknowledgments on p. ix constitute an extension
of this copyright page.

Cover image: Poems of Sadness, Angel Island Immigration © Christopher Michel

Bloomsbury Publishing Plc does not have any control over, or responsibility for, any
third-party websites referred to or in this book. All internet addresses given in this
book were correct at the time of going to press. The author and publisher regret any
inconvenience caused if addresses have changed or sites have ceased to exist, but
can accept no responsibility for any such changes.

A catalogue record for this book is available from the British Library.

A catalog record for this book is available from the Library of Congress.

ISBN: HB: 978-1-3503-3602-5
PB: 978-1-3503-3601-8
ePDF: 978-1-3503-3603-2
eBook: 978-1-3503-3604-9

Series: Readers' Guides to Essential Criticism

Typeset by Newgen KnowledgeWorks Pvt. Ltd., Chennai, India

To find out more about our authors and books visit www.bloomsbury.com
and sign up for our newsletters.

CONTENTS

Contents

ACKNOWLEDGMENTS

This book project has taken roughly four years to evolve into its current shape, but its roots are more extended and can be traced, for example, to the various Asian American literature courses I have taught or the numerous conference papers I have delivered over the years. The book has benefited more directly from the dialogues that I had carried out (sometimes via email) with colleagues or friends since I started drafting the manuscript in the beginning of 2018. These exchanges became grounds for my consideration of what to prioritize in my review of the field and how to present its overlapping discourses to the book's diverse and shifting audiences. For individuals interested in my thoughts about or actual work on the book, I want to thank Steve Sumida, Saree Makdisi, Brian Kim Stefans, Eric Jager, Ursula Heise, Harryette Mullen, Mitchum Huelhls, Louise Hornby, Tara Fickle, Jeff Cabusao, Keith Camacho, David Yoo, Kyeyoung Park, Lane Hirabayashi, and Omar Zahzah.

The book's launching, revision, and finalization involve the efforts of two presses: Red Globe Press from Palgrave Macmillan, the initial home for my book; and Bloomsbury Academic that my book migrated to subsequently and where it became published. It was a genuine pleasure working with Nicolas Tredell, consultant editor of the Essential Criticism series, who took an interest in my research and whose insights and patience were crucial to the book's readiness for final submission. The comments made by the anonymous reader assigned to review my book manuscript were detailed. Molly Beck, Palgrave's executive editor of literature, oversaw my book's transfer to its new home. I am very grateful to Ben Doyle, the publisher for Literary Studies at Bloomsbury, for the care and team efforts he provided during the book's integration, editing, production, and distribution. I wish to thank in particular several graduate students at UCLA who lent invaluable support to my work on this book at different stages of its development: Sharon Chon for her competent assistance in helping gather materials; and Lika Balenović and Lauren Higa for generously taking on the task of formatting the finished manuscript and double-checking its sources and citations.

INTRODUCTION
UNFINALIZING THE *AIIIEEEEE!*
MOMENT: A HISTORICIST VIEW OF
THE FIELD

Asian American literary studies—inaugurated in 1974 through the publication of *Aiiieeeee!*, a major literary anthology edited by Frank Chin, Jeffrey Chan, Lawson Inada, and Sean Wong—has been a burgeoning area of humanistic inquiry marked by its history-conscious, multidisciplinary, and transnational commitments. Both theoretically and in terms of textual analyses, the field's scholarly output has rapidly grown, reflecting the increasingly heterogeneous nature of Asian American populations, communities, and cultural productions. But surprisingly few published books or anthologies have introduced the evolving Asian American literary discourse by engaging the conditions, contingencies, and immediate or long-term effects of its major debates. Instead, most studies seem busying themselves with identifying new developments, fresh angles of attack, or emerging intersections as the field continues to expand beyond its early premise, hence foregrounding only part of the complex work done by Asian American critics. This book presents Asian American literary studies somewhat differently. First, it gives prominence to a range of key concerns that have consistently come to the fore and mark Asian American critical practice as an ongoing negotiation for a more nuanced and more adequate representation of its interests; second, it attempts to strike a balance between or among the diverse positionalities it surveys, with attention paid not only to familiar arguments but also less often recognized intellectual contributions. This study makes no claim to resolve the ideological tensions that surround the Asian American debates it covers, but it does hope to create an opportunity that, in its provisional and limited way, allows a greater degree of interaction, exchange, and circulation of critical opinions that make Asian American literary criticism a truly open, dynamic, and multi-accentual dialogue.[1]

A set of broadly conceived questions shapes this study: What constitutes Asian American literature or Asian American literary criticism? What are its founding ideals and the contexts of their rearticulation into different political commitments? Furthermore, what is the nature of the field's shift from its earlier group- or nation-based identity quests to its current investment in post-ethnic or post-racial imaginaries? To what extent does the field's transnational critique of the existential conditions facing Asian Americans—as many testify to undergoing social abjection or racial melancholia—work to rectify such conditions in a social-material sense? And to what extent does this critique, often enacted as a form of epistemological struggles, end up extricating Asian American critics from the need to work through the force field of the American nation-state, which give rise to their sense of alienation in the first place? Beyond identity issues, what might "literary form" mean in the wake of New Criticism? Are the methods of post-humanist theory historically specific enough for investigating the complexity of Asian American experience, affect, and literary artistry? How do we define the social function of Asian American literature under the all-encompassing premise of cultural studies, which, in its penchant for textualizing the social and political, tends to dissolve a minimal level of distinction between an imagined world and an empirically verifiable reality? Can the Asian American literary profession still maintain its capacity to identify, value, and encourage socially grounded literary knowledge under the influence of market-driven critical fashions or an individualistically based academic star system?

In this study, Asian American literature is understood as a discourse constructed out of its engagement with and articulation through a specific set of historical contingencies of the 1960s and the 1970s: racial tensions in the wake of the assassination of Martin Luther King, mounting protests against the US role in Vietnam, the impacts of the Third World Liberation Front struggles for decolonization and self-determination, identity politics, community work, feminism, counterculture, and intermittent resurgences of political conservatism. From today's point of view, it seems obvious that Asian American literature's initial self-insertion into public awareness through the effort of *Aiiieeeee!* did not lead to this literature's full-fledged incorporation into the cultural establishment.[2] Instead, the critical agendas advanced by this anthology—and modified through the arguments made in its 1991 sequel *The Big Aiiieeeee!*—have become a site of prolonged and uncompromising debates among Asian American writers and critics because of their obvious limitations: that is, the editors' male-oriented conception of

"Asian American cultural integrity," their rigid distinction between "racist hate" (blatant racial discrimination) and "racist love" (assimilation in stereotypical terms), their privileging of the English language as the only legitimate tool for counterhegemonic struggles (Chin et al. 1974, vii, xxv–xxvi), and, more serious, their obliviousness to Asian American women writers' concerns and contributions. One ironic outcome of such debates is that, although the editors played a central role in promoting a fledgling Asian American literary sensibility in the 1970s, they are not formal participants in the discourses of professionalized Asian American criticism, whose subsequent emergence and gradual attainment of respectability tend to be justified by those working from within as a motivated effort to become the counterpoint for almost everything that *Aiiieeeee!* represents.

Within this context, it is important to recognize that what the *Aiiieeeee!* editors intended to communicate to their readers of the 1970s were not subtle or objectivist messages. On the contrary, they were self-consciously confrontational and disruptive, while they unabashedly presented as irrefutable evidences or counterevidences what professionalized literary criticism gingerly avoids: that is, the empirical or the positivistic. Illustrating this pragmatic aspect of the *Aiiieeeee!* editors' approach is a personal view shared by Frank Chin in 1976, which goes as follows:

> Think of being born to people who have no culture, no literature, no writing, no writers, except in some past across an ocean. In 200 years and all your generations of white people living and creating new American experience and know-how, not one word, not one joke, not one book … A white American writer would feel edgy if all the books ever written in America were by blacks, browns, reds, yellows, and all whites had ever published were cookbooks full of recipes for apple pie and fried chicken.

He continues: "That's what I grew up with. A literary tradition of cookbooks and autobiographies by the children of Christian converts and Pocahontas yellows whites call progressive for marrying out white. I grew up told no one knew anything else about yellow writing because there was nothing else to know" (Chin [1976] 1979, 253–4). Chin's detailing of a form of cultural racism that he, as a fifth-generation Chinese American, had been subjected to since his childhood is conducive to an alternative understanding of the nature of the rhetoric that the *Aiiieeeee!* editors indulge in: that is, their claims of being charged with a historical mission to restore an "organic" and "exclusive" sense of Asian American "cultural integrity" characterized by a recognizable style of "masculine qualities of originality, daring, physical courage, and creativity" (Chin et al. 1974, xxvi, xxx). For, once considered through the lens of Chin's story, such claims could no longer be readily taken for a sure sign of the editors' determined adherence to nativist or anti-feminist agendas. Rather, they may be seen as a reflection of how the editors' oppositional vision was shaped by the limitations of their times and their immediate social experiences. Likewise, the editors' strongly worded objection to some Asian American writers' appropriation of Chinese cultural resources, as well as their insistence on a "real" versus "fake" distinction about what constitutes authentic Chinese folk traditions (Chin 1991, 3), seems to provide further evidence of how far they are willing to go in using empirical knowledge to justify their otherwise insightful critique of the negative effects of American orientalism in the decades leading up to the publication of their anthology.

Much of what was brought up and addressed by the editors of *Aiiieeeee!* (as well as *The Big Aiiieeeee!*) has since then been complicated and transformed by sophisticated Asian American literary criticism, with insights and findings obtained from institutionally sanctified procedures and protocols. Yet, a disproportionate amount of the revisionist energy has been spent on refuting some of the most untenable aspects of the arguments made in *Aiiieeeee!* or *The Big Aiiieeeee!*,[3] while little effort is devoted to examining the inconstancies or contradictions in academy-based Asian American theoretical assertions or claims. This asymmetrical approach to the *Aiiieeeee!* moment in professionalized Asian American criticism is theoretically provocative, especially in view of two problematic tendencies that it implicitly fosters in the realm of devising or applying periodization methods: namely, that of a premature suspension of engagement with the formative years of the field centering on the ideology of *Aiiieeeee!*, and, as a consequence, that of an unwittingly *de facto* acceptance of a presumed severance between the past and the present of Asian American literary history.[4] The persistence and ongoing effect of such tendencies then present the occasion for a critical redescription of how the cultural forces that enabled *Aiiieeeee!*'s voicing of its concerns relate to those touched off by its polemic, and for fashioning strategies in ways that might contribute to a reversal of the communicative breakdown at this crucial juncture of the field's evolution. My contention is that the positions taken by the editors and those assumed by their opponents are neither simple nor definitive when analyzed as conflictual modalities of a peripheral consciousness that is given rise to and continually reshaped by the unfolding social dynamics directly or indirectly influencing its evolution.

To illustrate such processes, I draw on aspects of Jean-Paul Sartre, Raymond Williams, and Paul Smith's theoretical work on the internal workings of cultural emergence, which in one way or another point to the possibility of reconceptualizing the *Aiiieeeee!* moment as an ideologically open, though by no means ideal, way of conducting opposition in the ongoing coming into being of an Asian American literary presence in the larger realm of American culture. In a series of writings published in France in the immediately post-Second-World-War years, Sartre proposes a doctrine of literary praxis that is premised on what he calls "engaged literature" (*la littérateur engagée*), a concept traceable to his prewar commitment to the activist ideals of a "non-authoritarian" politics and his postwar search for existential conditions still open to socially symbolic literary interventions (Ungar 1988, 5, 7). Central to this doctrine is Sartre's motto: "To write is ... both to disclose the world and offer it as a task to the generosity of the reader" (Sartre 1988, 65). By this remark, Sartre suggests that the enactment of literary praxis involves not just the speaking subject's self-awareness of the historical conditions that necessitate her/his articulation, but also the reader's willingness to grasp the articulated word as an occasion for understanding the larger motives behind it, hence to entertain the possibility of giving fuller expression to what has been disclosed—which is always incomplete or inadequate—through reciprocal performances (Sartre 1988, 61, 66).

Sartre's theorization of the dialectic between the writer's yearning to express on an individual basis and the reader's imaginative participation in expanding the writerly vision toward a sharable direction is the internal logic of cultural emergence well suited for examining the complexity of minoritarian formations such as Asian American literary criticism. Important in this process, according to Williams, is a recognition of the "embryonic" nature of an articulation of dissent during its "pre-emergent" stage, which tends to be ambiguous in meaning and unpredictable in effect due to the speaking agent's overreliance on "practical consciousness" as the basis for political action (Williams 1977, 126, 130–3). Illustrating Williams's perspective on this stage of cultural emergence is the *Aiiieeeee!* editors' appropriation of the inexpressive mumbo jumbo of "aiiieeeee!"—originally a stereotypical characterization of a yellow man's whining, shouting, or screaming when he was "wounded, sad, or angry, or swearing, or wondering" (Chin et al. 1974, vii–viii)—as the main title for their anthology. In elevating this meaningless noise to the status of a literary

5

declaration, the editors convey a sense of the linguistic deprivation—as well as the utter lack of innate power to create—on the part of the aspiring Asian American writer who struggles to gain voicing in terms not defined by the dominant culture. But the arbitrary nature of their naming of their anthology—as well as the absence of functional idioms for decoding and legitimizing its implied significance—suggests that the political pressures they exert on the cultural establishment through their anthology may have done more to confuse its readers than to prepare the grounds for their conversion. Thus, Williams considers "latency" a more appropriate term for describing what can be accomplished during cultural preemergence. Williams's elucidation of this subtle stage of a minoritarian formation is highly suggestive to Asian American debates over the meaning and status of *Aiiieeeee!*: despite the anthology's lacking a sympathetic hearing from professionalized Asian American literary criticism, the imprint it has left on the conditions of the field's rise is permanent, only that its inadequately conceived initial agendas await their rearticulation into projects that would become sufficiently evident in their tendency and more attuned to the diversity of Asian American interests and experiences.

As I have been proposing elsewhere regarding the interrelated historical processes either anticipatory of or subsequent to the *Aiiieeeee!* intervention,

> the newness of recent Asian American literary articulations lies not in their inherent power of being contemporary nor in their actual severance from previous sources of resistance, but in their fuller expression, under more enabling (or seemingly more enabling) social conditions, of the possibilities of liberation problematically or incompletely envisioned by earlier Asian American realist and/or nationalist literary voices. In this sense, Asian Americans cannot move easily beyond the limitations of their past simply on the basis of new social formations. For historical transitions are always ambiguous, protracted, and unpredictable, constantly throwing up obstacles to development and frequently demanding recontextualization of current problematics in light of the past and re-examination of the past in relation to its residual forms in the present. (Ling 1998, 29)

In light of the theoretical possibilities broached by Sartre and Williams, I further suggest that the intellectual agent uniquely positioned to reconnect the signifying chain snapped by *Aiiieeeee!*'s protest and the ongoing controversy over its shortcomings is none other than the Asian American critic, given that this critic heeds the inner voice of Sartre's motto: "To write is … both to disclose the world and offer it as a task to the generosity of the reader." Worth emphasizing here is that the gist of this Sartrean counsel does not involve the possibility of glossing over the erroneous assumptions of the *Aiiieeeee!* editors' arguments or reviving the agendas of cultural nationalism. Rather, it connotes the ethics of participating in discourses that build upon, either in affiliation with or against the thrust of, the momentum unleashed by *Aiiieeeee!*'s oppositional move, whose fallibility gets acknowledged, from a Sartrean point of view, for the sole purpose of clarifying and further engaging the larger sociohistorical process of which it is but a partial or imprecise expression. In Asian American literary studies, such readerly generosity may be gainfully practiced, I assert, when the critic starts viewing the inadequacies of the *Aiiieeeee!* moment as representing primarily a contingent subaltern response to overwhelming power, without taking the editors' words unduly literally under the assumption that they were unaware of the charged rhetoric they deployed or the risk they took in publishing their angry anthology.

Essential to my retheorization of the scenarios of cultural emergence in the field is the question of what constitutes Asian American agency, which is formulated in the discussion here as an ongoing "social-semantic" construct—to use Williams's terminology (Williams 1977, 133)—one made up of demands from multiple sites and at varying intervals within a zone of shared subalternity. In this process, the certainty of a single assertion of self-interest or of a claim for representativeness is always subject to its disarticulation, as well as its reworking into more inclusive and more heterogeneous possibilities (Smith 1988, 100–2).[5] The clarity with which a knowledgeable Asian American subject speaks, in either declarative language or theoretically savvy terms, then anticipates its own displacement and supersession by the voicing of other subjective positions. The Asian American political will that becomes identifiable and executable in the course of such a multiply negotiated process, it should be pointed out, is very different from the Asian American double agent preferred by recent scholars in the field, who tend to locate political action in the psycholinguistic domain of meditations on injury, irony, or paradox. Such recognition of Asian American agency informs how polemics, controversies, or extreme positions are treated in this book: despite the fact that such moments can be severely disruptive, they are seen as unavoidable developments in an uneven formation process whose outcome, though open-ended and unpredictable, is rewritable through self-conscious interventions.

The content of this book is organized in eight chapters, with each focused on a topic outlined below. The survey and presentation of critical positions are contextualized to reflect how the field has been energized by its defining moments, major debates, and cross-cutting relationships with the trends in other disciplines. This study covers a substantial body of secondary materials generated over a period of several decades (including, among others, the perspectives of non-US-based scholars and scholars operating either within or beyond Asian American studies), which, taken together, contributes to recognizable trajectories or configurations of Asian American literary criticism. Chapter 1, "Race, Gender, and Class: Overlapping Formations," focuses on several ongoing critical undertakings that mark the evolution of the field since the early 1980s: the centering of gender, exploration of sexuality, pursuit of a politics of difference, and engagement with race and class relations as either symbolic or socioeconomic concerns. Chapter 2, "The Necessity and Fiction of 'Asian America,'" traces the field's transition from its earlier adherence to group-based identity politics to its subsequent commitment to forging multiethnic or interracial alliances. Chief among the issues examined are the premise of cultural nationalism, the postmodern vision informing versions of post-*Aiiieeeee!* pan-Asian ethnicity, the contested/protracted nature of the transition from the national to the post-national, and efforts to rethink Asian American literary studies as an ethnic-specific US minoritarian formation amidst the transformations made in the field. Chapter 3, "Intercultural and Generational Concerns," examines the diasporic and multilingual origins and ongoing practices of the field through engagement with its recurrent themes: such as the role of immigrant writing; textual strategy for intracultural comparison and translation; the problematic of the "model minority myth" and its attendant paradox of Asian assimilation; and controversies over interpretation of generational conflict depicted in literature. In this chapter, intercultural or comparative approaches to literature are treated as overlapping with but not necessarily the same as transnational literary criticism, a topic that will be contextualized in the surveys of Chapter 4. "The Transnational Turn," the chapter that follows, foregrounds key Asian American arguments for expanding the range and scope of the field's research or operation beyond the confines of the United States. Such efforts are presented as taking shape amid several interrelated conditions or developments: the field's internal critique of cultural nationalism, the ascendancy of postcolonial theory as a dominant paradigm for ethnic American literary studies, the popularization of US multiculturalism as a fetishized global vision in the decade ushered in by the dissolution of the Soviet Union, and the rise of Asian modernity as an important player in the new-wave global capitalism.

Chapter 5, "The Social Function of Literature," delves into a long-cherished, though less often synthesized, tradition in the field: namely, the emphasis on the social relevance of creative writing, as well as the extent to which literature can still be used to comment on Asian American histories and realities under today's circumstances. The chapter frames its survey of this aspect of the field's work by introducing discourses on the dual functions of literature—its cognitive (or historical) orientation and its emotional (or intuitive) appeal—with a perspective on how these literary functions are manifested in Asian American genre deployments and genre expectations. Within this formally oriented framework, the chapter samples a range of Asian American approaches to, controversies over, or arguments for/against literary resistance. Chapter 6, "Aesthetic Form," evaluates the formalistic turn in Asian American literary studies since the beginning of the twenty-first century. The surveys and discussions in this chapter pivot on a premise established in Chapter 5, that is, recent efforts to revive a formalistic approach to literature are constrained by two factors: the irredeemable decline of the aesthetic programs of the Anglo-American New Critical doctrines and a simultaneous dominance in literary studies of post-structuralist-influenced methods, whose main interest is more in ideology than in aesthetics. Within such contexts, this chapter surveys the existing formalistic practices in the field, with a focus on realist genres, poetry writing, and theatrical productions. Chapter 7, "Protocols and the Politics of Institutionalization," highlights several defining aspects of the Asian American literary profession since the late 1980s: its efforts to build reading communities for its evolving discourse, to fashion rationales for periodizing its history, to rethink disciplinary or methodological assumptions, and, since the advent of the new millennium, to engage in post-ethnic or post-racial politics. Chapter 8, "Emerging Interests," identifies major intellectual accomplishments in recent Asian American interdisciplinary work, especially that between traditional literary analysis, paraliterary knowledge (including ethical criticism), and digitally mediated interactivity. Showcased in the surveys of this chapter are food studies, critical refugee studies, critique of militarization, exploration of the relationship between biology and ecology, speculative literature, and the computational humanities. This book concludes with a short essay by its author, titled "Anti-essentialist Critique and the Asian American Literary Profession," which offers an assessment, on the basis of the surveys and discussions of the preceding chapters of this study, of what has come to be seen by more and more scholars as a disciplinary crisis in the field.

Two reasons make this book tentative. First is that the range and depth of Asian American literary criticism defy comprehensive mapping. This situation is further complicated by a tendency among critics to shift gears midway in their arguments due to the opening of new lines of inquiry, the availability of new possibilities, or the pressure of stronger tendencies. Whereas it is unproductive to track down the causes for each of such shifts, their contradictory results remind us that Asian American literary criticism is an ongoing conversation and should therefore be seen as such, even with respect to its seemingly definitive moments. Second is the limitation of my own critical methods, which are informed by a strong dose of deconstructive and postmodern education in my postgraduate training, and by my subsequent shift to versions of Russian formalism, genre studies, and referential concerns associated with the transition from realism to high modernism or early postmodernism. These theoretical inclinations shape my sense of critical values and lead to my appreciation for scholarship that I see as capable of not only navigating poststructuralist intertextuality but also attending to the conditions of literary creation and response in non-sociological terms. My take on things inevitably finds its way to the materials I select and present in this study, as well as how I contextualize and evaluate them as constituting the essential criticism in Asian American literary studies, a discourse almost five decades in the making when examined retrospectively.

CHAPTER 1
RACE, GENDER, AND
CLASS: OVERLAPPING FORMATIONS

Two years after the appearance of *Aiiieeeee!*, Frank Chin published a short story titled "The Eat and Run Midnight People," which gives an account of its Chinese American male protagonist's yearnings for a selfhood unburdened by the negative effects of his racialization as an American-born Asian, a narrative marked by its intense libidinal charge and peculiar masculine symbolisms. The story begins by placing the reader in the middle of the first-person narrator's stream of consciousness animated by his vision of the "night sea" surging onto the warm sandy beach of Maui (Hawaii), where he lies. To the narrator, the exhaling sea evokes two interrelated scenarios of a repressed Chinese American history that he intends to legitimize: it resembles "the wet flash of old men's Chinatown sneezes"; it also brings to mind the steam puffed out from an "ancient ship" sailing on the horizon, namely, the train that the old men's grandfathers used to ride during their participation in the construction of America's first Transcontinental Railroad in the nineteenth century. With these scenarios, Chin implicitly designates the narrator as a tough descendent of the Chinese railroad workers, a connection that the latter reinforces by imaginatively becoming part of the scene he conjures up, as "the phantom soldier of the water." What the narrator is about to combat is the antitype of Chin's dream of Asian American male heroism, which is visualized in the story as a naked, forty-three-year-old, and beer-drinking WASP woman showing up next to him amidst her "fleshy stomp and throb," interrupting the narrator's historical reflections.[1] Such intrusion by this prostitute-like white woman, from the narrator's point of view, must be punished according to the stringent code of his railroad memory. Accordingly, a significant portion of the story that follows is devoted to describing how the half-conscious narrator reclaims the erased Asian American heroic tradition in the United States by conquering the white woman's body. During this process, parallels are drawn between male sexual acts and the workings of the locomotive, and between male ecstasy and the Chinese immigrant fathers' triumphant ride home along the railroad tracks they had laid.

Centering Gender

The sexist rhetoric and vengeful tone of Chin's story convey an attitude of male aggression, which is found also at work behind the *Aiiieeeee!* editors' attack on Asian American women writers seen as deviating from their prescribed literary doctrines. This approach to ethnic awakening and community building cannot but invite serious responses from Asian American women scholars, whose complication and reworking of the oppositional agendas of *Aiiieeeee!* have fundamentally reshaped the direction and dynamics of the field since the 1980s. Early feminist interventions in the masculinist bias exhibited by Chin and other editors of *Aiiieeeee!*, however, were largely corrective, though not without an awareness of their disruptive potential in a fledging literary community still working to maintain a degree of internal unity and cohesion. Representative of this phase of the Asian American feminist work is Elaine Kim's 1990 critique of Chin's male-centered discourse, as follows:

> It is impossible for Asian American women to interpret their own experiences as women without airing the "dirty laundry." … What Frank Chin eulogizes as the "Confucian ethic of personal revenge, friendship, and military alliance" is basically just another old boys' club for male bonding; sworn brotherhoods have never spelled freedom for women. … By not questioning the legitimacy of patriarchy's closed universe, accepting instead his oppressors' definitions of "manhood" and subscribing to the notion that his sense of worth can be recuperated through sexual empowerment, the Asian American male writer can only seek the white male center for himself at the expense of women. Taking the dominant group's hierarchy of values as the point of reference will not restore Asian American men's displaced control. (Kim 1990b, 78–9)

Kim argues that the Asian American female writer "never ceases to be both her racial and gendered self," whose agency, once articulated into a political program, thoroughly "dissolves binary oppositions of ethnicity and gender" falsely maintained in Chin's unidimensional protest, therefore constituting a more effective intervention in the hegemonic power that surrounds Asian American cultural emergence (Kim 1990b, 91; Kim 1995, 13).

Amy Ling, who coins the term "Chinamerican literature" in 1981, has compiled an extensive inventory of how women had been subjugated in feudal China in her 1990 monograph *Between Worlds: Women Writers of Chinese Ancestry*. Underscoring the tension between modesty/reticence as an ideal established for women in traditional Chinese culture, and egoism/self-exposure that women's self-representation would require in the West, she contends that

> in order for a Chinese immigrant woman to write and publish a book in English, she must be something of a rebel, for writing, an act of rebellion and self-assertion, runs counter to Confucian training. Also, she has to possess two basic character traits: an indominable will and an unshakable self-confidence. She must also be propelled by the undeniable drive to communicate with the readers and speakers of the dominant language of the society into which she has been transplanted either because of the rightness of her cause or because of the force of her need to express herself. (Ling 1990, 14)

To substantiate her claims, Ling devotes a significant portion of her study to restoring and showcasing the pioneering work of Chinese women writers in North America during the twentieth century, especially that of Edith Maude Eaton (Sui Sin Far), a Eurasian writer of partial Chinese descent, who published poetry, fiction, and journalistic essays in Canada and the United States at the turn of the twentieth century. Ling's designation of Sui Sin Far's literary activity as a foundational moment in Asian American literary discourse is a significant move in her rewriting of the male-centered Asian American literary history envisioned by the editors of *Aiiieeeee!*. For it constitutes a compelling argument that the field was also pioneered through the artistic labor of women, a critical effort that inspires numerous Sui Sin Far studies both within and beyond the field across a wide range of interests.[2]

Within this context, King-Kok Cheung, author of a 1989 essay "The Woman Warrior versus The Chinaman Pacific," contributes to Asian American feminist theorical work from a uniquely bicultural perspective. She maintains: "It is impossible … to tackle the gender issues in the Chinese American cultural terrain without delving into the historically enforced 'feminization' of Chinese American men, without confronting the dialectics of racial stereotypes and national relations, … [and] without wrestling with diehard notions of masculinity and femininity in both Asian and Western cultures" (Cheung 1989, 234, 240). This bicultural/comparative critique of traditional Eastern/Western conceptions of the difference between masculinity and femininity in binaristic terms is essential to Cheung's reading of silence as a coded metaphor in her 1993 monograph *Articulate Silence: Hisaye Yamamoto, Maxine Hong Kingston, Joy Kogawa*. She shows, through close analyses of the writings by these Asian American women writers, that the significance of non-Western deployment and interpretation of silence lies, ultimately, in its refusal to privilege direct speech over insinuation, a tendency that she finds predominant in the positions both taken by the editors of *Aiiieeeee!* and assumed by most North American feminist scholars (Cheung 1993, 9). Shirley Lim, more interested in forging a linkage between US-based ethnic studies and Western feminism, urges instead for an "ethnic nuancing" of Euro-American feminist conventions, while designating Asian American women's writing as the exemplary site for refiguring female subjectivity as one capable of creatively responding to the demands of both gendered and ethnically specific imperatives (Lim 1993b, 572–3).

These early efforts to interrogate the masculinist premise of Asian American literary/cultural history espoused by *Aiiieeeee!* and modified by *The Big Aiiieeeee!* anticipated a burgeoning of Asian American scholarship, especially in the form of monographs, which use female gender as the starting point for advancing the field as an ethnic-specific literary enterprise. A partial list of such achievements would include Wendy Ho's *In Her Mother's House: The Politics of Asian American Mother-Daughter Writing* (1999); Rachel Lee's *The Americas of Asian American Literature: Gendered Fictions of Nation and Transnation* (1999); Traise Yamamoto's *Masking Selves, Making Subjects: Japanese American Women, Identity, and the Body* (1999); Patricia P. Chu's *Assimilating Asians: Gendered Strategies of Authorship in Asian America* (2000); Leslie Bow's *Betrayal and Other Acts of Subversion: Feminism, Sexual Politics, Asian American Women's Literature* (2001); Laura Kang's *Compositional Subjects: Enfiguring Asian/Asian American Women* (2002); Susan Koshy's *Sexual Naturalization: Asian Americans and Miscegenation* (2004); Denise Cruz's *Transpacific Femininities: The Making of the Modern Filipina* (2012); and, more recently, Pamela Thoma's *Asian American Women's Popular Literature: Feminizing Genres and Neoliberal Belonging* (2013). At about the same time, anthologies by and about Asian American women mushroomed in the 1980s and 1990s, which include, among others, *Making Waves: An Anthology of Writings by and about Asian American*

Women, collectively authored by Asian Women United of California (1989); *The Forbidden Stitch: An Asian American Women's Anthology,* edited by Shirley Lim and Mayumi Tsutakawa (1989); *Home to Stay: Asian American Women's Fiction,* edited by Sylvia Watanabe and Carol Bruchac (1990); *The Politics of Life: Four Plays by Asian American Women,* edited by Velina Hasu Houston (1993); *Unbroken Thread: An Anthology of Plays by Asian American Women,* edited by Roberta Uno (1993); and *Our Feet Walk the Sky: Women of the South Asian Diaspora,* edited by The Women of South Asian Descent Collective (1993). Such coordinated efforts to reorient the field toward gender-focused literary criticism culminate in the publication of two collections of essays dedicated to Maxine Hong Kingston's highly acclaimed 1976 feminist narrative *The Woman Warrior: Memoirs of Girlhood among Ghosts*: Shirley Lim's edited volume *Approaches to Teaching Kingston's The Woman Warrior* (1991); and Sau-ling Wong's edited book *Maxine Hong Kingston's The Woman Warrior: A Case Book* (1999).

The Woman Warrior's newly achieved status as the most canonized Asian American text in the United States since its publication can be ascertained by its winning the 1976 National Book Critics Circle Award for best nonfiction, its being rated as "the most widely taught book by a living author on American college campuses," and its bringing Kingston "the rare title of Living Treasure of Hawai'i conferred by a Buddhist group in 1980" (Chu 2001, 88). But the accolades that Kingston has received for her memoir are also accompanied by its controversial receptions both in mainstream American culture and among members of the ethnic community. Anglo-American readers typically praise *The Woman Warrior* stereotypically, affirming, rather than unsettling, orientalist assumptions about Chinese American culture and experience—responses that frustrate Kingston herself (Kingston 1982, 56–65). Such misappropriations of *The Woman Warrior* by non-Asian American readers then give rise to criticisms of Kingston's intention of writing this book, especially by the editors of *The Big Aiiieeeee!* who castigate her for misrepresenting Chinese culture and Chinese American males, as well as for "selling out" Asian American interests for her acceptance by the cultural mainstream (Chin 1991, 9, 27–8). This is the context in which Kingston's 1980 nonfiction *China Men,* often seen as a sequel to *The Woman Warrior,* is increasingly used by Asian American critics as a platform for negotiating the seemingly irreconcilable politics between race and gender formations in the field. For example, Elaine Kim suggests in her 1982 monograph, *Asian American Literature: An Introduction to Asian American Writings and Their Social*

Contexts, that *China Men* is about "the reconciliation of the contemporary Chinese American and his immigrant forefathers, nourished by their common roots, strong and deep, in American soil. Kingston's men and women are survivors. The reconciliation between the sexes is not complete, but Kingston demonstrates that Asian American writers can depict with compassion and skill the experiences of both sexes. The men and women of *China Men* and *The Woman Warrior* are vivid and concrete refutations of racist and sexist stereotypes" (Kim 1982, 212–13). In a discussion of Kingston's adaption of aspects of Chinese mythology for the plot design of *China Men*, David Leiwei Li also maintains: "The socially enforced feminization of Chinese American manhood leads to another discovery when one begins to perceive the myth and the book in general as a male story envisioned by a female writer, a spokeswoman who voices her fellow men's valor and anger and redeems them from cultural misconception and historical obscurity" (Li 1990, 488). Along the line, Donald Goellnicht suggests that *China Men* be seen as "an act of attempted reconciliation between daughter and father, just as *The Woman Warrior* was an act of reconciliation between daughter and mother" (Goellnicht 1992, 205).

Despite these constructive efforts to ease the tensions between male and female positions during the gender debates over *The Woman Warrior*, the decades of the 1980s and much of the 1990s, as Shirley Lim points out, still belong to "a stage for women who claim, not the minor representation given in the 1970s' anthologies, but all the attention. Men are present in the work but often appear as aggressors or as ignorant of women's needs" (Lim 1993b, 577). This means that the actual practice of gender-based Asian American literary criticism would persist along the line described by Lim, at least for the period of time she designates, despite the simultaneous availability of feminist theoretical formulations characterized by subtlety and sophistication, as exemplified in the bicultural approaches to Asian American women's writing used by King-Kok Cheung. Hence, Rocío Davis finds Rachel Lee's 1999 rereading of Carlos Bulosan's *America Is in the Heart*—in which Lee criticizes the author for his depiction of the female characters as either "exoticized women" or "expendable foes" (Lee 1999, 12, 33–7)—inadequate, in that such a critique of Bulosan's representation of women, Davis argues, "diverts attention from the central focus of the novel, the history and price of early Filipino labor immigration," rather than shed light on the critical potential of the methods of feminism (Davis 2000, 1004). Jinqi Ling raises similar questions about Lisa Lowe's interpretation of Louis Chu's 1961 realist novel *Eat a Bowl of Tea* as a master narrative of "masculinist generational symbolism" (Lowe 1991, 34), arguing that such a rendering of the meaning of the text is based more on generalizations about the existence of a culturally based Chinese male essence than on a historicized reading of the lasting effects of America's anti-Chinese legislations on the New York Chinatown bachelor society that Chu describes with irony and ambivalence (Ling 1998, 76–7). Further manifesting the reactive impulses in gender-focused studies of Asian American literature is an argument advanced by Patricia P. Chu in her 2000 monograph *Assimilating Asian Americans*. She suggests, on the basis of a thematic survey of the writings of Bulosan, Younghill Kang, Milton Murayama, and John Okada, that a thread of "a common anxiety" unites these male authors' imaginary, and that the persistent operation of this male ethos is "not simply about Asian American manhood but about the construction of such manhood in the form of real and literary fatherhood—in short, a racialized anxiety of authorship in America." Chu then asserts that "for Asian American male writers the struggle to establish their masculinity is linked to the struggle to establish their literary authority and a literature of their own" (Chu 2000, 27–8).

Exploration of Sexuality

The question of sexuality becomes increasingly theorized in this context, especially among scholars committed to exploring gender differential, female subject formation, and intersectional relationships. Rachel Lee, for example, articulates a representative view of how sexuality allows a better understanding, as well as a more productive exploration, of such interrelated conditions or processes. She points out that "gender opposition, gender difference, and gender hierarchy become convenient ways for understanding, interacting, and reinforcing opposition, difference, and hierarchy more generally and an array of social relationships crisscrossed by racial, class-based, regional, and national differences." The problematic of such approaches to gender, Lee further suggests, lies in their tendency to obscure not only gender's embeddedness in the politics of nation-states and neocolonial situations, but also the unequal relation between the sexes, both within and beyond the Asian American community, family, and subjectivity. Recognizing that racial inquiry alone is unable to effectively interrogate such a "crisis and knotty barriers confronting" Asian Americans, she emphasizes that "gender and sexuality" are "instrumental to the ways in which Asian American writers conceive of and write about 'America'" (Lee 1999, 3–12). From an Asian American queer male perspective, David Eng urges that "the investigation of racial formation in Asian American studies must include a systematic consideration of sexuality," because this critical category underscores "the disparate ways in which race, gender, and sexuality come together in various configurations to secure and organize a genealogy of Asian American male subjectivity." He advises that "we must vigilantly pursue the theoretical connections between queer studies—with its focus on (homo) sexuality and desire—and women's studies—with its focus on gender and identification—in relation to the production of Asian American male subjectivity" (Eng 2001, 15–16). Reflecting on the critical potential of foregrounding Asian American male sexuality through the medium of literary representation, Stephen Sohn speculates that the "body of the queer Asian American in textual representations [would] become infused with a sort of political value that simultaneously redefines queer sexuality from an Asian American perspective, visibly presents this queer sexuality, and affirms the importance of freeing queer bodies from societal strictures and governmental regulations to explore desires and sexual proclivities" (Sohn 2006, 102).

Prior to these articulations of the importance of sexuality in recent critical discourse, several factors prevented Asian American critics from swiftly embracing sexual politics as a site for exploring identity or subject formation. First, as Helena Grice and Crystal Parikh observe, Asian American feminists were faced with a series of structural impediments both within and outside the ethnic communities in the 1980s and much of the 1990s, such as entrenched patriarchal ideology, common perceptions of race as an overriding issue for people of color, and communal pressures on women whose individual pursuits were in tension with the emphases of group-based projects (Grice and Parikh 2014, 170–1). Second, as Traise Yamamoto points out, the female body had historically been seen as a "profoundly problematic site" for dealing with questions of subjectivity among many Asian American scholars, because it "serves as both the locus for projected otherness and as the referent of specularity." Asian American women writers had therefore been reluctant to make a "direct, explicit" connection between feminism and the female body (Yamamoto 1999, 74). The question of specularity, according to Stephen Sohn, has been a particularly vexing source of Asian American queer male anxiety. He observes: "Queer visibility requires the public presence of the body in space, whether that space is textually produced or physically constructed. However, queer visibility is in itself fraught with dangerous possibilities ranging from hate crimes, dismissal from family units, and other such discriminatory consequences" (Sohn 2006, 101).

Sohn's concern derives in part from his awareness of a commonly held perception among Asian American males about their experiences with emasculation or feminization in the US context, a complaint that often works to reinforce Asian patriarchal values and practices under conditions of immigration or diaspora, while it also reproduces the heterosexual logic of orientalist ideologies. The social implication of this paradox, as Surabhi Kukkè and Svati Shah testify, is that Asian American queer activists, frequently seen as sexual deviants by other Asian Americans, suffer homophobia in their own communities in "severe" and "violent ways," yet no measures have so far been taken to protect their safety (Kukkè and Shah [1999] 2000, 133). Thus, Richard Fung emphasizes the urgency to unsettle the heteronormative assumptions not only in society but also among Asian American queers themselves, with the reminder that "there are competing and somewhat contradictory sexual associations based on nationality," which range from the "kinky," through the "available," to the "sexless" (Fung 1996, 182). Only by probing into the external and internal constraints on the Asian American queer male identity, suggests Crystal Parikh, can his presence be recognized as "a troubling subject who transgresses ... [arbitrarily enforced masculine/feminine] boundaries, while also revealing the imbrication of race and nation in the articulation of gendered identities" (Parikh 2002, 883). Embodying the gains of this period of exploration and legitimization of Asian American sexuality is a series of essay collections published since the mid-1980s, such as *Between the Lines: An Anthology by Pacific/Asian Lesbians of Santa Cruz*, edited by C. Chung, A. Kim, and A. K. Lemeshewsky (1987); *Lotus of Another Color: An Unfolding of the South Asian Gay and Lesbian Experience*, edited by Rakesh Ratti (1993); *The Very Inside: An Anthology by Asian and Pacific Islander Lesbian and Bisexual Women*, edited by Sharon Lim-Hing (1994); *Asian American Sexualities: Dimensions of the Gay and Lesbian Experience*, edited by Russell Leong (1996); *Q & A: Queer in Asian America*, edited by David Eng and Alice Hom (1998); *Queer Papi: Gay Asian Erotica*, edited by Joe Tran (1998); and *Take Out: Queer Writing from Asian Pacific America*, edited by Quang Bao and Hanya Yanagihara (2000).

In this process, the category of sexuality not only expands the scope of Asian American scholars' gender analyses, but also allows them to differentiate diverse Asian American political imperatives that take the form of bodily pleasure and for pursuing alternative forms of Asian American subject formation beyond heteronormative logics or assumptions (Ting 1998, 65–9). The beginning of the twenty-first century witnessed the publication of two pathbreaking monographs on Asian American male sexuality and queer politics: Daniel Kim's *Writing Manhood in Black and Yellow: Ralph Ellison, Frank Chin, and the Literary Identity* (2005); and, shortly before it, David Eng's *Racial Castration: Managing Masculinity in Asian America* (2001). The former is a comparative analysis of the intertwined sexual and racial logics that inform Ellison and Chin's respective literary outputs. Paying close attention to the grammar and syntax of "gendered and sexualized rhetoric that men of color use to underscore racism's dehumanizing effects," Kim argues that Ellison and Chin have the tendency to represent the racial discrimination experienced by the male characters in their writings in terms of how women are perceived and treated in traditional societies, thus inadvertently equating white racism with homosexuality. This conflation, Kim suggests, is central to the two writers' homophobic masculine discourses, as well as the programs of African American and Asian American cultural nationalisms, a problematic that he considers stemming from the mentality and value of the working-class communities of color in the pre-1960s period (Kim 2005, 7, 37).

Eng's book is more geared toward developing a psychoanalytic method applicable to Asian American queer studies. He contends that traditional psychoanalysis pays little attention to the question of racialization and, consequently, ends up reinforcing the social hierarchies that regulate Asian American sexual desires and practices. Seizing on a brief mention of the primitive man with "dark origins" in Freud's writings, Eng argues that the question of Asians' racialization has long been structured in the imaginary of psychoanalysis as an essentially Eurocentric method. He argues:

> Psychoanalytic theory can help us understand the important lesson that sexuality is not natural—that it is resolutely cultural and constructed. We need to expand this valuable axiom into the field of Asian American and ethnic studies to insist that psychoanalysis at once describes, marks, and produces social differences other than sexuality. Feminism and queer studies—as both intellectual and political projects—cannot proceed without an active engagement of psychoanalysis on these radically and racially modified terms. In this new form, psychoanalytic theory might provide a rich set of conceptual paradigms for the investigation of Asian American racial formation in relation to specific epistemologies of sexuality and sexual development. (Eng 2001, 14–15)

Eng's elevation of psychoanalysis as a key method in Asian American discourses on gender and sexuality is an important move, while it also leads some scholars to see psychoanalytically influenced literary analyses as *de rigueur* in the field, a view that will be historicized in the following subsection of this chapter.

Essentialism and Difference

A theoretical framework that Asian American critics frequently draw on in making the shift toward gender and sexuality analyses is the post-structuralist critique of essentialism, a common textual strategy today, but an eye-opening conceptual frontier when it was first introduced to the field in the early 1990s. Such critique is a key aspect of Lisa Lowe's pathbreaking 1991 essay "Heterogeneity, Hybridity, Multiplicity: Marking Asian American Differences," in which she makes a complex anti-essentialist move by simultaneously foregrounding and problematizing the assumptions that underlie deconstructive theory's conception of difference. She argues:

> Binary constructions of difference use a logic that prioritizes the first term and subordinates the second; whether the pair "difference" and "sameness" is figured as a binary synthesis that considers "difference" as always contained within the "same," or that conceives of the pair as an opposition in which "difference" structurally implies "sameness" as its complement, it is important to see each of these figurations as versions of the same binary logic. My argument for heterogeneity seeks to challenge the conception of difference as exclusively structured by binary opposition between two terms by proposing instead another notion of difference that takes seriously the conditions of heterogeneity, multiplicity, and nonequivalence. (Lowe 1991, 31)

Lowe's attempt to pluralize a hierarchically conceived Western idea of difference received explicit endorsement by Dorinne Kondo, a cultural anthropologist by training and the author of a 1995 article titled "Poststructuralist Theory as Political Necessity." In so aligning herself with Lowe's critical effort, however, Kondo makes a contrary move vis-à-vis the Western notions of difference that Lowe finds wanting: she emphasizes the continuing relevance of the founding premise of Jacques Derrida's deconstruction. The latter is well-known for his attack on the Enlightenment thinkers for their "illusory" investment in external grounds as the ultimate source of human representation and cognition (Derrida [1967] 1976, 159–60), as well as for his simultaneous demonstration, through the workings of the *différence* (his neologism that superimposes differentiation and deferment), that such "external grounds are always internally, linguistically generated" (Pecora 1992, 63). From this perspective, Kondo maintains that "experience—considered not as unmediated and inviolable, but as a theoretical abstraction and discursive production—becomes the instantiation of the workings of larger forces; discursive practices are inseparable from … 'social institutions' and the powers of the 'state' and 'political economy.' A poststructuralist perspective would *interrogate* the genealogy of such binaries as 'the subject' and 'structure' " (Kondo 1995, 96).

Dissolution of the subject/structure (or the inner/outer) distinction—a conflation more in dispute during debates over deconstructive methods—has somehow escaped Lowe's interrogation of Western binaries and, as a consequence, found its indirect return at the heart of her culturally based heterogeneity argument. It is from this little-troubled Derridean ground of difference that Kondo poses (in an article published before Lowe's 1991 essay) the following questions to scholars of Asian American studies: "If 'inner' processes are culturally conceived, their very existence mediated by cultural discourses, to what extent can we talk of an 'inner, reflective essence' or an 'outer, objective world' except as culturally meaningful, culturally specific constructs? And how is the inner/outer distinction itself established as the terms within which we must inevitably speak and act?" (Kondo 1990, 12–13). Notably, both Lowe and Kondo consider poststructuralist-influenced feminism practiced by women of color best able to address Asian American concerns beyond essentialist constructions of difference, a theoretical stance that has influenced several theory-oriented monographs in the field since the beginning of the twenty-first century. For example, Leslie Bow's *Betrayal and Other Acts of Subversion* advances a politics of infidelity—as a "pervasive figuration" in Asian American writing by women—for a feminist critique of the nation, modernity, and ethnocentrism (Bow 2001, 11). Laura Kang posits in *Compositional Subjects* that Asian American women are a "productive figuration" characterized by "their multiply delineated specificity and their scattered appearances … across a diverse range of discursive terrains" (Kang 2002, 21). Kandice Chuh declares in *Imagine Otherwise* that " 'Asian American,' because it is a term in difference from itself—at once making a claim for achieved subjectivity and referring to the impossibility of that achievement—deconstructs itself, is itself deconstruction" (Chuh 2003, 8).

Not all Asian American critics are persuaded by such formulations of Asian American difference, however. For example, Traise Yamamoto points out in her discussion of Japanese American women's works that "for the raced subject, an ontology and epistemology based on fragmentation not only pose seriously political problems but also tend to subvert the attempt to integrate the several and disparate aspects of being and bring them to bear on a sense of self" (Yamamoto 1999, 75). Anne Lacasmana is similarly concerned about the implications of a conceptual/theoretical overprivileging of "ludic feminism" informed by academy-based postmodernist epistemes, especially its tendency to obfuscate the "systemic, structural crisis" of capitalism, which demands "a politics of representation for radical transformation" from people of color as a collectivity (Lacasmana 1998, 41). Jeffrey Cabusao comments on the conceptual limits of hybridity by underscoring a distinction between cultural hybridity (namely, intersectional differences in linguistic terms) and social hybridity (that is, unequal relations of power as a form of existential condition). He argues that, in collapsing her analysis of capitalism into that of culture, Lowe inadvertently sidesteps the material histories of both colonial violence and anti-colonial struggle, so far as the Filipino and Filipino American experiences are concerned (Cabusao 2011, 127). Colleen Lye reacts to this anti-essentialist turn in the field by pointing out some of its unintended consequences, observing:

The current feminist preoccupation with the problem of essentialism, converging with "post-Marxist" theoretical developments in general, should be understood as the outgrowth of the need to challenge earlier theoretical formulations for their racial, sexual, geographic, and class omissions. However, the radical critique of what was the starting point of the feminist project—the attempt to define "woman"—appears to have altogether displaced its end point: the emancipation of women. Although antiessentialist feminist theorizing emerged out of the need to broaden and complicate a political agenda founded on naturalized assumptions about identity, the concern with identity categories, *identity as category*, seems to have hegemonized the content of the feminist political agenda itself. (Lye 1995a, 277)

Lye's intervention in Asian American anti-essentialist debates is important for its evocation of some of the less often considered contexts for the rise of a postmodern politics of difference in academy-based theoretical work. One such context is highlighted by Stuart Hall in his 1985 analysis of a connection that he discerns between the ascendency of poststructuralism in Western humanistic discourses and the decline of Marxism worldwide since the 1970s, at a time when he, a sociologist by training, was still tentative in his engagement with semiotic models. For Hall, this coincidence points to a structural asymmetry in Western theoretical development: that is, there is an overabundance of sophisticated theorizing of subject formation based on linguistic paradigms (psychoanalysis and sexuality studies among them), but a scarcity in well-developed theoretical models for analyzing socioeconomic matters or processes (such as class and the production of social relations). He states:

> The question of reproduction has been assigned to the Marxist, (male) pole, and the question of subjectivity has been assigned to the psychoanalytic (feminist) pole. Since then, never have the twins met. The latter is constituted as a question about the "insides" of people, about psychoanalysis, subjectivity and sexuality, and is understood to be "about" that. It is in this way and on this site that the link to feminism has been increasingly theorized. The former is "about" social relations, production and "hard edges" of productive systems, and that is what Marxism and the reductive discourses of class are "about." (Hall 1985, 102–3)[3]

Reflecting on the implications of such imbalance in theoretical models adopted for recent Asian American studies, Arif Dirlik observes that a refocusing from grand concepts or large structures of domination to the internal dynamics of human desires often goes hand in hand with a celebration of the politics of difference and, along with it, a flourishing of "methodological individualism" in the field. What this tendency inevitably translates to, he cautions, is a marginalization of historicized research, whose veracity can no longer be verified in the presence of sophisticated theorization on textual fluidity or arguments about the omnipresence of discursive power. From this perspective, Dirlik considers the hybrid Asian American subjectivity fashioned out of linguistic paradigms politically ambivalent at best since the performance of this subjectivity is already "overdetermined, conditional, and as much the product of sentiment and emotion as of reason" (Dirlik 2007, 2–3).

Race and Class Revisited

A few years before Hall published his 1985 essay in which he reflects on the pros and cons of the semiotic turn in Western humanistic and social science theorizing, he shifted the focus of his own research from its prior emphasis on class formation to race relations, with an explicit purpose of diversifying the critical agendas of orthodox Marxism, another of his intellectual affiliations at the time, because the latter was often criticized for its tendency to reduce the issue of race to an aspect of class struggle. As an alternative, Hall proposes: "One needs to know how different racial and ethnic groups were inserted historically, and the relations which have tended to erode and transform, or to preserve these distinctions through time—not simply as residues and traces of previous modes, but as active structuring principles of the present organization of society" (Hall 1980, 339). This shift in Hall's research orientation, though necessary as a corrective to orthodox Marxism's habitual assimilation of race into class, ironically opens the door to an emphasis on race in lieu of any direct engagement with class as a socioeconomic manifestation of race relations. As race is seen more and more as a discursive construction without its economic referent, it has become hardly representable according to some poststructuralist theorists, even with regard to those suffering from the most primitive form of urban exploitations.

This is the climate under which Michael Omi and Howard Winant's 1986 classic *Racial Formation in the United States: From the 1960s to the 1990s* becomes increasingly problematized by Asian American literary scholars for its applied approaches. For example, Viet Thanh Nguyen criticizes the book's emphasis on "class as the only difference that counts" for racial identities to the neglect of how alienation and race relations in capitalism can be expressed through sexual desires, gender differences, interethnic encounters, generational gaps, and post-national affiliations (Nguyen 2008, 1558, 1560–1). James Lee, taking issue with the sociological "language of prophecy" in Omi and Winant's study, states: "We look for resistance as figures of agency in our texts, not as a relentless life practice, a practice toward life, which sometimes exceeds the tools we're been given in our analytical labor." Lee then asserts that literary study, in its capacity to serve as an "archive of feeling" and "compel" its readers to do what they "would not do on their own," can be a better ground for imagining "a racial future worthy of securing" (Lee 2008, 1550, 1553, 1555). On the basis of these arguments, Susan Koshy suggests that "literature is more receptive to the contingencies of racial formation: the opacities of otherness, the partial light in which action and agency unfold, the ineluctable gap between intervention and outcome, and the temptations and perils of authenticity and full description" (Koshy 2008, 1542–3, 1545).

Emblematic of the new trend of symbolic condemnation of racism in the field is David Eng's 2008 article titled "The End(s) of Race." In it, race is understood as a psycholinguistic juncture of "haunting" with "political and aesthetic effects," or an "affective mood" that revolves around the "logic of the ghost characterizing Derrida's analysis of capital." Eng provides a context for his reworking of race in this way, observing: "Today we inhabit a political moment when disparities of race, not to mention gender, sexuality, and class, apparently no longer matter; they neither signify deep structural inequalities nor mark profound institutional emergencies. Yet we continue to struggle with the political, economic, and cultural legacies of empire and its constructions of race as one significant project of Euro-American modernity" (Eng 2008, 1479, 1486–7). Anne Cheng's 2000 monograph *The Melancholy of Race: Psychoanalysis, Assimilation, and Hidden Griefs* is another notable attempt along the line. This study aims to reveal the injurious effects of the Asian American subject formation process by paying particular attention to "the more immaterial, unquantifiable" dimensions of its mechanism relative to the operation of the "racial othering" apparatuses of American law. Proceeding from within the linguistic labyrinth of Freudian psychoanalysis, Cheng designates what she calls the melancholia of race as constitutive of a "nexus of intertwining affects and libidinal dynamics," or a "web of self-affirmation, self-denigration, projection, desire, identification, and hostility," which, she argues, works to perpetuate Asians' feelings of alienation or abjection in American society. Similar to Eng's characterization of race as a form of ghostly haunting on the Asian American psyche, Cheng's dissection of racial melancholy does not include a discussion of how to engage with or work through the social determinants mainly responsible for the existence of such a psychic condition, except for noting that knowledge of the traumatic nature of it may constitute a step toward un-suturing the dilemmas facing Asian Americans (Cheng 2000, 6, 17).

Commenting on the limitations of academy-based semiotic criticism of race,[4] bell hooks reminds scholars that racism also has a basic sociopolitical dimension whose impact on Black people needs to be named in terms specific to the population and the conditions of their subjugation (hooks 1992, 345–6). Henry Louis Gates similarly suggests, from a self-reflexive poststructuralist point of view: "Race is a trope of ultimate, irreducible difference," whose significance lies not only in its being "the emblem that links racial alienation with economic alienation," but also in "the difference it makes" through recognition of and serious attention to such a connection in literary criticism (Gates 1986, 1, 5, 6). Teasing out the implications of the question of racial alienation in terms of its intertwined relationship with economic alienation, however, means a reengagement with the issue of social class and, for some, even with Marxism, a possibility that has been viewed with increasing skepticism in academy-based theoretical work since the early 1980s. Hence, Christopher Newfield notices that important recent humanistic critiques of the US capitalist economy do not generally talk about "economics in enough detail to explain its impact on culture or vice versa" because the authors of such studies do not want to appear operating in the Marxist camp (Newfield 2008, 1126, 1130). Lurking beneath the performative contradictions called attention to by Newfield vis-à-vis recent critiques of capitalist economy is a literary dilemma. That is, as Fredric Jameson puts it, a "breakdown of the signifying chain" has taken place in contemporary reading practice, which since the early 1980s, has shifted from its traditional interpretive focus on the signifier–signified relationship to that of "a rubble of distinct and unrelated signifiers." What Jameson refers to is what he considers the corrosion, displacement, or disappearance of "the historical referent" in literary studies due to the poststructuralist critique of realist representation as an emblem of essentialism (Jameson 1991, 26–7). Under the circumstances, empirically concrete knowledge has been linked to instrumental (or means-end) rationality, while reasonings about the socially constructed nature of evidential knowledge are used to validate arguments that deny the existence of extratextual reality.

Despite such theoretical and practical challenges facing scholars committed to socially engaged literary studies, careful analyses of race and class dynamics have never been entirely absent from the cognitive map of Asian American criticism. For example, E. San Juan has consistently argued that race and class are central to grasping America's late capitalist culture and social relations, stating:

Concrete investigation of various historical conjunctures is needed to answer how the reproduction of social relations operate through race insofar as capitalism … articulates classes in distinct ways at each level (economic, political, ideological) of the social formation. In effect, the schematics of race and its use to ascribe values, allocate resources, and legitimize the social position/status of racially defined populations (in short, racism) centrally affect the constitution of factions of black, Asian, or Hispanic labor as a class. Put another way, the class relations that ascribe race as social/political/economic positioning of the subject (individual or collective) function as race relations. (San Juan 1992, 47–8)

The race-class nexus that San Juan formulates in this argument is a major referential frame for his wide-ranging literary or cultural criticism centering on anti-colonial artistic productions, especially the writings of Carlos Bulosan, well known for his portrayal of Filipino immigrants' participation in class struggles through broadly based labor movements.

Alan Wald, an expert on the Jewish and African American literary leftism of the Depression era, pioneered the study of the Chinese American proletarian writer H. T. Tsiang's interwar literary activities. Wald takes a special note of Tsiang's realist depiction (in his 1937 novel *And China Has Hands*) of New York Chinatown as a racialized ghetto, as well as the "surrealist features" of his representational style, which Wald likens to the "Marxist playwright Bertolt Brecht's use of 'alienation' effects" in the latter's experimental work during the rise of German modernism (Wald 1996, 341, 343–4). Since the beginning of the twenty-first century, Floyd Cheung and Julia Lee have done significant work on updating Asian American scholarship on Tsiang's literary contributions. For example, in his examination of the Chinatown conditions described in *And China Has Hands*, Cheung focuses his attention on the author's realist detailing of the surroundings of this ethnic ghetto as one made up of "a host of complex, diverse communities"— with each "beset with its own internal cleavages"—as well as his "sober-eyed account" of the "hardscrabble existence" of the laundry worker Wong Wan-Lee, the novel's male protagonist who eventually becomes a union activist (Cheung 2003, 11–12). Lee reads the same novel by paying close attention to its portrayal of Pearl Chang, a biracial female character with Chinese and African American backgrounds. Lee argues that, although Pearl's mixed racial identity is frequently seen as "the most troubled symbol" for unionized struggles centering on the Chinatown laundry workers, the "combination of her female body and hybrid ethnicity [also] excludes her from virtually all the privileges of white American males—and even from the few privileges accorded to ethnic American males like Wong [Wan-Lee]." The presence of this biracial character in the novel thus "complicates" not only the author's somewhat unidimensional "vision of class revolution" but also the novel's "political stance" of critiquing exploitative labor and American capitalism (Lee 2005, 81–2, 95).

Yoonmee Chang's 2010 monograph *Writing the Ghetto: Class, Authorship, and the Asian American Ethnic Enclave* is explicitly concerned with the relationship between race and class. The goal of this study, as she indicates in its introduction, is to reverse the tendency in recent Asian American cultural studies "to mute socio-political critique" of "racially segregated" communities and the "resultant class inequality." In formulating her argument, Chang presents the idea of class in a two-pronged fashion: as "an aggregation of [measurable] sociological indices" in terms of class inequity and class hierarchy, and as an indeterminate discursive process animated by the "symbolic, affective, and semiotic dimensions" of class consciousness. She suggests that the "illegibility of Asian American ghettoization" in recent Asian American criticism reflects the bias of "culturalist epistemologies," which work to displace the "ethnographic" detail of racialized socioeconomic realities undergone by lower-class Asian Americans (Chang 2010, 1–2, 13–17). Christine So's 2007 monograph *Economic Citizens: A Narrative of Asian American Visibility* indirectly takes up the question raised by Chang regarding the "illegibility of Asian American ghettoization," by focusing on "the images of money, commodities, buying, lending, banking, and selling" described in Asian American literary works produced from the 1940s to the beginning of the twenty-first century. So does not equate such images with the legibility of Asians' racialization per se, however. Rather, she uses them to explore the abstract process of "economic exchange" that conditions Asian Americans' everyday life under capitalism, observing that "despite the promise of economic exchange as a means toward social integration, Asian Americans are in the end unable to escape the economic circuits that keep them as tightly contained as Chinatown's boundaries." From this perspective, she argues: "Mapping race along the axis of economic exchange enables the articulation of a striking narrative of Asian American identity formation—one that demonstrates the power and ubiquitousness of the economic realm as a means of bringing people into relation with one another, and one that maps the strict and confining limits of economic circulation for racialized Americans as a pathway into abstract citizenship" (So 2007, 3, 5, 8).

So's argument for the need to examine economic/financial logic—through which Asians' racialization is articulated into the cognitive realm—finds a notable parallel in Iyko Day's 2016 study *Alien Capital: Asian Racialization and the Logic of Settler Colonial Capitalism*. Using the familiar Asian stereotypes ingrained in the North American popular imagination—model minority and yellow peril—as a launching point for her analysis, Day suggests that these stereotypes have always functioned as "complementary aspects of the same form of racialization, in which economic efficiency is the basis for exclusion or assimilation." Conversely, she adds, the abstract economic logic of capital can make its operation manifest only through Asians' concrete experiences of being present and subjugated in the West through the racial identities imposed on them. From this perspective, Day emphasizes that "the contemporary economism of Asian racial form [be it model minority or yellow peril] does not represent a break from the past but rather is part of a continuum of settler colonial capitalism and its racial formations" (Day 2016, 6–7). In formulating her argument in this way, Day has spelled out, from an economic perspective that she shares with So, a fuller implication of Colleen Lye's concept of "Asiatic racial form" as a cultural-materialist trope.[5] Day observes:

> It is the "inorganic quality of the Asiatic body" that manifests the "intangibly abstract" threat of finance capital. Reflecting on the role of economic tropes embedded in racist representations of Japanese American success in agriculture in the early twentieth century, a success mirrored by Japanese Canadians in the British Columbia fishing industry, Lye points to what she calls "the economism of Asiatic racial form—a form in which economic interests are not masked but are the primary medium of race's historical expression." (Day 2016, 6; Lye 2005, 122, 124, 130)

In this chapter, the categories of race, gender, sexuality, and class are examined as interrelated and non-hierarchical constructs open to ideological reformulations; they are also recognized as power relations that can be experienced socially and economically. The critical opinions surveyed in this chapter highlight the historical contingencies that necessitate their articulation into distinct or seemingly coherent ideologies, as well as their subsequent complication and reworking into more reflexive stances or politics. One context evoked during the survey of this chapter is an uneven theoretical development that Stuart Hall discerns in academy-based Western intellectual discourses since the 1970s, namely: a paucity in sophisticated theory on socioeconomic issues and an overabundance of theory on human desire and sexuality, in the wake of the Marxism-inspired social movements worldwide. Hall's highlighting of the existence of such ideological/institutional constraints on developing historically grounded research methods today is very suggestive. For it invites scholars to consider the possibility that truly innovative work in ethnic literary studies may lie under the circumstances not in that readily responding to well-rehearsed protocols of semiology, but rather in that able to reintroduce historicism to the discursivity of the dominant postmodern episteme, without at the same time falling back on unmediated empirical approaches to literature, including the utilitarianism of vulgar Marxism.

Chapter 2 extends the survey in this chapter to an exploration of Asian American critical efforts to diversify the agendas of identity politics, to move beyond a pan-Asian imaginary long cherished in the community, and to build multiethnic textual alliances at emerging intersections. Chief among the issues to be examined are the premise and operation of cultural nationalism, which shaped the horizon of expectations of Asian American creative and critical discourses from the mid-1970s to the dawn of the1990s.

CHAPTER 2
THE NECESSITY AND FICTION OF "ASIAN AMERICA"

In a 2010 special issue of *Modern Fiction Studies* (*MFS*) dedicated to "Theorizing Asian American Fiction," the guest-editors of the volume—Stephen Sohn, Paul Lai, and Donald Geollnicht—describe the evolution of Asian American literary and cultural studies as comprising of three overlapping stages:

> the cultural nationalist phase of the late 1960s to the late 1970s, the feminist phase that dominated from the late 1970s through about 1990s (and still ongoing), and the transnational phase or diasporic phase from about 1990 on. The cultural nationalist phase was epitomized by Frank Chin and the *Aiiieeeee!* editors with an emphasis on racial identity politics founded on American nativity and the English language, and on the project of "claiming America" in decidedly masculinist, militaristic, working-class fashion. The feminist phase (ushered in by Maxine Hong Kingston's *The Woman Warrior* in 1976) opposed Frank Chin's masculinist ideology, despite the similarities of their projects in "claiming America"; it later broadened out to deal with the complexities of gender and sexuality more generously, culminating in extensive present engagements with queer studies. (Sohn, Lai, and Goellnicht 2010, 2)

This mapping of the field offers a convenient starting point for the survey in this chapter, which is primarily concerned with issues either arising from or closely associated with Asian American cultural nationalism, a complex topic that the editors analyze in more or less definitive terms.

Within this context, two little examined assumptions that inform the editors' characterization of cultural nationalism also help set stage for the discussions to follow. First, the editors consider the cultural nationalist phase of Asian American literary studies a "decidedly masculinist, militaristic, and working-class based" formation, one diametrically opposed to the feminist and diasporic phases of the field that they simultaneously recognize as "overlapping" developments. Second, the editors imagine the shift from the cultural nationalist to the transnational phases of Asian American literary studies in somewhat developmental terms, without paying adequate attention to the circumstantial constraints that make either a cultural nationalist or a diasporic claim more a rhetorical gesture than a politically substantive move. The survey in this chapter goes beyond the scope of the editors' mapping of this crucial period in the field's evolution by introducing a wider range and greater variety of critical opinions, with an emphasis on cultural nationalism as a historically contingent and internally complex ideology, as well as a long-drawn and multiply negotiated process structurally connected to other social dynamics or formations.

Cultural Nationalism

Lisa Lowe sets the tone for the field's critique of cultural nationalism in her influential 1991 article "Heterogeneity, Hybridity, and Multiplicity," by designating the project of *Aiiieeeee!* as an emblem of racial, masculinist, and nativist essentialism, while urging for a diasporic conception of Asian American subjectivity from postcolonial and poststructuralist perspectives. Lowe especially underscores the dangers of a cultural nationalist politics that "relies upon the construction of sameness and the exclusion of differences" in the ethnic community, whose collectivity, she maintains, is by nature "unstable and changeable, with its cohesion complicated by intergenerationality, by various degrees of identification and relation to 'homeland,' and by different extents of assimilation to and distinction from 'majority culture' in the United States." From this perspective, she argues that Asian American culture—as "a fluctuating composition of differences, intersections, and incommensurabilities"—is ontologically resistant to the totalizing ideologies of cultural nationalism that structurally replicates the agendas of US modernity (Lowe 1991, 27, 29, 39). In many ways, the alternative vision that Lowe articulates about the future of Asian America as an inherently "open, plural, and dynamic" process of ongoing formation represents a major turning point in the field's subsequent shifts and transformations. Hence, Anita Mannur and Allan Punzalan Isaac look back at Lowe's 1991 article appreciatively in recognition of its long-lasting contributions to the field, emphasizing that it "offers a conceptual vocabulary to think through the multiple differences that structured Asian American cultural, social, and political formations"; and it expands "the framing possibilities for Asian American cultural production and analysis" as the field was poised for significant shifts in the twenty-first century (Mannur and Isaac 2015, 324–5).

Asian American feminist critics who participated in trailblazing the field in the 1980s and the 1990s responded to Lowe's call for a paradigm shift in the field equally enthusiastically. For example, Elaine Kim states, in reference to the significance of Theresa Ha Kyung Cha's modernist text *Dictée* that is paradigmatic of Lowe's diasporic conception of a post-national Asian American subjectivity, as follows:

> I am searching for a space where "women" and "Korean" might work together. … Refusing to be drawn into an opposition between "woman" and "Korean" or between "Korean" and "Korean American," Cha creates and celebrates a kind of third space, an exile space that becomes a source of individual vision and power. … She foregrounds a highly specific cultural context, inserting Korean, Korean women, and Korean American women into the discourse, thereby opening the space for an individual search for selfhood as well as a non-reified, non-essentialized collectivity. (Kim 1994, 7–8)

King-Kok Cheung vividly illustrates the game-changing nature of Lowe's theoretical intervention by observing:

> A significant switch … has occurred in Asian American literary studies. Whereas identity politics—with its stress on cultural nationalism and American nativity—governed earlier theoretical and critical formulations, the stress is now on heterogeneity and diaspora. The shift has been from seeking to "claim America" to forging a connection between Asia and Asian America; from centering on race and on masculinity to revolving around multiple axes of ethnicity, gender, class, and sexuality; from being concerned primarily with social history and communal responsibility to being caught in the quandaries and possibilities of postmodernism and multiculturalism. (Cheung 1997, 1)

For Shirley Lim, the theoretical breakthrough made by Lowe would inevitably translate to the construction of "a confrontational relation between place and identity and compose a tradition of 'global literature' complexly differentiated from the tradition of nationally bounded and divided identities that has conventionally organized our understanding of 'world literature'" (Lim 1997, 299).

Sau-ling Wong's 1995 article "Denationalization Reconsidered: Asian American Cultural Criticism at a Theoretical Crossroads" is a major attempt to reassess the trend started by Lowe's deconstructive critique of cultural nationalism and endorsed by a growing number of scholars in the field. She contends:

> I have found myself raising questions about the consequences of an uncritical participation in denationalization, as if it represented a more advanced and theoretically more sophisticated (in short, superior, though proponents rarely say so directly) stage in Asian American studies. A developmental or maturational narrative about reconfigurations in Asian American cultural criticism, whether implicitly or explicitly presented, to me poses some serious risks. … [that is,] unwitting subsumption into master narratives (despite a mandate to subvert master narratives built into the ethnic studies approach), and depoliticization occluded by theoretical self-critique. (Wong 1995a, 12)

Jinqi Ling's 1998 monograph *Narrating Nationalisms: Ideology and Form in Asian American Literature* represents another serious attempt to retheorize cultural nationalism beyond the linguistic protocols of deconstruction. Recognizing the "structural deficiency" and ideological limitations of this phase of Asian American literary history, he maintains that the *Aiiieeeee!* editors' unidimensional insertion of racial difference in masculinist terms matters to the field only insofar as it is understood as a historically contingent move and, in retrospect, as able to produce a strategic "breach" in the cultural establishment, to reveal "additional possibilities for engagement," and to create "a precondition for the adoption of more flexible and tactical positions" that supersede those of its own (Ling 1998, 12–14, 25–7). He considers Lowe's designation of heterogeneity, hybridity, and multiplicity as the "points of origin" and "fundamental condition" of the totality of Asian American experiences (Lowe 1991, 31–2; Lowe 1995b, 42) an undertheorized hypothesis in that it fails to give an account of how the emancipatory scenario of differences she envisages is reached through socially based struggles and made to serve progressive ends in historically specific terms, especially under conditions of "fundamental power imbalance" such as that facing the proponents of cultural nationalism in the 1970s (Ling 1998, 8). Commenting on the implications of Asian American desire for inclusion into the US nation-state in the pre-1965 period, Christine So suggests that such "entry into the state's apparatuses and its institutions and corporations," even if realized, "does not necessarily mean that racial difference has been contained, co-opted, and managed. Instead, we see ... an anxiety that permeates all exchanges between margin and mainstream—the presence of a racial excess that can neither be specifically quantified, exactly accounted for, nor fully erased" (So 2007, 5–6). Pamela Thoma similarly designates Asian American "cultural citizenship" as a space where meaningful interventions in the hegemony of America's neoliberal capitalism can be made through efforts by women writers of color, who reformulate the terms of their belonging by transforming, both in words and through ideological transcoding, the conventions of "popular narrative genres" of "the market place," as a major venue for reproducing the values and attitudes of American nativity or nationalism (Thoma 2013, 4).

Despite its commonly held perception as a symbol of masculinist and racial essentialism in the field, cultural nationalism contains in its body politic an irrepressible feminist presence and contributions, as testified to by quite a few Asian American women scholars, most notably, Maxine Hong Kingston, who invents the idea of "claiming America" shortly after the successes of her 1976 feminist work *The Woman Warrior*.[1] Thus, Jennifer Ting reminds recent critics of cultural nationalism: "The racial formation called 'Asian American' emerged, in part, through the written discussion of sexuality" during the cultural nationalist period. She further points out:

From *Gidra's* front-page article, "Yellow Prostitution," to *Bridge's* special issue on women (1978), sexuality saturates this writing. Although we tend to think of the Asian American movement press primarily in terms of writing about racial and/or class politics, it was not unusual for these newspapers, magazines, journals, and books to write about sexual desire, to use sexual metaphors in their anti-imperialist and antiracist analysis, to celebrate sexual activity and the flaunting of bourgeois mores, and to denounce sexual exploitation. (Ting 1998, 67)

This underreported aspect of cultural nationalist struggles receives serious consideration by Laura Kang, the author of *Compositional Subjects*, who details, from an explicitly poststructuralist perspective, Asian American women's "syntactical formulation" of their "gender ontology" and "compositional" subjectivity through community-based publications they sponsored during the 1960s and the 1970s. Kang argues that contemporary versions of sexual difference often cited by scholars in the field are but "distinct offshoots" of the Asian American "figure of destabilizations" already at work in the "agonistic intersections of the feminist, antiracist, and anti-imperialist social movements" (Kang 2002, 2–3, 5, 11). Ting and Kang's efforts to reintroduce the cultural nationalist struggles staged by Asian American feminist scholars—and to make visible the sites and structures of their resistance effaced by generalized discussions of *Aiiieeeee!* and cultural nationalism—find ready echoes in the case studies conducted by other scholars, such as Michiko Owaki's examination of the "intersubjective" connectedness of the body, sexuality, identity, and the ethnic community in Janice Mirikitani's movement poetry (Owaki 2001, 43, 54); Daryll Maeda's discussion of Asian American women's efforts to transform gender hierarchy by creating women-centered spaces or operating mechanisms despite the pervasive masculinist assumptions and practices in the movement (Maeda 2009, 95); and Colleen Lye's analysis of a range of Asian American women's texts that reflect the conflicting tendencies of the rise of postmodern cultural studies via high theory and community-based activism inspired by visions of the Third World Liberation Front struggles in the long 1960s (Lye 2014, 213–14).

Within the broader context of the survey in this subsection of the chapter, David Leiwei Li's cultural criticism seems most consistent in its designation of this phase of Asian American literary history as a US-specific phenomenon. For Li, the contradictions confronting Asian Americans both in the movement era and at the present moment—their admission into the American system by way of racially based legal instrumentality and their acquisition of US citizenship in the form of racial abjection and social alienation—cannot be fully comprehended without a critical dissection of the self-justifying mechanisms of the American nation-state and its accompanying neoliberal regimes. Hence, he acknowledges the legitimacy of cultural nationalist contestations in nativist terms, while skeptical of the field's overinvestment in the centrifugal forces of a post-national or a diasporic transformation of the field as a whole (Li 1998, 1–4, 17). To a certain degree, Li's empathy for cultural nationalist struggles, as well as Sau-ling Wong's objection to the denationalizing tendencies in recent Asian American theorizing, does represent, as several scholars have pointed out, the last major attempt in the field to align Asian American literary agendas with those of cultural nationalism (Chen 2011, 885; Chiang 2009, 109; Koshy 2000, 118; Lee 2012, 5–6). At the same time, this consensus in the field is also symptomatic of a larger shift in ethnic studies worldwide since the mid-1990s, which is marked, as Stuart Hall observes, by its practitioners' awareness of "the passing away of what at one time seemed to be a necessary fiction," namely, ethnic particularism. Hall, who spearheads this post-national shift, urges scholars conducting ethnic studies to "*decouple ethnicity*" from its "equivalence with nationalism, imperialism, racism and the state" (Hall 1995, 225, 227).[2] In line with his general move toward a postmodern revamping of ethnic studies, Asian American literary critics start identifying links in the field suspicious of what Paul Gilroy refers to as "ethnic absolutism" (Gilroy 1992), another way of saying, as it were, "racial essentialism" or cultural nationalism. One of the ready targets for criticism in this context is community-based self-representation through the medium of realist literature, a topic that will be explored in the survey of Chapter 6.

Despite the obvious limitations of cultural nationalism, it should be noted that the national question connotes very differently to Marxist critics or critics sympathetic to a Marxian understanding of the role of the nation as an indispensable stage of historical materialism. For example, Alan Wald reminds that "the single most influential theoretical work" for analyzing cultural nationalism of the 1960s should be "Frantz Fanon's *The Wretched of the Earth* (English translation, 1966), which unambiguously argues that the re-establishment and valorization of the culture of the oppressed is only a preliminary step to the achievement of a truly international culture." Recognizing that many "poorly thought-out—and even foolish—things were said and done" in the "fervor of the 1960s," he suggests that "the declaration of cultural independence that occurred in the 1960s on the part of racially-oppressed minorities involved a crucial polemic against liberal notions of assimilation and integration" (Wald 1981, 20–1). Tim Libretti reacts to recent post-national arguments by commenting on their evasion of the actual politics of transnationalism, arguing: "Post-ethnic ideology attempts to sweep the concrete and material realities of the various national entities or constituencies existing as Third World pockets within the US under the well-worn rug of national unity, figuring people of color in the same vein as European ethnic immigrants, as people waiting to be absorbed or assimilated into the 'American' way." He contends that the impulse of post-ethnic discourse in "forgetting nationalism ... seems to be a desire not so much to move beyond ethnicity through historical process and struggle but rather to avoid ... [the] difficult and controversial steps [of transforming

American society and making it 'truly postethnic'] by returning nostalgically back to some imagined pre-ethnic or pre-racial moment in 'American' cultural history, a moment of cultural purity before the national identity was threatened with contamination by people of color" (Libretti 1999, 5–6).

Arif Dirlik complicates the debate between Marxism and postmodernism over the national question by suggesting that certain questions raised by postmodernism may in fact be beneficial to Marxism, which is urgently in need of updating its program and expanding the range of its epistemological instruments to maintain its relevance in the age of global capitalism. At the same time, he makes explicit his commitment to the basic arguments of Marxism, advising: "We need to ask not just whether or not Marxism is relevant to providing some of the answers, but what we stand to lose if we ignore the kinds of answers it has to provide" (Dirlik 2007, 16). Within this context, Terry Eagleton offers by far a most illuminating analysis of the evolving concept of nationalism by tracing it to its anti-colonial and anti-imperial origins, while pointing out the limitation of approaching this question from a detached cosmopolitan perspective:

> Given the partial failure of national revolution in the so-called Third World, post-colonial theory was wary of all talk of nationhood. Theorists who were either too young or too obtuse to recall that nationalism had been in its time an astonishingly effective anti-colonial force that could find nothing in it but a benighted chauvinism or ethnic supremacism. Instead, much post-colonial thought focused on the cosmopolitan dimensions of a world in which post-colonial states were being sucked inexorably into the orbit of global capital. In doing so, it reflected a genuine reality. But in negating the idea of nationhood, it also tended to jettison the notion of class, which had been so closely bound up with the revolutionary nation. Most of the new theorists were not only "post" colonialism, but "post" the revolutionary impetus which had given birth to the new nation in the first place. (Eagleton 2003, 10)

Beyond Pan-Asian Ethnicity

Susan Koshy's 1996 article "The Fiction of Asian American Literature" has remained a major frame of reference in recent Asian American critical debates because of its close attention to what has happened in the field since

Lisa Lowe's 1991 theoretical intervention. In this article, Koshy discerns a glaring contradiction between what she finds to be a "highly stratified, uneven, and heterogeneous" condition of Asian American experience revealed by postmodern analytical methods, and the restrictive East-Asia-centric operating principles that continually shape the definition of "Asian America" fashioned out of the political agendas of the 1960s and the 1970s. The prime symptom for this ongoing dilemma, in her view, is the common practice in the field of keeping adding new elements to its existing body of work, rather than transforming the field in ways that are strategic to its growth, thereby perpetually deferring Asian American literary studies from coming into being (Koshy 1996, 315–16). Despite the warnings advised by Koshy, however, this "additive" approach has not only persisted but also become normalized over time. In this process, as Christopher Lee observes, there has emerged a "'catch-up' to the world" mentality—even a sense of "moral" urgency or responsibility for being inclusive—among Asian American critics committed to visions of heterogeneity (Lee 2007, 2–3). Prior to the publication of Koshy's 1996 essay, two serious attempts had been made to expand the parameters of the field's practice. First is Elaine Kim's 1995 essay "Beyond Railroads and Internments: Comments on the Past, Present, and Futures of Asian American Studies," in which she urges Asian Americanists to "imagine new conceptual frameworks" beyond Chinese exclusion and Japanese internment as foundational events of Asian American history (Kim 1995, 18). Second is Jessica Hagedorn's 1993 edited volume *Charlie Chan Is Dead: An Anthology of Contemporary Asian American Fiction*, which includes the creative work of forty-eight writers with diverse backgrounds as a way of showcasing a vastly expanded definition of "Asian America" (Hagedorn 1993, xxx). What distinguishes Koshy's contribution from those of her predecessors is her willingness to engage the emerging problematics in contemporary Asian American critical practice, as well as her attempt to reset the terms for Asian American debates beyond a routine reference to the polemical—and by no means influential—positions of *Aiiieeeee!* and *The Big Aiiieeeee!* as the only ground for advancing new visions or arguments about the field's development.

The need to rethink what constitutes Asian American literature under the new circumstances necessarily involves a reassessment of established paradigms that have continually shaped the field's self-perception and day-to-day performance. One aspect of the critical work conducted along this line is concerned with teasing out, interrogating, and reinventing the idea of "pan-Asian ethnicity," which has been used to mobilize community-based activism both during and after the social movement era. Yen Lê Espiritu's 1992 sociological classic, *Asian American Panethnicity: Bridging Institutions and Identities*, has received certain scrutiny in this context. With this book, Espiritu seeks to expand the synthetic potential of the term "panethnicity" (in recognition of its bureaucratic origin and categorical ambivalence) by reworking it into a theoretical paradigm for describing not only how Asian Americans "of diverse national origins can come together as a new, enlarged panethnic group," but also how they simultaneously become part of a spontaneous, open-ended, and multiply negotiable formation unfolding amidst multiple contradictions (Espiritu 1992, 3). A point of tension in the ensuing debates over Espiritu's semiotically valenced mapping of contemporary Asian American panethnicity involves an argument advanced by E. San Juan, who notices a methodological affinity between her mapping of the field in such terms and Lisa Lowe's hypothesis of the emergence of a "new historical bloc" in the post-1965 Asian American communities and populations, and that both are based on interpretations of data compiled from the experiences of Asian Californians (San Juan 1998, 160, 165–6; Espiritu 1992, 104). San Juan's concern can be affirmed by a quick perusal of Lowe's own account of this aspect of her Gramscian imaginary—the basis of her argument in the 1991 article. She states: "The first reason to emphasize the dynamic fluctuation and heterogeneity of Asian American culture is ... to arrive at a different conception of the general political terrain of culture in California," since it has "become commonplace to consider it an 'ethnic state,' embodying a new phenomenon of cultural adjacency and mixture," and "the fundamental condition of heterogeneous differences" (Lowe 1991, 28, 34, 39).

Stephen Sumida's 1998 essay "East of California: Points of Origin in Asian American Studies" was published in the context of this subtle aspect of the debates in the field. In this essay, Sumida calls attention to the limited applicability of the idea of pan-Asian ethnicity based on a California model, while reminding readers of his essay that "Asian America has a long and widespread history in what is now the United States." He argues:

The name "East of California" not only acknowledges but exposes, critically, a regional boundedness of a field where Asian American studies of the West Coast have been assumed to be not regional but unbounded, central, and broadly paradigmatic, even while at the same time some consider that region to have exceptional conditions and qualities that empower it in the field (e.g., in claims, especially during the 1980s, that California is the first and precedent-setting multicultural state). Working with the evidence of the Asian/Pacific American history and culture of the South and Midwest reveals certain limitations of a California paradigm ... The expression "East of California" itself both inscribes and plays with notions of centrality of the West Coast in Asian American studies. (Sumida 1998, 85–6)

San Juan provides additional reasons for his reluctance to endorse Asian American panethnicity imagined from an exclusively Californian perspective, by taking issue with Lowe's formulation of Asian Californians as a "new historical bloc." He contends that "East Asians, on the West Coast in particular," have long been "instrumentalized" by the US dominant bloc as "a buffer race" to "breathe new life into the assimilationist syndrome," for "multiplicity serves as the theoretical wedge to displace the organizing category of class, founded on the unequal division of social labor and therefore unequal power, as the ordering principle of U.S. capitalism" (San Juan 2009, 80–1).

The social experience and cultural production of Asian Pacific islander Americans constitute a notable exception to post-*Aiiieeeee!* formulations of pan-Asianism according to a West Coast imaginary. An early attempt to resist the continental definitions of Asian American collective identity or politics was documented in Candace Fujikane's study of the birth of a Hawaiian American consciousness, which is marked by two pivotal events that took place in 1978. First was the publication of *Talk Story: An Anthology of Hawaii's Local Writers* (edited by Eric Chock), a book distributed at the "Hawaii's Ethnic American Writers' Conference" held in that year. Second was the simultaneous launching of a local literary journal *Bamboo Ridge: The Hawaii Writers' Quarterly*. Both events serve to highlight the specific histories, cultures, and social concerns in Hawaii, and to underscore "the difficulty of 'fitting'" Hawaiian literary articulations into the frameworks used to analyze continentally based Asian American social and cultural experiences (Fujikane 1994, 26, 29). Sumida's 1991 monograph *And the View from the Shore: Literary Traditions of Hawai'i*, which focuses on the uneven dynamics of the local and colonial histories that at once situate and motivate participants in Hawaiian literary activities, represents a major detailing of the internal complexities of Hawaiian American literary production since the early twentieth century (Sumida 1992).

In a more recent examination of how Asian Pacific islander American experiences relate to either pre- or post-*Aiiieeeee!* prescriptions for what constitutes Asian American studies, Susan Najita advances an "oceanic" perspective, emphasizing: "The study of the Pacific poses peculiar problems because of its decentered rhizomatic geography, its myriad cultures and languages, and most of all, its history of multiple and different neo-colonizations that have produced a region that does not fall neatly within the paradigms of American Studies, Commonwealth Studies, or Pacific Studies." Skeptical about the recent moves made in postcolonial American/ Asian American studies toward extending its scholarship to include Asian Pacific Studies, she argues for a comparative but "island-centered" approach with an emphasis on "indigenous nationalisms and claims to land," especially the "relation between the nation and its false promise of modernization and development" (Najita 2014, 167–8). Along the line, Keith Camacho reminds readers of Asian American culture that "Pacific Islanders seldom figure prominently in discussions of the United States empire, itself a frequently disavowed apparatus of white economic, military, and political supremacy. Whether construed as products of genocidal removal, national amnesia, or political marginalization, Pacific Islanders frequently remain at the fringes of this nation-state. Yet they play vital roles in the making and unmaking of the empire from the late nineteenth century to the present" (Camacho 2011, ix).

Many Filipino American scholars have compelling reasons for distancing themselves from pan-Asian ethnicity as an umbrella term both before and after Lisa Lowe's 1991 initiation of a paradigm shift in the field. For example, Oscar Campomanes contends that the Philippines is the only Asian country "drawn into a truly colonial and neo-colonial relation with the United States," a history that makes the Filipinos' incorporation into the United States socioeconomic system qualitatively different from that of other Asian groups. Within this context, he considers Filipino Americans' underrepresentation in Asian American studies reflects, more than anything else, the field's indifference to the historical and contemporary conditions facing the Filipino American community, an attitude that, he emphasizes, partially explains why many Filipino Americans refuse to join in the claims on America (Campomanes 1992, 52). Regarding the issue of underrepresentation, Eleanor Ty further points out: "In the 1960s and early 1970s, another kind of invisibility occurred: there were still not as many Filipinos in the United States as there were Chinese or Japanese, and the reality of these numbers created a different kind of liminality for Filipino Americans within Asian American groups" (Ty 2015, 372). From this perspective, Sarita See asserts: "Filipino America is strangely and structurally invisible, and its position at the crossroads of race and empire has everything to do with that invisibility" (Ty 2015, 372).

E. San Juan argues more forcefully that the conceptual framework of panethnicity conceals "the ethnic chauvinisms and class cleavages, hierarchy and conflicts generated by the operation of U.S. racializing politics or inherited from imperil divide-and-rule policies." This concealment, he maintains, promotes a neoconservative cultural entrepreneurship open to utilitarian and opportunistic bourgeois ethos associated with the Pacific Rim "tigers," an implicit acceptance of the "model minority" stereotype, and an alignment with forces opposing affirmative action and social programs for the disadvantaged (San Juan 1998, 160–1). Reflecting the field's failure to confront the consequences of colonial legacies that continually shape the Filipino condition in shifting contexts is the 1998 controversy over Lois-Ann Yamanaka's AAAS (The Association for Asian American Studies) award for her novel *Blu's Hanging*, which led to Filipino American protests across the country for the inclusion in its portrayal of stereotypes of Filipinos. The ensuing debate over the controversy tends to revolve around its perception as a reflection of either disciplinary entrenchment (such as that positing literary representation against its sociological reduction) or an academia–community divide (thereby an issue of accumulation of cultural capital by the former at the cost of the latter). Darlene Rodriguez and Seri Luangphinith historicize the controversy differently by linking it to the dehumanizing effects of colonial impositions on the Filipinos living in Hawaii, effects that they consider continually played out in Yamanaka's fictionalized portrayal of "the most provincial places like the Kalihi Valley," the setting of the novel's interethnic tensions—a lingering colonial legacy that, during AAAS's granting Yamanaka a book award in 1998, became a political trigger for the Filipino American protests (Rodriquez 2000b, 199–200; Luangphinith 2015, 393, 395).

Sentiments of alienation are registered additionally among scholars who pursue certain emerging areas of inquiry and find their investments in tension with the parameters and practices of pan-Asianism. For example, Dana Takagi complains that Asian American gay and lesbian social organizations are teetering on the margins between the white gay community and the Asian American community at large (Takagi 1996, 21); Mark Jerng calls attention to the "uneven and sometimes uneasy" entry of the study of transracial Asian adoptees into established Asian American studies, as well as the "tensions within the lines of filiation and affiliation that constitute the Asian American subject" (Jerng 2014, 21–2).[3] In this process, Louisa Schein and Va-Megn Thoj articulate a concern that can be shared by other Hmong Americans who find themselves "[e]verywhere minoritized" in their exilic existence in the United States: that is, they are frequently made to feel both an outsider of "the alternative modernity of Asia" and an "immigrant misfit" in the political equation of the ethnic community/hierarchy of which they have become a part (Schein and Thoj 2008, 1756). Further contextualizing the existential tensions alluded to by Schein and Thoj, Linda Võ observes:

> While Asian Americans, mainly Chinese and Japanese, during the anti-War Movement of the late 1960s and 1970s saw the killing of their "Vietnamese brothers and sisters" as a reflection of their own dehumanization, they were unsure of what to make us once we arrived on American shores. These activists had worked hard to situate themselves as "Americans," so some reacted by disassociating themselves from these FOB (fresh off the boat) foreigners. Asian American Studies scholars also struggled to figure out how to incorporate these newcomers into their teaching, research, and theories; unfortunately, this inclusion still remains underdeveloped or neglected. (Võ 2003, ix)

As a result of concerted efforts to historicize and make visible the fissures, absences, or discrepancies in the various pan-Asian paradigms proposed over time, the past two decades have witnessed the publication of a number of important book-length studies that significantly depart from the coalitional politics either promoted by the editors of *Aiiieeeee!* according to pre-1965 Asian immigrant experiences, or reinscribed by Lisa Lowe on the basis of a post-1965 Californian imaginary. These studies include, among others, Rajini Srikanth's *The World Next Door: South Asian American Literature and the Idea of Home* (2004);[4] Susan Najita's *Decolonizing Cultures in the Pacific: Reading History and Trauma in Contemporary Fiction* (2006); Mark Jerng's *Claiming Others: Transracial Adoption and National Belonging* (2010); Jodi Kim's *Ends of Empire: Asian American Critique and the Cold War* (2010); Anita Mannur's *Culinary Fictions: Food in South Asian Diasporic Culture* (2010); and Cathy Schlund-Vials's *War, Genocide, and Justice: Cambodian American Memory Work* (2012).

Comparative Race and Ethnicity Studies

The theoretical landscape that has emerged from the field's internal critique of the limitations of cultural nationalism and different versions of pan-Asian ethnicity is both complex and enabling. But the transition from the national to the post-national in Asian American literary studies does not take place instantaneously in a clear-cut fashion. As Colleen Lye suggests, the field has yet to go through "a standoff" phase during this shift—which is marked by its contingent investment in a "multiracial model [that is continually] limited by a national horizon"—before it reaches a stage of development when "a historical background for conducting cross-racial analysis" is no longer readily available and an explicitly post-racial and post-national "diasporic model" prevails (Lye 2008a, 1732). What Lye suggests is that once Asian American literature becomes diasporic or transnational in its actual practice, its traditional emphasis on race relations and the consequences of racialization—which is tied to the problematics of American laws governing Asian immigration, assimilation, and acquisition of US citizenship rights—would give way to concerns that are meaningful only in the social contexts or cultural conventions that Asian American studies migrate to. Hence, Joseph Keith considers comparative race studies constituting a key transitional methodology for the field before it grows out of "the limitations of prior models of racial or ethnic solidarity based on cultural nationalist and identitarian forms of subjectivity and collectivity." Keith recommends this method in terms of its potential to recognize "the forms and legacies of alliance, antagonism, analogy, with respect to other racial minorities, that have been central to conceptions of Asian American subjectivity," and to give a sense of "how those conceptions have changed over time and place" (Keith 2015, 183–4).

An early form of comparative race or ethnicity studies is proposed by Shirley Lim, who considers aspects of Hisaye Yamamoto's writing from the 1940s through the 1950s containing an embryonic paradigm that anticipates some of the contemporary critical practices on the concern in the field. She observes:

> Hisaye Yamamoto's short stories construct a multicultural and poly-Asian society missing in works by her contemporaries. Besides the Japanese American subjects that form the major characters of her fiction, Chinese Americans appear as victims of racism ("Wilshire Bus") or as economic exploiters ("The Brown House"); Italian Americans appears as alcoholic lovers ("Epithalamion"), and Filipino Americans as field hands and romantic interest ("Yoneko's Earthquake"; "Seventeen Syllables"). Yamamoto's stories foreshadow the present and future of an Asian American literature in their

inclusiveness of representation and in their recentering from an ethnocentrism countering a cultural other that is Anglo and white to a critique of ethnocentrism that presents the other as ethnically multiple. (Lim 1993a, 159–60)

King-Kok Cheung's 1997 edited volume *An Interethnic Companion to Asian American Literature* represents a more substantive effort to reorient the field toward multiethnic and comparative directions, with an informative introductory essay that reviews major denationalizing trends and critical positions. The essays of this collection are quite diverse in their coverage based on specific ethnic or national origins or under such foundational categories as race, gender, class, and sexuality. Specifically included in the volume are individual chapters on South Asian American, Vietnamese American, Filipino American, and Hawaiian literatures. The book's somewhat conventional organization thus points to Cheung's implicit adherence to Sau-ling Wong's cultural nationalist conception of building an Asian American literature's "textual coalition," as well as her own negotiation between the sweep of her interethnic claims and her awareness that "cultural nationalism, far from being dissipated by growing heterogeneity, has taken plural forms." Further illustrating Cheung's negotiation with these tensions is her attempt to keep a balance between "simultaneous claiming and disclaiming of both Asia and America" (Cheung 1997, 3–4, 10, 26–7).

The first decades of the new millennium have seen the publication of a number of book-length literary studies dedicated to examining interracial or interethnic relations along the lines described by Joseph Keith. Spearheading this trend is James Kyung-Jin Lee's *Urban Triage: Race and Fictions of Multiculturalism* (2004), which brings into dialogue the literary works of African American, Asian American, Chicano, and white authors through its critique of the 1980s neoliberalism. In a similar vein, Grace Hong's *The Ruptures of American Capital: Women of Color Feminism and the Culture of Immigrant Labor* (2006) analyzes the writings of Hisaye Yamamoto, Toni Morrison, Helena Maria Viramontes, and Jessica Hagedorn, among others, through the lens of women of color feminism as an all-encompassing analytical paradigm. Several monographs produced in the same period are focused on the dynamics of Afro-Asian relationship, following the examples set by Vijay Prashad's *Everybody Was Kung Fu Fighting: Afro-Asian Connection and Myth of Cultural Purity* (2001) and Bill Mullen's *Afro-Orientalism* (2004). These works include, among others, Daniel Kim's *Writing Manhood in Black and Yellow* (2005); Daryl Maeda's *Chains of Babylon: The Rise of Asian America*

(2009); Leslie Bow's *'Partly Colored': Asian Americans and Racial Anomaly in the Segregated South* (2010); Julia Lee's *Interracial Encounters: Reciprocal Representations in African American and Asian American Literatures, 1896–1937* (2011); and, beyond an Asian-Black dynamic, Stephen Sohn's *Racial Asymmetries: Asian American Fictional Worlds* (2014), a study of how Asian American literature becomes "Othered to itself" through its adoption of the point of view of Chicano/a characters that occupy the central plot of Asian American literary writings.

Key to building multiethnic or interracial textual alliances, as mentioned earlier in this chapter, is a comparative method that, according to Joseph Keith, has "sought to think not only in terms of the parallels but also to think the difference *between* and *within* racialized, gendered, and sexualized collectivities." Keith believes that the significance of this analytic lies mainly in its capacity "to render legible and combat the new racisms and shifting structures of racial difference" as the field has evolved into its twenty-first-century configurations (Keith 2015, 186–7). During this process, several critics have voiced reservations about analyzing Asian American experiences depicted in literature by relying too heavily on frameworks of interethnic comparison or cross-referencing. For example, Viet Thanh Nguyen warns: "The fiction of ethnic equivalence that forms the foundation of interethnicity must be disposed of in order for us to more clearly understand Asian America as a hegemonic construction, built in response to the dynamics of racial formation, and complicit in reproducing racial formation's management of power through an inadequate representative categorization that ignores issues of domination, rivalry, antagonism, and inequality" (Nguyen 1998, 239). Jinqi Ling highlights the affinity of the interethnic approach to the "reductive interpretive procedure of homology, or structural parallelism" as a key ingredient in the French philosopher Lucien Goldmann's structuralist Marxism. He suggests that this method, in its "attempt to construct discursive relationality among disparate literary works linked by their comparable *mentalité*," does little more than "relegate the significance of individual literary works and their respective traditions to a secondary rung of the unifying structure" assumed by the critic. He cautions that this comparative method may end up "reproducing, through its emphasis on the exteriority of literature, the functionalist bias of structuralism" (Ling 2012, 27). To a certain degree, the views of Nguyen and Ling resonate with an observation articulated by Colleen Lye about "the limits of the notion of parallel minoritization," which she considers typified in Claire Jean Kim's theory of "racial triangulation of Asian Americans."

Kim's theoretical model, simply put, pivots on a distinction that she draws between the racializing processes experienced by Asian and African Americans respectively; that is, the former's suffering from "civic ostracism" and the latter's experiencing "relative devalorization" (Kim 1999, 105–38). This interpretation, Lye argues, problematically designates "Asian ostracism as deriving from a white supremacist ideology that had already been put in place by the contradictions of a slave republic," hence preventing effective conceptualization of Asian American politics because of the community's relegation to "a second order racism" (Lye 2008a, 1733–4).

Rethinking Asian American Specificity

The interethnic or interracial tensions or antagonisms insufficiently registered through the application of comparative paradigms are the focus of several studies during the past two decades. For example, Daniel Kim observes that both Ralph Allison and Frank Chin have a tendency to privilege virility as an effective mode of combatting racism that brings about "'the castration' of men of color." In focusing on this aspect of the Afro-Asian interaction, Kim underscores "a complex competitiveness" between Allison's conception of "American Negro" nationalism informed by "latent orientalism" and Chin's uncritical borrowing from Black-authored texts to fashion an Asian American version of cultural nationalism in masculinist terms. What Kim reveals through such an analysis is "interracial antagonism rather than solidarity" at the core of Afro-Asian alliances (Kim 2005, xvii–xix). Julia Lee's discussion of the "reciprocal representations" in early Asian American and African American texts is similarly suggestive of the "incredible diversity and surprising ambivalence" of these interracial dynamics. Commenting on the goals of her 2011 monograph *Interracial Encounters*, she states: "I ask what kinds of Afro-Asian representations emerged in light of the shifting levels of economic exploitation, physical violence, and political exclusion from the nation's imagined community that each group endured in the early twentieth century. In other words, Afro-Asian representations are informed by the specific discourses that the early twentieth century's national anxieties surrounding citizenship and global relations produced" (Lee 2011, 3–4).

Still another example along the line is David Palumbo-Liu's interpretation of Jean-Marc Giroux's photo of Koreatown during the 1992 Los Angeles riots. Commenting on the hierarchy of interethnic presences in the image captured by the photo, he observes that

> an Asian body occupies the foreground in the narrative; blacks are present as second-level images (Malcolm X on the t-shirt). Whites, however, are invisible, ... Thus, what is missing in the narrative implicated by this photo/text is any inquiry into the structure of an economic system that historically has placed Asians against blacks and Latinos, and exploits that antagonism in order to construct a displaced rehearsal of a simplified white/black, purely "racial" antagonism. To begin to account for this elision of whites and the restaging of race relations without whites (but nonetheless containing the *function* of a white supremacist ideology channeled through the historically convenient body of Asian America), one must understand the continuity of the function of Asian Americans in the recent U.S. imaginary. (Palumbo-Liu 1999, 185–6)

What the perspectives of Kim, Lee, and Palumbo-Liu serve to foreground is the racially defined socio-structural relations that pit people of color against one another in the United States. They also evoke a position adhered to by E. San Juan who has long argued that "the schematics of race and its use to ascribe values, allocate resources, and legitimize the social position/ status of racially defined populations (in short, racism) centrally affect the constitution of factions of black, Asian, or Hispanic labor as a class." He therefore cautions against "the banal pragmatic-instrumentalist humanism" characterizing "the dominant paradigm in mainstream comparative cultural studies," one that "preaches that we are all the same and can all partake of the wealth of the transnational boutiques" (San Juan 1992, 47–8, 108–9). San Juan's comments, though made from a different critical locus—and primarily concerned with promoting coordinated collective struggles by all people of color in the United States—provides an associative context for clarifying the diverse Asian American positionalities surveyed in this section of the chapter, namely, how to restore a sense of specificity for contemporary Asian American literary studies as a collective project, which seems at the present moment on the verge of losing its binding force under the pressures of various multicultural and comparative initiatives. Two book-length studies of Asian American literature have stood out for their contrasting responses to this pressing Asian American concern: Christopher Lee's *The Semblance of Identity: Aesthetic Mediation in Asian American Literature* (2012) and

Colleen Lye's *America's Asia: Racial Form and American Literature, 1893–1945* (2005).

The former uses Theodore Adorno's post-identity concept of "semblance"—a fiction of reality construed through the introspective logic of modernist aesthetics in the form of montage, pastiche, parataxis, or parody—to suggest a symbolic solution to the field's disciplinary contradictions. He suggests that the field's "subject [formation], however exhausted or embattled, might finally be reanimated in a reconciled future" as a "Utopian promise" (Lee 2012, 144). Lee's reliance on a little historicized modernist moment—that is, Adorno's aesthetic retreat from engagement with the diachronic function of literary artistry during the realism debate of the 1930s—in tackling the practical issue of the operability of the field as an academic discipline is an inadequate move in that it displaces such a practical concern into the speculative realm of lag, deferral, or future reconciliation, hence inadvertently evading the identity question that he raises with a degree of urgency. By comparison, Colleen Lye's 2005 monograph is both more focused and more effective in its rethinking of the mission of the field that appears diffused, rather than consolidated, by its growing awareness of methodological intersections or possibilities. She states in the introduction of her book:

> A historical approach to racial representation has the advantage of being able to account for the specificities of different marginalized groups, whose stereotypical attributes are located in the shifting dynamics of social relations and social conflicts. A historical approach also helps us to maintain a healthy skepticism toward the "evidence of experience" and toward the temptation to think that the articulation of minority subjectivity can be separated from the history of racialization or can express an independent rejoinder to it. At the risk of ignoring new social history's call to document subaltern experience and agency, this book returns to the study of racism and power of racialization efforts. (Lye 2005, 4)

Lye's emphasis on the importance of using a historical approach to investigate Asian American subject formation in the larger contexts of Asians' racialization brings into focus a key argument that she makes in her monograph, that is, how "Asiatic racial form" gains its shape and negatively affects the lives of Asian Americans under specific and specifiable socioeconomic conditions. Conceptualized to show the range and pattern of Western hegemonic constructions of Asia in the shifting dynamics of the global marketplace, this concept promises multiple lines of inquiry and heralds a wide range of critical outcomes. Within the context of the discussion here, it performs a uniquely strategic function of reviving the current state of Asian American literary studies, whose growing reliance on comparative methods as a privileged way of envisioning and gauging contemporary development of Asian American studies seems to have contributed to de-emphasis, rather than enhancement, of the social and historical relevance of the field. This is precisely where Iyko Day finds Lye's concept of "Asiatic racial form" working at its best. She observes that this concept shows why an "Asian American analogical dependence" on an examination of anti-blackness (Lye's words) is inadequate for theorizing the racial formation of Asian Americans. For such analogical dependence "constrains our ability to elaborate the specificity of Asian racialization that isn't merely a by-product of a foundational antiblackness" and it "fails to clarify the way contemporary expressions of political liberalism and white supremacy seem to diverge so starkly from those of the late nineteenth-century," thus leaving unanswered the question of whether contemporary "Asian American mobility confirms the persistent power of white privilege or whether it represents the detachment of whiteness's symbolic power from material power" (Day 2016, 23).

This chapter has surveyed a range of critical opinions on the internal complexity, the historical role, and the obvious limitations of the cultural nationalist period in Asian American literary studies. It has also examined two contemporary versions of Asian American coalitional politics informed by postmodern imaginaries—a California-based pan-Asian ethnicity (or a new historical block) model and an interethnic/interracial paradigm indebted to comparative studies—both premised on anti-essentialist principles and developed in rejection of *Aiiieeeee!*'s race- and class-based identity politics. One perspective emerging from the survey of this chapter involves assessments the field's shift from its adherence to the legacies of cultural nationalism to the associative politics of post-nationality as a negotiated and long-drawn process, during which the *Aiiieeeee!* moment is shown to be an imperfect antithesis to, rather than a passive copy of, the ideologies of American nativity and bourgeois nationalism. The last subsection of this chapter reviews recent scholarship that offers nuanced readings of race and class relations described in Asian American literature, with an emphasis on the specific histories, conditions, and inner logics of the field as a minoritarian formation both embedded in and distinct from other ethnic literary discourses in the United States. To provide a sense of how and why Asian American literature came into being in the first place, Chapter 3 will look into its diasporic/immigrant roots, multicultural and multilingual practices, generational dynamics, and growing pains.

CHAPTER 3
INTERCULTURAL AND GENERATIONAL CONCERNS

In several essays published during the first half of the 1990s, Sau-ling Wong comments extensively on the historical role of Asian immigrant writing (especially its non-Anglophone productions) from a bicultural or comparative perspective, reacting to what she sees as a growing marginalization of this type of literary output in the field. Noteworthy in this process is her characterization of immigrant writing as a phenomenon closely associated with the work of "first-generation" writers, who, upon "arriving in the United States in adulthood, possess an already well-formed sense of self that, even under challenge by a new environment, allows them to envision full, adult participation in society." Based on this observation, she suggests that the cultural memory, artistic drive, language use, and angle of representation in immigrant writing starkly differ from those shaping the literary imaginaries of American-born Asian writers (Wong 1992, 123–4). Wong's reflections on Asian immigrant literature pave the way for this chapter's survey, while they also contextualize several premises basic to the discussions to follow. First, we can assume that Asian immigrants who arrive in the United States as children and undergo the pressures of assimilation share more with American-born Asians in terms of psychic structure and social value than with their immigrant parents. Second, serious examination of immigrant literature—often written with Asian ethos and non-Western values—would require a level of bilingual and cross-cultural proficiency that, with few exceptions, is generally unavailable to American-born or American-reared generations of Asians. Thus, King-Kok Cheung considers it less likely for American-born Asians to truly "avail themselves of a diasporic identity" (Cheung 1997, 9). Third, the peripheral status of immigrant writing in contemporary Asian American literary criticism seems to show the extent to which the agendas of the field are being shaped by the concerns of American-born and American-reared scholars, who tend to see immigrant writing, as Wong points out, as "less than fully

American" and hence less effective in addressing urgent concerns faced by the profession (Wong 1991a, 142). Margaret Hillenbrand, a Sinologist who advocates for greater attention to the non-Anglophone literature written in Sinic languages, provides a list of complaints often lodged against immigrant writing by US-born or US-reared scholars, as follows: its propensity to enact "textual retreat" to homeland politics, its "ethnocentric" or "chauvinist" undertone, its tendency to generalize about American society, or its resort to rhetorics of "xenophobia" when challenged (Hillenbrand 2013, 49).

Writing Immigrants

Despite the marginal status of immigrant writing in recent Asian American literary studies, aspects of it—such as the Angel Island poems inscribed on the barrack walls of the immigration detention station at the San Francisco Bay (1910–1940)—are enduring legacies to the field. This is an area of research conducted by the historian Him Mark Lai who, in collaboration with Jenny Lim and Judy Yung, has resurrected, annotated, and translated these Chinese-language poems as the first material evidence of the "pioneering spirit," "vitality," and "indomitability" of the early Chinese immigrants in the United States (Lai, Lim, and Yung 1980, 8, 27–8). Commenting on the significance of the recovered Angel Island poems, the historian John Kuo Wei Tchen describes the efforts made by Lai and his colleagues as constituting a "Herculean" feat of global proportion, which, in his view, is tantamount to "chipping away the consequences of exclusion and limitations imposed on Chinese Americans," and laying the foundation for a new field of study amid "the shaky relations between China and the United States" during the Cold War (Tchen 2011, vii–xi). Since the early 1990s, there has been a growing interest among Asian American literary scholars to explore the historicity and textual substance of these poems, especially by paying attention to three aspects of their meaning making: the material conditions of their inscription, the bicultural nuances of their encoding, and the aesthetic innovations attempted by their anonymous authors. Exemplifying such efforts are several essay-length analyses: such as Sau-ling Wong's "The Politics and Poetics of Folksong Reading: Literary Portrayals of Life under Exclusion" (1991b); Cynthia Wong's "Anonymity and Self-Laceration in Early Twentieth Century Chinese Immigrant Writing" (1999); aspects of Xiao-Huang Yin's 2000 monograph *Chinese American Literature since the 1850s* (2000, 35–42); Yunte Huang's "Angel Island and the Poetics of Error"

(2009); and Shelley Wong's "'I Seek Out Poems Now Incomplete': Writing from the Angel Island" (2014).

Karl Lo, a former librarian of East Asian Studies, pioneered the research on Chinese vernacular presses run by prominent intellectual exiles in North America and Hawaii during the first half of the twentieth century, as well as their influences on how Chinese Americans viewed themselves in relation to their ancestral land at the time (Lo 1984, 172, 176). This line of inquiry has been significantly expanded in recent studies of the Chinese immigrant writers publishing in English, such as Yan Phou Lee and Yung Wing who produced the earliest book-length Chinese American autobiographies in the United States during the late nineteenth century (Cheung 2005, 24–40); of Lin Yutang who wrote extensively—as an essayist, linguist, and non-fiction writer—about the turbulent Sino-American relations since the First World War (Zhou 2014, 57–93; So 2016, 122–65); and of Chiang Yee, the Chinese painter and travel book writer residing as an exile in Britain and the United States from the 1930s to the 1970s (Zheng 2010). Marlon Hom initiates the study of Chinatown-based bilingual literary production by focusing on two aspects of its early activities: the development of Cantonese folk rhymes in the late nineteenth and early twentieth centuries, and the Chinese-language immigrant writing that flourished in the 1930s and the 1940s (Hom 1982, 75–6, 87–8; Wong 1988). The latter dimension of Hom's research has been revived, both thematically and in analytical method, through recent scholarly attention to writings that appeal to the bilingual readers in Taiwan, mainland China, and the United States. This emerging literary interactivity across the Pacific, according to Wen Jin, witnesses not only increased dialogues between the three reading communities, but also ideological tensions among them, such as that over the selection, evaluation, translation, or dissemination of texts, because of the existence of divergent academic politics (Jin 2006, 572).

Scholars in the field generally locate the inaugural moment of Japanese immigrant literature in the decade of the 1890s, when Sadakichi Hartmann and Yone Noguchi published experimental poems written in English in New York City. This turn-of-the-century burst of Japanese poetic energy in urban America has generated considerable interests among recent scholars who see the phenomenon as symptomatic of Asian American writers' participation in a nascent American literary modernism (Park 2008, 96–7). Following this brief experimental phase in early Japanese immigrant writing in English is the extensive creative activity carried out by Japanese immigrants who settled in the American Pacific West from the 1920s to the 1930s. During this period, *issei* formed groups to write *haiku* and *senryu* in Japanese; *nisei* published poems in English through community-based bilingual or English-language literary magazines (such as *Reimei* and *Leaves)*. According to Traise Yamamoto, this pre-Second-World-War formation of a Japanese American literary discourse, though disrupted by the internment of Japanese Americans from 1942 to 1945, did not entirely vanish. Instead, *nisei* writers continued to practice their craft by composing stories and poems for various camp publications (such as *Trek*, the *Poston Chronicle*, the *Manzanar Free Press*, and *All Aboard*), and, after the war, publishing them in the English sections of community-based Japanese-language newspapers (such as *Rafu Shimpo, Ho Kubei Mainchi, the Pacific Citizen*, and *Crossroads*), although little of this writing circulated in the wider public sphere before the 1970s (Yamamoto 1999, 198–9).[1] The maturation of Japanese American political consciousness during the war, as Garrett Hongo suggests, anticipates a "fervent time" for Japanese American literary productivity in the 1970s and the 1980s (Hongo 1993, xxvii), which culminates in the publication of numerous recovered or newly written narratives or poems with an explicit intercultural or generational focus. Such writings include Toshio Mori's *Yokohama, California* ([1949] 1985); Monica Sone's *Nisei Daughter* ([1953] 1979); John Okada's *No-No Boy* ([1957] 1974); Milton Murayama's *All I Asking for Is My Body* ([1959] 1975); Mitsuye Yamada's *Camp Notes and Other Writings* (1976); Janice Mirikitani's *Awake in the River* (1978); Garrett Hongo's *Yellow Light* (1982); and, somewhat belatedly, Lawson Inada's *Legends from Camp* (1992).

Korean immigrant literature gains its shape through two substantial efforts to trace its origins and map its subsequent developments: one by Sammy Edward Solberg (S. E. Solberg) and the other by Kun Jong Lee. The former situates this literature's rise in the 1920s along narrative and poetic tracks, while designating its practice as "firmly rooted in the Korean immigrant experience." According to Solberg, Korean immigrant narrative—pioneered by Sö Chae-p'il, Il-Han New, and Younghill Kang—culminates in Ronyoung Kim's 1987 novel *Clay Walls*, and Korean immigrant poetry—begun with the works of Jaihium Kim, Ko Won, and Chungmi Kim—peaks in Theresa Cha's *Dictée* (1982) and Cathy Song's *Picture Bride* (1983). One shortcoming in Solberg's study is that it mainly focuses on Korean immigrant writing in English (often through available translations) and the literary production of the US-born generations of Koreans, to the neglect of Korean-language immigrant writing, except for a cursory reference to *Ulim* (*The Echo*) and *Munhak Segye* (*The Literary Realm*), two bilingual literary journals operating in Southern California during the 1960s and the 1970s (Solberg 1988, 20, 22). Kun Jong Lee's 2008 review of Korean-language American literature is in this sense an important effort to fill the gap in Solberg's study. Of the various findings presented in Lee's review, the following are significant: first, he pinpoints "A Song in Commemoration of the Establishment of the Public Association," published in *The United Koreans* in 1906, as the first Korean-language weekly in the continental United States. This newspaper, observes Lee, played a prominent role in disseminating nationalist ideologies among political exiles or in soliciting contributions from immigrant writers who submitted short lyrics, prose, fiction, poems, Christian hymns, translated work, and folk songs/ballads during Japan's occupation of Korea (1905–45). Second is the continuation of this tradition among Korean immigrants to the United States in the post-1965 period, when an increasing number of immigrant literary societies have been established through regional and national networks. Lee considers Korea-based scholars specializing in the study of Korean-language American writing contributing most substantially to a broadening of the purview of Korean American literature from a unique Korean perspective, and to "the renaissance of Korean-language [American] literature in the second half of the twentieth century" (Lee 2008b, 16–22).

Oscar Campomanes's 1992 essay "Filipinos in the United States and Their Literature of Exile" provides by far the most comprehensive review of Filipino American literature since Kai-yu Hsu and Helen Palubinskas include excerpts of early Filipino/Filipino American writing in their 1972 anthology *Asian-American Authors*.[2] In this essay, Campomanes characterizes Filipino American literature as fundamentally shaped by its authors' "exilic experience and perspective, exilic identity and language, and exilic sensibility and attitude toward history and place," in contrast to "the immigrant ethos" that animates the majority of mainstream Asian immigrant writing. Tracing Filipino American literature to its formative years, he reports: "There is the pioneering generation consisting of Bienvenido Santos, N.V. M. Gonzalez, Jose Garcia Villa, and Carlos Bulosan for the period of the 1930s to the 1950s; a settled generation that matures and emerges, after Penaranda, Tagatac, and Syquia, may be called the 'Filips' [Filipino Americans raised in the U.S.]; and the politically expatriated generation of Epifanio San Juan, Linda Ty-Casper, Ninotchka Rosca, and Michelle Skinner from the 1970s to the present." Campomanes observes: "Nearly all the emergent writers are women [such as Ty-Casper, Rosca, and Skinner], and this amplitude of women writing is a development observable for the emergent literatures in the United States and postcolonial world" generally (Campomanes 1992, 55–6, 70). Several studies published since then have supplemented Campomanes's mapping of early Filipino American literary history. For example, Augusto Espiritu offers a perspective on the formative years of N. V. M. Gonzalez's creative career as a period marked by the author's commitment to constructing an "allegory of decolonization" (Espiritu 1998); Darlene Rodriguez details Al Robles's community-based poetic networking, by which the poet weaves together immigrant ethos, American-born sensibility, and the internationalist spirit of the 1960s and 1970s (Rodriguez 2000a); and E. San Juan interprets Philip Vera Cruz's life history as an immanent coming into being of an imaginary of "the power of the multitude" and "productive cooperation" of "associate labor" (San Juan [1995] 1996, 137).[3]

The existing scholarship on South Asian immigrant writing has been predominantly concerned with its production in English, despite the fact that this literature is continually written in the native tongues of India, Pakistan, Sri Lanka, the Maldives, Bhutan, and Nepal. Katu Katrak offers a rationale for this linguistic preference in US-based South Asian American literary studies, stating: "One advantage of studying only English language writers" is that such an emphasis would provide a sense of "the cohesiveness of language, literary forms, and thematic concerns" for a discourse fragmented by its internally diverse articulations of the "loss of a homeland," its bewildering "uses of memory and indigenous folklore as sustaining mechanisms in alien environments," and its variegated expression of desires for "reconciliation and hope in creating new spaces of belonging" (Katrak 1996, 122–3). South Asian American literature started to make an impact on North American literary scenes in the late 1980s, a rise to prominence anticipated by two waves of South Asian immigration to North America: one in the late nineteenth century and early twentieth century, and the other since 1965. Closely associated with such visibility are the works of Bharati Mukherjee, Michael Ondaatje, Sorab homi Fracis, and Jhumpa Lahiri, to name only a few representative figures. Commenting on the designation of English as the primary language for South Asian American literature from a different standpoint, Asha Nadkarni calls attention to an implicit "Indian hegemony" in the South Asian community and its "tendency to erase the ethnic, religious, and national diversities" among South Asian American populations. She argues that South Asian American texts "do not simply represent the sites of the North American diaspora as one's of hybridized possibility." They also reflect the power dynamics that shape "the triangulation of U.S. and British empires," as well as the operation of US neoliberalism and state power, hence "the imbrication of the domestic and the global" as an ever-present thread of South Asian American literary productions (Nadkarni 2015, 356, 360).

Since the mid-1990s, the bicultural emergence and evolution of Southeast Asian American literature has been a most salient aspect of the field's growth. Monique Truong, the novelist and the critic, has played a pivotal role in bringing two strands of first-generation Vietnamese-language writing to public awareness: its pre-1975 phase of immigrant literature marked by a preference for "orally communicated" narrative forms (such as folklore and song lyrics); and its post-1975 phase of refugee literature distinguished for its testimonial forms employed to enhance the writer's "dual role as survivor and storyteller" (Truong 1993, 28–9, 31–40; Nguyen 2013, 146; Janette 2003). Anh Thang Dao-Shan and Isabelle Thuy Pelaud provide an additional perspective on Vietnamese refugee writing, which they consider simultaneously promoting "alternative memories" in exile so that they can relate to the conditions of displacement undergone by "other people of color" in the United States (Dao-Shan and Pelaud 2015, 470–1). In this process, several scholars emphasize the conditions of Southeast Asian refugee literary production, which, they point out, often involve mainstream culture's misrepresentation of the consequences of the American war in Southeast Asia or the nature of the communist violence and genocide in countries such as Cambodia during the 1970s. Along this line, Sody Lay cautions that the Cambodian refugee tragedy "not be unearthed, butchered, and put back together like some kind of literary Frankenstein" (Lay 2001, 182). Louisa Schein and Va-Megn Thoj also contend that "the collective [American official] effort to forget the many culpabilities of the United States in the Southeast Asian wars" is turning Hmong and Laotian Americans into an "anathema of identity signifiers" (Schein and Thoj 2008, 1756). It is from this perspective that Cathy Schlund-Vials emphatically argues: "Cambodian, Lao, and Hmong American authors render visible the cause-and-effect relationship between the Cold War, the Vietnam War, and discernible 'refugee-ness,'" which marks a "Southeast Asian American artistic mode" as "refugee aesthetics" (Schlund-Vials 2015, 486).

Cultural Translation

The multilingual origins and ongoing investments of Asian immigrant writing not only mark this body of literature as inherently diasporic, but also represent an essential aspect of its ideological reproduction in largely

Eurocentric cultural environments. Presupposed in this observation is the role played by the Asian American critic as one uniquely positioned to provide informed translation of non-Western cultural idioms used in such texts into their English equivalents, so that the cross-cultural nuances of the former could appeal to, rather than alienate, readers dependent on the latter in accessing their meaning and significance. In this context, Stella Bolaki's working definition of cultural translation—which is formulated from her reading of Maxine Hong Kingston's *The Woman Warrior*—seems speaking more or less directly to the concerns foregrounded in the survey of this subsection. She observes: "Translation allows a form of mobility that is bound by debt to the 'original,' and that at the same time is enriched by coming into contact with another idiom or culture; therefore it can open the way for new configurations and constructions of American identity that makes room for creative fusion that does not destroy difference" (Bolaki 2009, 40). From a writerly point of view, Shirley Lim further suggests, also in reference to the bicultural contents and allusions in *The Woman Warrior*: "The linguistic survival of first language expressions, whether actual or translated into English," indicates the writer's "awareness that there exists in the original language itself certain values, concepts, and cultural traits which are discoverable in English" under conditions of immigration or acculturation (Lim 1987, 54; Lim 1993b, 578).

Stephen Yao, a practitioner of bicultural poetic studies, attaches strategic importance to such "discoverable" cultural traits in Chinese immigrant writing, convinced that they have become indispensable to the renewal of Asian American literary reproduction in the age of increased global migration and border-crossing. For him, this

> approach to "Asian American literature" … not only takes into account the substantive differences among the various distinct linguistic and cultural traditions underlying the category of "Asian American," but … also seeks to explain how the specificities constituting those differences help to shape the parameters, dynamics, and significance of literary production by people of Asian descent in the United States under evolving conditions of its production and reception. (Yao 2010, 8)

Such awareness of being in possession of an intellectual tool for addressing the cognitive limits of Anglo-American linguistic traditions or cultural imaginaries was an important catalyst for a period of unprecedented growth in Asian American literary scholarship from the early 1980s to the mid-1990s. In this process, two intracultural idioms—"talk-story" and "silence"—generated wide appeals among readers of Asian American literature, whose enthusiastic responses to them lead to highly innovative work.

According to Wendy Ho, "talk-story" has two origins: it is traceable, on the one hand, to the Cantonese folk tradition in rural China and, on the other, to the local oral traditions in Hawaii. Ho considers this orally mediated narrative device crucial to early feminist recovery of submerged histories embedded in other time frames because it creates bonding between the immigrant mother and her American-born daughter (as is the case with the writings of Maxine Hong Kingston, Amy Tan, and Fae Ng). At the same time, she also takes note of the confounding effects that this narrative strategy may produce on readers differently predisposed in American culture, politics, and ethnic relationships (Ho 1999, 27–8, 35–42; Ho 1991). This ambiguous aspect of the mother-daughter bonding is the focus of numerous studies that explore the doubleness of telling and layered listening in woman-centered bicultural literary analyses. Beyond the formulaic mother–daughter relationship basic to talk-story as a stock device in feminist Asian American narratives, this rhetorical instrument can be found also at work in writings that thematize colonial bondage, ethnic genocide, social movement, or war memory, such as Wendy Law-Yone's *The Coffin Tree* (1987); Gary Pak's *A Ricepaper Airplane* (1998); Kao Lalia Yang's *The Latehomecomer: A Hmong Family Memoir* (2008); and Karen Tei Yamashita's *I-Hotel* (2010).

"Silence" is a semantically complex metaphor with multiple implications and diverse contextual overtones. One type of silence (such as that evoked in the works of Marilyn Chin, Garrett Hongo, Li-Young Lee, and David Mura) often connotes self-prohibition imposed by family members of the Second World War generations seeking "survival in a hostile environment." Such silence, according to these writers, not only "robs sons and daughters of a knowledge of their own history and origins," but also gets "passed on from one generation to the next," thus placing the families "in a void of cultures, where they can feel paralyzed by an inexplicable shame and guilt" (Slowik 2000, 221–3). From this perspective, Stan Yogi argues: "*Nisei* silence about significant events in their lives would leave their *sansei* children without a complete sense of self-understanding," a gap tantamount to "collective social amnesia" that must be rectified (Yogi 1996, 245–6). Approaching silence from a broader bicultural perspective, King-Kok Cheung is reluctant to see it as an unambiguous sign for deprivation. Instead, she considers it more suggestive of cross-cultural wisdom that favors "non-verbal communication and indirect speech," in contrast to verbal assertion or expressive immediacy core to Western cultural conventions. Therefore, she believes that silence can also be articulate, especially in the writings by Asian American women, whose deliberately executed "textual ellipses, non-verbal gestures, authorial hesitations" constitute a feminist "art" of "reticence" (Cheung 1993, 4, 28). Cheung's reworking of the meaning and implication of silence has led to further practices among scholars working on Asian American women's texts, such as reading inarticulation as a form of authorial disguise or self-masking (Yamamoto 1999, 151–2); interpreting voicelessness as "the language of trauma" (Hill 2003, 150–4); comprehending quietness as an expression of female anxiety (Schueller 1989, 423); and redefining gossip (*chismis* in Tagalog) as a socially denigrated speech act subversive to the gender hierarchies under colonial or neocolonial conditions (Grice 2004, 183–4, 193).

Bicultural representation or interpretation of Asian male sexuality constitutes a particularly suggestive aspect of the recent work on intracultural translation, because this concern remains inadequately theorized by scholars who rely on Western analytical methods in making sense of perceived Asian males' emasculation or feminization in the United States context. Sau-ling Wong's comparative approach to this issue is eye-opening. She observes:

> When we cross cultural boundaries, the provisionality of previously naturalized, smoothly functioning categories [of race, gender, and sexuality] becomes suddenly visible. ... In Chinese immigrant writing, ... the meaning of sexuality is rich and fluid. At once irreducibly private, intensely communicative, and fraught with public implications, sexuality is invoked and endlessly modulated by writers to enact a number of conflicts between private tendencies and social influences—conflicts not peculiar to immigrants but certainly exacerbated by their precarious economic and cultural situation. If any single "idea" about sexuality emerges as central in these fictional couplings and uncouplings, it is that heterosexual fulfilment free of demeaning compromises signals an idealized state of fullness of being—ethnic dignity without practical failure, power without callousness, self-actualization without social irresponsibility—which seems to be the end point of the immigrant's recentering efforts. (Wong 1992, 111, 113)

Within the context of Wong's critique of the limitations of Western definition of male sexuality, King-Kok Cheung makes a somewhat different move. She uses the *"shusheng"* (a male poet scholar) figure depicted in many Chinese literary or theatrical classics as a model for refashioning Asian American masculinity from "both cultural nationalist and feminist standpoints." She suggests: "He is seductive because of his gentle demeanor, wit, and poetic or artistic sensibility; he prides himself on being indifferent to wealth and political power and seeks women and men who are his equals in intelligence and integrity. Such a model not only counters the cultural invisibility of Asian Americans but offers a mode of conduct that breaks down the putative dichotomy of gay and straight behavior" (Cheung 2000a, 264).

Notable efforts to apply techniques of cultural translation can also be identified in Cheng Lok Chua's reading of Chinese herbal tea as a symbol of reviving male potency in Louis Chu's 1961 novel *Eat a Bowl of Tea* (Chua 1982, 45); Juliana Chang's formulation of an "interlingual poetics" that alters "the shape and sounds of dominant languages" (Chang 1996, 93–4); Mariam Beevi's analysis of the ordeal undergone by the female protagonist in Le Ly Hayslip's *When Heaven and Earth Changed Places* as a parallel to that in Nguyen Du's *The Tale of Kieu* (Beevi 1997, 27–36); Walter Lew's interpretation of Younghill Kang's *East Goes West* in terms of the author's translation of Korean cultural idioms into the American vernacular of the 1930s (Lew 2001, 171–90); and Josephine Nock-Hee Park's theorization of how the vision and tonality of Myung Mi Kim's modernist poetry gains its "ordering logic" from Korean diction and ethos (Park 2006, 235–6). A somewhat contentious issue emerging out of this process concerns the extent to which non-Anglophone languages should be emphasized in assessing the field's early and recent literary productions. Shu-mei Shih, for example, urges that American literature written in Sinitic script (whether based on Mandarin, Cantonese, or Minnan dialect) be granted a status equal to that of American literature written in English, against two competing cultural homogenies that she considers working to marginalize Sinophone literature: that of US-centrism and that of China-oriented Han-centrism (Shih 2014, 330–1). Steven Yao, who has done significant work on bicultural criticism, chooses instead the English language as a basic tool for conducting this type of research in the US context, under the assumption that English would allow "a linguistically informed examination" of the subjects under study and a realistic sense of what can be accomplished in a predominantly Anglophone environment (Yao 2010, 7, 9). Reflecting on the prospect that English-language readers would remain the majority audience for Asian American literature in North America, Christopher Lee reminds cross-cultural translators that, in attempting "to render multilingual realities into an English-language literary form," they must constantly negotiate the tensions between the demands of Anglophone literary conventions and audience expectations, and the different values and motives that shape the Asian imaginaries or linguistic idioms rooted in other time frames (Lee 2015, 129–31).[4]

Model Minority and the Paradox of Assimilation

Beyond the imperative of cross-cultural negotiation in the textual domain, a social issue that frequently confronts Asian American scholars and demands their critical response is mainstream society's habitual misrepresentation of their ethnic community as a model minority—an ironic reversal of the older yellow peril stereotype often assigned to their immigrant forebears. Robert Lee traces the origin of these rotating Asian stereotypes in the American popular imagination to several political measures taken by the US state to contain perceived domestic threats in the early phase of the Cold War: a "Red Menace" from unionized activities, a "Black Menace" from civil rights struggles, and a "White Menace" from the alienated middle-class suburbia. Lee emphasizes that by not directly targeting Asian Americans, these measures implicitly single out Asians as a recognizably traditional, apolitical, and self-reliant ethnic group, thereby creating the false impression that they were somehow exempt from America's social, economic, and cultural subjugations (Lee 1999, 145–61).

The film critic Peter Feng probes into the underlying logic of such elevation of Asians to an "honorary white status" in a period of heightened racial tensions in the United States, suggesting that behind the creation of the model minority stereotype is a calculated attempt at "attributing economic successes and failures to cultural factors and thus denying the existence of structural inequities that systematically disfranchise people of color" in America's capitalist system (Feng 2002, 2). This is the context in which Yoonmee Chang forcefully argues that

the core of the myth is the belief that Asian Americans possess unique, productive cultural values and ethics, such as of hard work, devotion to family, and commitment to education, that distinguish them as a race. This racial distinction makes them a group that distinctively does not suffer under class inequity but readily, and inherently, transcends it. The linear relationship between race and class inequity, that being racially different has negative class effects, is derailed for Asian Americans. For Asian Americans the conventional relationship between race and class inequity is inverted. (Chang 2010, 5)

A key factor that contributes to such an inversion of the traditionally understood relationship between race and class inequity in the United States is the die-hard yellow peril stereotype that characterizes Asians as inscrutable, sneaky, and secretive. This underside of the model minority myth, observes Peter Feng, is chiefly responsible for Asian Americans' being made to serve as a routine outlet for "resentment from both white 'haves' and non-white 'have-nots,' as evidenced in the widespread destruction of Korean American stores in the L.A. Riots" (Feng 2002, 2).

A particularly traumatizing result of such workings of the model minority stereotype is that Asian Americans—members of the American-born, American-reared generations in particular—find themselves often confronted with two irreconcilable realities: their full awareness of the unquestionable nature of their participation in American cultural norms, and their constant reminder of the impossibility of their full acceptance by the country of their birth because of their Asiatic backgrounds. Commenting on this paradox from a personal perspective, David Palumbo-Liu observes that the model minority stereotype imposes a "double duty" of "assimilation" on generations of Asian Americans like himself, for it is "producing a subject who has those 'memories' implanted in his or her psyche, and yet those memories, dispositions, intuitions serve only to remind him or her of the gap that lies between them and those memories—in other words, of their borrowed, not shared, nature" (Palumbo-Liu 1999, 300). Yoon Sun Lee echoes Palumbo-Liu's sentiment by underscore a related irony, that is, although Asian Americans are rarely referred to as people of color in the United States, they are at the same time "too colored to be counted among the European ethnic immigrant groups. … Both exotic and banal, familiar and foreign, neither reliably racial nor merely ethnic, their position relative to the material and ideological bases of American ordinariness continues to shift in response to national and global exigencies" (Lee 2013, 4).

Thus, Anne Cheng argues that the racial grief felt by Asian Americans is not only a result of explicit or implicit racism toward them in the public domain, but also a psychic condition for them to imagine subject formation as a personal experience. Behind this "diligent system of melancholic retention" that assumes both material and immaterial forms, she emphasizes, is the operation of America's racial state whose instrumentality "appears in different guises. Both racist and white liberal discourses participate in this dynamic, albeit out of different motivations. The racists need to develop elaborate ideologies in order to accommodate their actions with official American ideals, while liberals need to keep burying the racial others in order to memorialize them" (Cheng 2000, 4, 6, 11). David Eng and Shinhee Han approach the question of racial melancholia by linking its effect to the conditions that lead to disability and mental health, in recognition of "the disturbing patterns of depression" among "a significant and growing number of Asian American students" with whom they interact on a regular basis. They suggest that the students who undergo such experiences suffer two kinds of losses: a "loss of whiteness as an ideal structuring the assimilation and racialization processes of Asian Americans," and a simultaneous loss of "identification and affiliation with 'original' Asian cultures." Eng and Han describe the sentiments voiced by these students as a "politics of mourning." They reflect:

If the losses suffered by the first generation are not resolved and mourned in the process of assimilation … then the melancholia that ensues from this condition can be transferred to the second generation. … If so, mourning and melancholia are re-enacted and lived out by their children in their own attempts to assimilate and to negotiate the American Dream. Here, immigration and assimilation might be said to characterize a process involving not just mourning or melancholia but intergenerational negotiation between mourning *and* melancholia. (Eng and Han 2003, 343–4, 352–3)

Noteworthy in this process is Tina Chen's 2005 monograph *Double Agency: Acts of Impersonation in Asian American Literature and Culture*, which is explicitly focused on scenarios associated with the underside of the model minority stereotype, that is, the perception of Asians as sneaky, inscrutable, and secretive. In the introduction of her book, Chen states: "Given the pervasive ideas of Asian Americans as somehow never 'American' enough, the very nature of Asian American identity might be thought of as *one that requires one to impersonate fundamentally oneself.*" What Chen intends to show is that the subversive potential of Asian American selfhood may be best realized through a performative reenactment of the inconsistent and contradictory voice of Asian American speaking or interpretive agency (Chen 2005, xvii–xviii). Emblematic of the critical vision that Chen articulates is a chapter in her book that offers a close analysis of the role of "the double agent" in Chang-rae Lee's 1995 novel *Native Speaker,* a case study that has generated a considerable interest among scholars in exploring the dualistic cast of Asian American subjectivity.[5]

Heidi Kim intervenes in Asian American critiques of the model minority myth and its related assimilation problematic in important ways. She urges critics to locate the "specific historic sites of cultural unease or social anxiety" and to demonstrate "how Asian Americans were uniquely affected" by the processes they identify (Kim 2016, 17). Within the purview of this critical investment, Jennifer Ho observes: "Of all the major racial groups in the United States, Asians in America have had to self-consciously transform themselves into Americans. It is not taken for granted that someone with Asian physical features is native to the United States. Instead, Asian Americans experience an ongoing tension of looking 'different' from those deemed to be 'typical American'" (Ho 2005, 3–4). Dorothy Wang links such Asian American predicament to the irony of how the US identity of many Asian Americans is often betrayed by their perfect command of the English language, their native tongue. Wang underscores the fact that her generation of Asian Americans is always under intense pressures to assimilate and prove their "Americanness" through "the imperative to master English," but they are also seen at the same time "as utterly alien to Americanness and to the English language" because of the unchanging "view of them as culturally and linguistically unassimilable." From this perspective, she argues: "Like all groups of minority Americans, Asian Americans have experienced unique forms of racial interpellation in the United States, but unlike other minority groups, 'Orientals,' 'Asiatics,' and 'Asians' in particular came to exemplify a racialized form of constitutive and immutable alienness from what it means to be 'American'" (Wang 2014, 24–8). For David Leiwei Li, what this generationally inflected Asian American dilemma ultimately points to is the triumph of American neoliberal democracy, in which the idea of Asians' US citizenship has become a necessary fiction invented for an "optimal realization of market rationality and individual accountability," hence serving to obscure, rather than expose, the differential treatments given to people of color in the United States (Li 2012, 5).

Breaking the Tradition

Lisa Lowe's 1991 essay "Heterogeneity, Hybridity, and Multiplicity" begins with scenarios from Janice Mirikitani and Lydia Lowe's respective poems, both thematizing their American-born female speakers' attempts at "disruption and distortion of traditional cultural practices." In the first example, a *nisei* daughter resists her *issei* mother's "repressive confinements" of her desire for self-determination to "the tedious practice of diminution" and a mandate for "silences of obedience." In the second, a Chinese American daughter defies her mother's demand for "filial duty" and compliance with familial "stratification among Asian women"—an enforcement of Confucian hierarchy that replicates the structure of capitalist economy subordinating Asian female immigrant subjects (Lowe 1991, 24–5). These scenarios of generational conflict are foregrounded at the beginning of her essay to set the stage for Lowe's feminist critique not so much of the Asian family tradition, against which the American-born daughter rebels, as the linear and binary logic of its ordering principles evocative of the oppressiveness of Asian American cultural nationalism.

Lowe's exhibit is Louis Chu's 1961 novel *Eat a Bowl of Tea*, a family narrative set in New York Chinatown's bachelor society at the start of the Cold War. The gist of Lowe's argument is that Chu's novel exemplifies a "masculinist generational symbolism, in which a conflict between nativism and assimilation is allegorized in the relationship between the father Wah Gay and the son Ben Loy. ... Way Gay wishes Ben Loy to follow Chinese tradition, and to submit to the father's authority [by marrying a 'nice Chinese girl and having sons], while the son balks at his father's 'old ways' and wants to make his own choices. ... Chu's novel figures the conflict of nativism and assimilation in terms of Ben Loy's sexuality," with "its oedipal resolution in a Chinese-American male identity," a "third" alternative emerging out of the choice between two cultural binaries (Lowe 1991, 26, 34–5). Lowe's using the symbolism of generational conflict to urge for a break from traditional practices in Asian American studies, as shown in aspects of the surveys in the previous chapters, is premised on her perception of the pre-1965 Asian American social experiences as a somewhat neatly homogeneous process of co-optation by or absorption into American nativism. This perception strongly informs her assessment of the Asian American cultural nationalist period and her promotion of Teresa Cha's modernist text *Dictée* as the model for a paradigm shift in the field.

Within the context of Lowe's call for a generational revolt in favor of a post-1965 Asian American politics of difference, Erin Ninh's 2011 monograph *Ingratitude: The Debt-Bound Daughter in Asian American Literature* represents a somewhat paradoxical move, for it is both inspired by and working against Lowe's 1991 generational thesis, by focusing on the post-1965 Asian American immigrant family—which is not a concern in Lowe's argument—as the target of its interrogation. In this study, Ninh describes the Asian "immigrant nuclear family as a special form of capitalist enterprise" that invests in educational and professional achievements as the best conduits for their American-born children to gain upward social mobility, while it inculcates in them Asian values of diligence, docility, and filial piety. This mode of parenting, Ninh maintains, inadvertently forces second-generation Asian Americans to align with the requirements for model minority and to convert the Asian American immigrant family into "a productive unit—a sort of cottage industry, for a particular brand of good, capitalist subject" (Ninh 2011, 2). She argues:

What we call intergenerational conflict is at the bottom a conflict of interests, as such, symptomatic of a social and economic unit whose agents are differently vested in power. Such conflict appears apolitical only when its language of filial piety and affect—suffering and guilt, devotion and anger, trauma and disownment—is allowed to be spoken in isolation from the politics of the family. An understanding of generational dynamics as implicated by and participating in a racialized, gendered, and material history is by no means reductive of cultural politics, but even fully accountable to them. (Ninh 2011, 6)

Elsewhere, Ninh suggests, based on her rereading of several Asian American narratives of generational conflict, that "Asian American family stories not only tend to follow a tired formula but this formula is a politically conservative one." For the Asian American model minority subject being produced in this process, she asserts, is "far from being a 'myth'"; it is "as familiar to us as a family" (Ninh 2015, 114–15).

The implications of Lowe and Ninh's critiques of the tradition of Asian American studies via the trope of generational conflict remain to be assessed. Stephen Sumida, vigilant to tendencies to assimilate generational conflict described in Asian American literature into other kinds of distinctions, urges critics to consider why generational conflict—a common theme in literature worldwide—has become so embattled and irreconcilable in Asian American literary criticism, and how "it is possible to generalize so enormously about such Asian American family rifts that may not inhere in either the literary works or the field of Asian American literary studies" (Sumida 1986, 64–5). Sumida finds it especially ironic that poststructuralist-influenced Asian American critics are no less prone, compared with those they see as committing the error of essentialism, to reproduce the logic of "dualism and binarism" in their treatments of the relationship between first- and second-generation Asian Americans, and that, led by theory, these critics routinely reduce literary contents to naïve sociological presumptions (Sumida 2008, 33–5). Sumida's skepticism about theoretical constructions of abstract opposition between Asian America's past and its present based on literary depictions of generational conflict finds an affirmative parallel in the perspective articulated by David Palumbo-Liu regarding what he finds to be a wrong-headed shift toward a "fetishization of the present" in recent Asian American cultural studies. This trend, he suggests, is discernable in the context of two commonly adopted approaches to history by these critics. "First, the notion that our sense of time has become flattened out: we dwell entirely in the present, dismissive of both the past and future as being contaminated by master narratives of the historical or the teleological. Second, in practice the object of scrutiny tends almost always to be the contemporary, or close to it" (Palumbo-Liu 1995c, 58).

This chapter has examined several concerns that fall under bicultural and generational categories in order to illustrate the field's diasporic origins and multilingual traditions, as well as its ongoing investment with immigrant writing in the post-1970s contexts. Some of these concerns—such as the paradox of Asians' assimilation and the persistence of Asian stereotypes in American culture and workplace—not only serve as reminders of unresolved contradictions that continually vex the ethnic community, but also point to directions where fresh possibilities emerge and new momentums build up, especially a transnational turn of the field starting from the mid-1990s, the focus of the next chapter. The discussion in the present one thus ends by raising several questions in anticipation of such a shift in the topic of discussion. One may ask, for example, what are some of the internal and external conditions that make the field's transnational move inevitable, as both a US-based critical undertaking and a form of extraterritorial engagement? To what extent is the transnational turn of the field a result of Asian American critics' disillusionment with the false promise for assimilation granted them by the American neoliberal democratic system?

What specific roles do bilingual competence and intracultural translation play in this process? What constitutes a transnational Asian American critical subject? Are there any limits to the grand theoretical vision of Asian American transnationality? These are some of the issues that will be looked into, explored, and hopefully clarified through the surveys and discussions in the next chapter.

CHAPTER 4
THE TRANSNATIONAL TURN

There has been a general consensus among scholars that a transnational Asian American literary discourse, which became fully established by mid- or late 1990s, had grown out of two internal critiques of the field's limitations since it was institutionalized in the wake of *Aiiieeeee!*'s publication. First is its failure to develop in ways that can adequately reflect the unprecedented sociodemographic transformation of the ethnic community and a simultaneous diversification of the sites and forms of its cultural activities. Second is its apparent lagging behind in theoretical development that would allow the field to transcend the conceptual limits of a cultural nationalist emphasis on race, class, and ethnic community as the guiding principles for the field's self-reproduction. Within this context, the argument advanced by Lisa Lowe in her 1991 "Heterogeneity" article had remained, until the dawning of the second decade of the twenty-first century, a most generative ground for Asian American literary scholars to imagine the field's transnationality. As suggested in the surveys of Chapter 2, such a transnational imaginary, though abundantly theorized throughout the 1990s, did not materialize right away because the field had yet to go through an interethnic or interracial phase in its evolution, whose agendas would be shaped by both the emergent possibilities promised by cosmopolitan epistemology and the residual influences of the existing US minoritarian politics.

What remains to take place in this process is the crystallization of two conditions external to the field by the end of the decade. First is the dissolution of the Soviet Union (1989–91), which ushered in more than a decade of US-dominated world order and allowed a triumphant American ideal of neoliberal democracy to assert itself as the justifying ideology for a new wave of global capitalism, both socioeconomically and in the realm of culture, liberal arts, and the humanities. Second is a simultaneous ascendency in academy-based Western humanistic and social science discourses of anti-imperial and post-national theoretical models, especially postcolonial criticism, which, by late 1990s, had established itself as the standard-bearer for cutting-edge ethnic American literary and cultural studies. The confluence of these internal and external factors is the overall climate under which an Asian American transnational project took shape and became a source of new intellectual energy for the field's ongoing transformations. Under the circumstances, more and more scholars in the field started to see Asian American literature as no longer rooted in the United States, while continued global migration and border-crossing enabled this literature to be perceived as "simultaneously local and transnational, rather than only as a subordinate category of American literature" (Ling 2006, 1–2).

Planetary Presence

Retrospectively, the field's expansion beyond its cultural nationalist confines may be seen as taking place along three overlapping, though temporally uneven, trajectories. First is its inadvertent translation, through the cultural spread of a post-Soviet-era global capitalism emanating from the United States, to a transnational literary undertaking through its enthusiastic adaptation by the educational apparatuses or establishments in different parts of the world. Second is its self-conscious opening up, at different stages of the field's growth, to a study of Asian diaspora in the entire American continent, with the predominantly Anglophone North America deemed to be the logical first choice for its hemispheric inclusion. Third is its motivated investment in the Asia-Pacific region as a key reference point for rethinking US-based Asian American literary studies, in repudiation of the cultural nationalist claim that Asian American subject formation is predicated on Asia's exclusion. These interrelated tendencies in the field's transnational shift will be surveyed in the first two subsections of this chapter, while the two remaining subsections are devoted to reviewing scholarship that complicates the work done in the initial phase of the field's transnational turn and points to new possibilities and directions.

The question of how Asian American literary studies—a community-based minority discourse in the United States—acquires its international popularity in the post-Soviet era tends to be assumed, rather than carefully historicized, by Asian American literary scholars because of the common perception among them that this literature's new-found prominence in the global community of letters unambiguously affirms Asian Americans' unhindered access to the social or spatial heterogeneity theoretically promised them. Such a sentiment is evident in Jessica Hagedorn's 1993 renaming of contemporary Asian American creative practice as a version of world literature, in Shirley Lim's call for Asian American academics to occupy "the leading edge" of such "globally circulating discourses" (Quayum and Lim 2003, 86); and in Amy Ling's comparison of an emerging Asian American globality to a "culture smorgasbord to which all the peoples of the world would be invited to partake of whatever catches their eyes and pleases their palate" (Ling 2002, 235).

Other Asian American critics are cautious about what they witness. For example, Jefferey Santa Ana calls attention to a 1993 special issue of *Time* magazine that features "The New Face of America" with a computer-generated female image of mixed race as a prime symbol for global capital's growing preoccupation with cultural pluralism. He observes: "The editors at *Time* believe that we have entered a new era in which the assimilation of immigrants into the United States changes the 'complexion' of the average American" and that the new face they have created constitutes "a compelling reason to celebrate the hybrid racialization in America, which the editors explicitly link to America's status as the leading world power" upon the dissolution of the Soviet Union (Santa Ana 2004, 15–17). Sue-Im Lee problematizes the new language of a "globalist we" as an ironic signifier for the emerging ethos of "the global village," which she considers tantamount to "the latest rendition of imperialist … universalism" that emphasizes a "global intimacy and shared fate" among populations who find themselves caught in disparate socioeconomic conditions while struggling with the consequences of the leveling forces of global capital (Lee 2007, 503). Noting a resonance between this version of transnationalism and Aihwa Ong's concept of "flexible citizenship," which describes elite Asian cosmopolitans moving freely between Asia and the West, Iyko Day remarks somewhat sarcastically: "What Lisa Lowe observed as the 'Heterogeneity, Hybridity, Multiplicity' of Asian Americans in 1991 has never been more actively realized than today" (Day 2007, 71).

Such responses to the field's newly achieved global profile clearly point to the ambiguous nature of its transnationality, while they also serve to foreground a set of specific conditions under which Asian American literature migrates to other countries or regions since the mid-1990s. According to Helena Grice, Asian American literature arrived at European institutions of higher education in two primary ways: through texts available to a general reading public and through texts that appear on university and college curricula. Each means of dissemination remains to a large extent under the control of the publishing industry, which involves both large commercial presses (such as Penguin USA) and small American publishers (such as The Women's Press). Grice suggests that the academic contexts in which Asian American literature is embedded are quite diverse across Europe: it may be a component of Philosophy, Comparative Literature, Modern Languages, Women's Studies, or English (including American Literature) departments. But the central conduit is the long-established American Studies program (such as those in Belgium, England, Germany, Spain, Denmark, Netherlands, Italy, Sweden, and Poland), an institutional base that came into being during the 1950s and became transformed into that of multiculturalism since the new millennium (Grice 2014, 280–1). Rocío Davis and Sämi Ludwig offer a perspective on the central role that academic networks—workshops, regional or national conferences, and the activities sponsored by the European Association of American Studies (EAAS)—have played in establishing or maintaining ties among European scholars dedicated to Asian American literary studies (Davis and Ludwig 2002, 10). Taken together, the introduction of Asian American literature to Europe is marked by several defining moments: the 1996 official adoption of "European perspectives on Asian American Literature," the title for a special issue of the short-lived UC Berkeley-based journal *Hitting Critical Mass* (quoted in Grice 2014, 281); the 1998 publication of Lina Unali and Christopher Leigh Connery's coedited volume *Talk-Story in Chinatown and Away: Essays on Chinese American Literature and on US-China Relations*; and, into the twenty-first century, Robert Lee's 2008 monograph *Multicultural American Literature: Comparative Black, Native, Latino/a, and Asian American Fictions*, which provides a comprehensive review of the field in multiple contexts.

At about the same time, Asian American literature finds its second home in Asia through various teaching and research initiatives supported by traditional departments, newly established academic centers, conferences, professional organizations, or academic journals. The geographical sites witnessing a burgeoning of such activities in Asia are quite diverse; they include Burma, India, Cambodia, Thailand, the Philippines, Vietnam, Malaysia, and Indonesia. But this long list of hosting countries has gradually dwindled to a small number of financially well-off East Asian entities, such as Hong Kong, Taiwan, Singapore, Japan, and, since the beginning of the twenty-first century, the mainland China, which was undergoing a period of rapid economic growth and fast expansion of its humanities education. Unlike the way Asian American literary studies is introduced to Europe through the established channels of American Studies programs as an evolving field tied to academic careers—a venue strengthened by the Anglophone publishing industry, such as that in England, which is already transnational—Asian American literature's entry into Asia was spearheaded by US-based Asian American scholars with bilingual and bicultural backgrounds. Reflecting on Taiwanese scholars' initial engagement with Chinese American literature, Pin-chia Feng observes that local scholars with similar bilingual or bicultural skills tend to see themselves as uniquely positioned to introduce this line of study to home audiences. Such a perception of shared linguistic heritage and affective affinity with Chinese American literature, Feng suggests, was a major cause for the popularity of this literature in Taiwan from the late 1980s to much of the 1990s because scholars believed that they could offer "innovative" and "enriching" interpretations of Chinese American texts from a local perspective (Feng 2014, 257, 263). Feng's observation about the tendency among bilingual Taiwanese readers of Chinese American literature to privilege the knowledge form and cultural premise native to them finds a resonance in an observation made by Walter Lim, a literary critic in Singapore, who notices that his students also have the tendency to focus primarily on the "Chinese" side of the "Chinese American equation" in this literature and to overlook literary content in need of different kinds of contextualization not readily available to them (Lim 2008, 138). Despite the cautions advised by Feng and Lim, however, penchant for reading Chinese American literature through a Sino-centric lens has remained predominant among the Chinese-speaking readers in Asia.

The second aspect of the field's transnational expansion revolves around the initial work done in Asian Canadian studies. In her 2004 monograph *The Politics of the Visible in Asian-North American Narratives*, Eleanor Ty calls for an "Asian North American" conception of Asian American literary studies, suggesting that "there are too many commonalities in the situation of Asian Canadians and Asian Americans to ignore and that a cross-border comparative reading is fruitful and long overdue, especially in our transnational and diasporic world" (Ty 2004, 26). Donald Goellnicht, who proposed "a strategic alliance" between Asian Canadian and Asian American studies in 2000 (Goellnicht 2000, 21), considers the inclusion of excerpts of Joy Kogawa's writing in Jessica Hagedorn's 1993 anthology *Charlie Chan Is Dead* an official initiation of Asian Canadian literature into the new transnational Asian American literary canon (Goellnicht 2015, 268). The Asian North American perspectives embraced by Ty and Goellnicht can be traced to the inaugural vision of such a transnational imaginary articulated in King-Kok Cheung and Stan Yogi's 1988 annotated bibliography of Asian American literature. This expanded notion of Asian American literary studies also receives a major updating in a recent historical analysis offered by Erika Lee, who argues, based on several cross-border anti-Asian race riots along the North-American Pacific coast in 1970, for the existence of a long-standing commonality between Asian Canadian and Asian American experiences (Lee 2007, 20). In this process, some Asian Canadian scholars have voiced reservations about making Asian Canadian studies mere "institutional attachments" to US ethnic minority studies, a move that, they argue, may result in downplaying the specificity of Asian Canadian studies. This is the position taken by Iyko Day, who asks, "in the effort to cite broad historical, disciplinary, and cultural parallels to justify a more expansive Asian North American framework, do we risk losing sight of the intersections of gender and sexuality which are so often sacrificed to make room for 'macro' theorizing that attend [sic] broadened transnational paradigms?" (Day 2007, 80). Along the line, Christopher Lee offers a pointed critique of the tendency in Asian American studies south of Canada to appropriate Asian Canadian resources and accomplishments in self-serving ways, a practice that, he contends, when "combined with the general dominance of U.S. academia" in Asian North American studies, is tantamount to an exercise of "intellectual imperialism" (Lee 2007, 3–7).

Meanwhile, significant progress has been made to incorporate the non-Anglophone Asian diasporas in South America into the agendas of Asian American transnational studies, especially through an engagement with Karen Tei Yamashita's novelistic representation of the knowledge forms, points of view, and affective force of the Global South. This Yamashita turn in the field is mainly centered on her 1997 novel *Tropic of Orange*, which describes a symbolic dismantling of the territorial borders separating the United States and Mexico, as well as an imagined showdown between Third World labor and First World capital personified in a wrestling match between two literary transfigurations: Archangel (representing the South) and SUPERNAFTA (embodying the North). Notable studies of this aspect of the Asian American transnational imaginary include, among others: Molly Wallace's discussion of the novel's dual engagement with an economic/universalist and a metaphorical/localized effects of NAFTA (the North American Free Trade Agreement) as a dominant signifier in the age of global capitalism (Wallace 2001); Alvina Quintana's analysis of Yamashita's participation in the rewriting of "*border Brujo*," a term invented by Guillermo Gómez-Peña, the well-known Chicano performance artist whose transgressive style has influenced Yamashita's construction of Archangel (Quintana 2002); Caroline Rody's exploration of the novel's symbolic warning of "the perils of the ethnically and nationally bounded imagination" and of "received" representational forms of ethnic identity or sense of belonging (Rody 2004); and Susan Thananopavarn's foregrounding of the demystifying power of a LatinAsian point of view that the novel adopts, which she considers working effectively to reveal repressed aspects of American history, such as colonial or imperial violence, Cold War militarism, cross-border race riots, and transnational human organ or drug trafficking catering to the needs of metropolis (Thananopavarn 2018, 107–32).[1]

In this process, fruitful efforts have also been made to trace the multiple roots and trajectories of Asian diasporas in South America from sociocultural perspectives. Examples along the line include Christine So's examination of the question of creolization in relation to the experiences of early Chinese immigrants in Guyana, Trinidad, and Jamaica (So 1989); Lane Hirabayashi's historicization of Japanese settlers' transculturation practices in Latin America (Hirabayashi 2002); Roshni Rustomni-Kern's chronicling of Indian migration to New Spain (Rustomji-Kerns 2002), and Cynthia Tolentino's mapping of the emergence of Asian America within the framework of "equatorial archipelago" formations (Tolentino 2014).

The Asia-Pacific Investment

The most significant work accomplished by Asian American critics during the field's transnational shift is their theoretical justification of a connection that they attempt to (re)establish between consequence of Asian American subject formation in the United States and that of Asia's subjugation during the global reach of US hegemony. In the process, they draw on two competing models in meeting the theoretical challenge. The first is postcolonial criticism, which foregrounds sensibilities of rootlessness, alienation, and psychological distancing as the basis for imagining border-crossing between the United States and Asia in non-essentialist terms. According to this model, Asia, though deemed indispensable as a transnational signifier, is inherently unrepresentable, therefore relevant to Asian American transnational arguments only in terms of its affirmation of the baseless nature of the model minority stereotype. The second is historicism, which emphasizes the need to situate the question of Asian American abjection within the larger context of East–West relations centering on Asia-Pacific, an approach adopted for the explicit purpose of tackling the schizophrenic results of Asians' racialization in the United States in materialist terms. Both theoretical positions are implicitly derivative from Asian American critiques of the model minority myth and the paradox of Asian assimilation, which have been surveyed in Chapter 3.

Exemplifying the first theoretical approach is a 2001 collection of essays coedited by Kandice Chuh and Karen Shimakawa, in which they declare:

> Postcolonialism's interrogation of the consequences of imperialism for both the (formerly) colonized and the metropole has effectively undermined binary epistemologies that give rise to essentialist conceptions of East/Other and West/Self. … Transnationalism is grounded in recognition of global movements of capital and related migration of peoples; as a theory, it both describes and interrogates the possibilities for inhabiting and co-opting this cross-border mobility for the sake of envisioning communities bounded not principally by national identifications and investments. These complementary discourses have decidedly undermined the stability of the Three Worlds model of global organization inherited from the Cold War era.[2] (Chuh and Shimakawa 2001, 5–6)

A notable feature of the transnational argument made by Chuh and Shimakawa is that the authors attempt to undo several binary distinctions that they find conceptually reductive: that between the East and the West, that between America and Asia, and that between the First World and the Third World. What emerges from such a deconstructive critique of the received geopolitical categories is a mode of "cross-border mobility" not only free of the referential constraints of Asia being evoked, but also lacking any executional potential for the "global movements" they recommend. As a consequence, this theoretical model energizes only a limited constituency of the field's initial imaginings of its post-national work.

By contrast, scholars adopting the second theoretical model inadvertently reactivate a classic argument of cultural nationalism, that is, the *Aiiieeeee!* editors' quasi-pragmatic designation of "dual personality" as the prime symptom for Asian racialization in the United States. Illustrating the point made here is an observation voiced by Juliana Chang in a 2007 article titled "Interpreting Asian American Identity and Subjectivity," in which she states: "Thirty-plus years after Ben R. Tong and the *Aiiieeeee!* editors made their critique of the notion of the Asian American 'dual personality,' the presumed opposition between Asian and American lives on. This pervasive paradigm of identity conflict is reminiscent of, even as it departs from, the figure of the tragic mulatto/a in the nineteenth century." Continually "pulled between Asian cultural tradition and American cultural modernity," Chang argues, the "American-born-and-raised" generations are particularly hard-pressed by the fact that, to them, the problematic of assimilation is unavoidable in any review of the predominant post-1960s representation of Asian Americans as a model minority (Chang 2007, 868). What Asian American transnational theorists have done with the *Aiiieeeee!* editors' "dual personality" argument is strategically essentialist (to evoke a concept from Gayatri Spivak):[3] they retain the logic of the editors' emphasis on the dualistic consequence of racialization for the Asian American psyche, while redefining the role of Asia from that of a cultural burden in the editors' formulation to that of a political necessity, thereby reversing the anti-Asia bias in cultural nationalism in ways that do not involve a wholesale dismissal of the *Aiiieeeee!* editors' contributions.

Such a strategic reversal of the cultural nationalist disinterest in Asia seems at work in Palumbo-Liu's pathbreaking 1999 monograph *Asian/America: Historical Crossings of a Racial Frontier*, in which he contends that the

> precise nature of "dual" personality cannot be grasped without a specific sense of the forces that create that schism, the assumptions that underlie the imputed *separateness* of the two realms of experiences, and the nature of the "wholeness" sought. Rather than assuming … schizophrenia, we should see that the separation of "Asia," "America," and "Asian America" is *itself* a psychic rationalization that, in seeking to simplify complex forms of identification and disidentification, blinds us both to the precise politics of separation, and, concomitantly, to their grounds for interpretation. The question behind cultural nationalism is therefore not the availability of a "nation" to secure "culture," but rather the historical materiality of a culture produced in a psychic space wherein a particular and contingent formation of the nation appears *in relation to* multiple identifications which are themselves driven by specific contingencies. (Palumbo-Liu 1999, 308, italics in original)

Colleen Lye further theorizes the stakes of such a refocusing on Asia in her 2005 monograph *America's Asia*, as follows:

The American identification of the Asiatic was not arbitrary; it was rooted in the material history of U.S. relations with East Asia. The antinomies of Asiatic racial form reflect the pattern of a modernizing China and Japan changing places as U.S. friend and enemy. At any given point in this history, their opposite status was necessary to the maintenance of U.S. security. ... [The] hegemonic construction of Asians—as civilizational threat or as testimony to the universal arrival of American democracy—paradigmatically derived from interlinked Chinese and Japanese examples. China's and Japan's modes of late modernization dually involved trans-Pacific labor migrations," while reflecting "the discursivity of a neo-colonialism that installed the East as a Western proxy rather than antipode." (Lye 2005, 9–10)

Somewhat at odds with the historicist thrust that marks the positions taken by Palumbo-Liu and Lye is Lisa Lowe's emphasis on the determining role of epistemology in her discussion of Asia's relevance to Asian American transnational criticism. She suggests that "the necessary precondition for the forging of an adequate set of methods for the project of 'mapping the Asian diaspora' " lies in a disruption of established academic "disciplines within the US university, that is, as ideological apparatuses for producing knowledge within and for the United States, whether the disciplinary foci are 'Asia,' 'America,' or 'Asian America.'" The problematic of such "disciplinary fields," Lowe maintains, is that they make Asia, the global frame for the US domestic construction of Asian Americans as national subjects, a referent/ signifier of "stability." Lowe's alternative to the static Asia, which she sees as an inevitable conceptual outcome of compartmentalized area studies, is what she calls a "post-1965 Asian immigrant subject." It is political agent that, by virtue of its incompatibility with any official categorization, is inherently disruptive of "the disciplinary paradigms" that "manage their objects of study" and legitimize the "occlusion of the 'Asian immigrant' " (Lowe 2001, 267–8). Lowe's complex and somewhat vague discussion of the urgency of pluralizing Asia as a referent/signifier in transnational Asian American studies clearly follows the logic of a poststructuralist critique of traditional notions of realist representation as a reductive or essentializing practice, and it is consistent with the discursive nature of her theoretical innovations generally.

The increased theorization of and attention to Asia as a key reference point for US-based Asian American transnational studies then leads Hyungji Park to assert: "Our new understanding of 'Asian American literature' must include practitioners who may live anywhere in the globe and be writing on themes that are far removed from the issues that dominate *The Woman Warrior*. It is humbling to remember that from the perspective of Asian diaspora, Asian American literature is one of its subsets" (Park 2015, 166). Eric Hayot, an expert in comparative literature and Asian studies, registers a caveat about placing undue weight on Asia in efforts to refashion Asian American literary studies. He suggests that a "postorientalist" rethinking of Asian ethnicity as "an effect of international relations" may open the door to gravitating the field toward comparative ethnic studies and bicultural studies—a move that he considers would in turn allow world literature studies to "gesture toward the profession's latest *bête blanche*" (Hayot 2009, 908–9). This is a similar context in which Margaret Hillenbrand argues for the centrality of the Sinophone texts written by Chinese immigrant intellectuals in the post-Fordist and post-Cold-War Asian American literary studies. She maintains that the "Sinophone medium and audience [both within and outside the U.S.] compel a deeper recognition" of its "carving of cross-oceanic conduits" through human activities, ethno-linguistic fertilization, and community building. Understood in this way, Sinitic texts are therefore dwelling "on the threshold … between America and the Sinophone world and belonging equally to both" (Hillenbrand 2013, 45–8, 49). Shelley Wong poses a set of questions about the interpretation of Angel Island poems based on similar grounds. She asks: "What difference, then, might it make to engage the Angel Island poems within the frame of the original Sinitic language of composition instead of through English translations? What difference might it make, that is, to the kinds of meanings or institutional status that we attribute to these poems? In the mobilizing of meanings across languages, what gets redirected or displaced in transmission?" (Wong 2015, 72).

Wong's questions are inspired in part by Yunte Huang's 2008 monograph *Transpacific Imaginations: History, Literature, and Counterpoetics*, which offers a reading of the Angel Island poetry through the Chinese poetic concept of *tibishi* (namely, the inscriptions of spontaneous responses on a particular placer), as part of the author's larger bicultural argument that Asia-Pacific has functioned as a "counterpoetic" space vis-à-vis Anglo-American literary traditions and practices since the nineteenth century (Huang 2008, 2, 4). Huang's 2008 book, which situates early Chinese immigrant writing (along with the poetry of Lawson Inada and the modernist narrative of Theresa Cha's *Dictée*) in an emerging field of "transpacific studies," has generated certain interests among Asian American scholars who pursue literary studies with a focus on Asia-Pacific (Suzuki 2014, 355–6). Notable among the Asian American responses to Huang's arguments is Tina Chen's 2011 review of his book, which recognizes the "new insights and assessments" yielded from the planetary sweep of its study, but also points out its obvious limitations. Chen observes:

> His eclectic range of texts is both welcome and disruptive insofar as this study concatenates the far-flung points of connection and disconnection dotting the transpacific, even as the book's separate parts do not necessarily cohere into a systematic articulation of the critical contours of transpacific space. Additionally, the absence of Native Pacific peoples in the book raises questions about the principals who are fighting to determine the meaning of the Pacific ... Huang's approach, which simultaneously seems to differentiate discursive modes such as the historical, the literary, and the counterpoetical even as such differences often collapse in the readings themselves, also makes clear that one of the problems of writing about the transpacific revolves around how to discuss productively an oceanic space of exchange, projection, and conflict whose abstraction makes it impossible to map. (Chen 2011, 891–2)

Huang's inadequate attention to the uneven histories and developments of the native populations of the Asian Pacific, as Chen suggests, bespeaks a related problem in his study; that is, its overlooking the multiple sites and forms of cultural nationalisms being pursued in the region historically— Filipino, Indonesian, Vietnamese, Singaporean, Korean, Chinese, Japanese, American, Hawaiian, among others—which would mark the Asian Pacific as a truly contested space of "political struggle "in a historically concrete sense.[4] As such, Huang's notion of "transpacific counterpoetics" gets perilously close to reinscribing a century-old dichotomy core to the comparative studies methods developed in China since the late Qing Dynasty.

Cautions and Dissonances

Eric Hayot also expresses doubts about whether US-based bilingual academics can be truly "on the inside of a language situation" of an Asian country that they relate to only on cultural or intellectual grounds (Hayot 2009, 909). The depth of this concern can be illustrated by a personal view of Diana Chang, author of *The Frontiers of Love* (1956), regarding some of the insurmountable obstacles to her becoming an insider of Chinese culture despite her bicultural upbringing and having lived in China during the formative years of her life. She believes that the measure for a Chinese American to become an insider of China is "to be found not so much horizontally—across the Pacific Ocean—but in the verticality of social strata and its diversity," to which recognition of her bilingual or bicultural competence in Western metropolis is no equivalence (Hamalian 1995, 39). In other words, US-based readers of Sinophone literature would not become reliable insiders of the Chinese language situation they embrace, unless they are truly embedded in its political and legal systems as alienated subjects. Hence, Hayot argues: "The danger of the new movement toward global American studies is that the final turn of its analysis becomes a revelation about the nature of the United States, or Americanness, so that the rest of the world becomes interesting only when it says something about us" (Hayot 2009, 910). David Li asks a different but no less important question regarding this issue, "can we simply turn the 'Asian' in 'Asian America(n)' into a regional signifier, denoting that land mass on the eastern edge of the Pacific, rather than keeping the 'Asian' in 'Asian America(n)' as a racial signifier, suggesting a specific historical identity and a set of social relationships within the United States?" (Li 2010, 101).

Some Asia-based scholars are similarly skeptical about the applicability of the transnational approaches developed out of US conditions to their own teaching or research needs. For example, Walter Lim points out: "We recognize almost immediately that so long as the target audience for the Asian American author remains the mainstream reader in the United States, Asian American literature's multiculturalist project will always, at an important level, cater to the voyeurism of the dominant gaze. It cannot be otherwise" (Lim 2008, 142). He emphasizes: "Because the space of the Orient is imagined and represented, it is never in precise alignment with perspectives held of it by the Asian subject, who finds himself or herself having to access the American context that constitutes the point of origin of the text's ideological production." From this perspective, he argues, the "ghostly alterity" of Asia in traditional Asian American studies, though currently attaining "a certain substantiality" in the US-based transnational imaginary, is ultimately tied to "the cultural logic of globalization" (Lim 2004, 160, 163). Underlying such reservations about shifting the site of Asian American literary studies to Asia-Pacific is the concern, especially among scholars based in the region, that such a move might just be a minoritarian version of US nativism masquerading as a critique of the American nation and Asian American cultural nationalism. This concern, though insufficiently registered among US-based Asian American literary scholars, has received serious consideration in Yasuko Takezawa and Gary Okihiro's coedited 2016 volume *Trans-Pacific Japanese American Studies: Conversations on Race and Racialization*. This volume is pathbreaking for being the first substantial cross-cultural effort that directly engages with a vexing but somehow repressed structural problem within transnational Asian American literary studies: namely, its latent US-centrism.

Takezawa and Okihiro raise this issue without rhetoricity in their introduction to the volume, by focusing on "the phenomenon of some U.S.-based Asian American scholars—domestic minorities in their home country—engaging in an imperial mission of uplift when they participate in a 'one-way teaching' process and demonstrate little eagerness to engage in mutual learning" (Takezawa and Okihiro 2016, 1, 8). At issue is the perception of a tendency among these US-based scholars to impose a "U.S.-centric framework"—with its assumptions about racial discrimination and racial stereotypes (as shown in its critique of the invidious workings of the model minority myth), and its rejection of Asia-centrism and cultural nationalism (through its promotion of the desirability of interracial or interethnic alliances)—onto their Asian Pacific readers, hence reducing them to "cultural incompetents whose deficiencies require remediation if they aspire to produce 'proper' reading" of Asian American texts (Nakamura 2016, 297; Takezawa 2016, 399). The objection voiced by these Asian Pacific scholars to the US leanings in transnational Asian American literary studies does not escape the attention of some US scholars aware of the risky nature of conducting bicultural crossings that involve incompatible national cultures and sociopolitical conditions. Mark Chiang, for example, takes issue with David Eng's interpretation of the queer politics in the 1993 Taiwanese film (directed by Anh Lee) *The Wedding Banquet*, as manifesting obvious US-centricism.[5] Chiang points out: "Eng's strategic reading of the film attempts to negotiate the mutual exclusions of racial and sexual communities and identities, yet it also operates within the context of US identity politics, which cannot account for the complexities of sexual and ethnic identities in the global system. What is occluded in a national reading is the way in which the closet self is reconstructed, in the course of the narrative, under the pressure of globalization. From an initial problematic of assimilation, in which it is a question of competing national identities, the choice gradually becomes recast as one between a national and a transnational/global identity" (Chiang 2002, 276).

Commenting on the conflicting agendas and uneven conditions that often become obscured during Asian American literary migrants' crossing to Asia-Pacific, Susan Koshy warns that "if the expansion of the field proceeds at this pace, without a more substantial investigation of the premises and assumptions underlying our construction of commonality and difference, we run the risk of unwittingly annexing the newer literary productions within older paradigms, overlooking radical disjunctions within more established formations like Chinese and Japanese literature, and perpetuating hierarchies within the field" (Koshy 1996, 317). The concern expressed by Koshy underscores a growing problematic in US-based Asian American transnational effort bent on decontextualized bicultural exchanges, namely, its possible absorption into "more established formations" like Chinese or Asian studies. Arif Dirlik is similarly vigilant to such tendencies in recent Asian American studies, observing: "The academicization of the field has been accompanied by the appearance of new kinds of problems (most notably, problems of identity that intellectually draw from postcolonialism and cultural studies) that call into question the perpetuation of community-based academic work. These questions are empowered by the changing composition of Asian Americans, who foreground their ties to Asia rather than to communities in the U.S." One of the new pressures that Dirlik identifies in this process has something to do with "Asian Studies programs, [which,] once disdainful of Asian American Studies, have recently discovered both intellectual and institutional reasons for absorbing Asian American Studies" (Dirlik 2003, 167–8). It is obviously out of a combination of the concerns voiced by Koshy and Dirlik that Jennifer Ho suggests that the transnational investment of Asian American literary studies, in shifting the sites of its critique to other locations of the world, inadvertently elevates ethnicity and downplays race in ways that obscure the core concerns of the field as a largely US-based intellectual formation (Ho 2013, 305–6). Along this line, Sau-ling Wong names the following tendencies in current Asian American transnational literary studies as potentially doing irreparable harms to the field: "decontextualization," "Asian national recuperation," "deminoritization," and "U.S. nationalist recuperation" (Wong 2004).[6]

In the meantime, scholars in the Asian Pacific wrestle with a different set of concerns confronting them, especially with regard to how Asian American literary studies can be conducted in ways that benefit the local intellectual community and home audiences. For example, Kuan-Hsing

Chen, a scholar in Taiwan, criticizes what he considers a complicit role played by the "native informant" at the receiving ends of the US-generated Asia-Pacific dynamic. This "academic broker," Chen suggests, uses his Western knowledge and Western connections to promote "self-interest," thus engaging in a coproduction of the erasure of US imperialist histories or practices in Asia-Pacific, while allowing his own transnational vision to be defined by US-based Asian American academics (Chen 2013, 176). What Chen problematizes here is a neoliberal by-product spawned by the post-Soviet global capitalism, namely, a false sense of cross-cultural intimacy or sharedness that Sue-Im Lee has called attention to, and, in the context of Chen's argument, an inadvertent translation of the political imperative of Asian American transnational critique to a practice of international careerism that is sustained, at least in part, by the principles of commercial exchange.

For US-based Asian American scholars, the issue remains, as Walter Lim suggests, that "representing diaspora can, at the end of the day, be a tricky business—much depends on whether the Asian American author can successfully extricate himself/herself from the orderings of the binaristic dominant/subjected and center/margin paradigm" (Lim 2008, 141). The paradox of the center/margin binary that Lim finds at work in much of the Western transnational literary imaginary has received a theoretical clarification from Françoise Lionnet and Shu-mei Shih, who observe that "when it stands as an end in itself, [such critique of binarism] seems only to enhance it; the center remains the focus and the main object of study. ... The ethical implications of this approach are important in that they prevent the reification of the other, one of the major pitfalls of identity politics. However, when seen from this perspective, the other continues to exist more as a promise than as a reality" (Lionnet and Shih 2005, 3).

Locating the Historical Referent

In a 1999 essay on migrant Asian women workers in the United States, Evelyn Hu-DeHart maps the history of transnationalism by focusing on its shifting priorities and practices. First, she differentiates between two phases of globalization: the pre-Second-World-War period characterized (especially in the United States) by "the outright acquisition of territories" during "the heyday of a maturing capitalism extending into imperialism." This phase of globalization, she maintains, triggered large-scale human displacement due to the outpouring of US capital and massive population movement into the country for labor-intensive plantation work, infrastructure construction, or back-breaking mineral extractions. The second period, she suggests, began during the Cold War (which witnessed the growing power of the "military-industrial complex" in the United States, and the wars in Korea and Vietnam), and reached a high point in a West-initiated global economic restructuring that transformed some of the global peripheries into new sites for Export-Based Industrialization (EBI). Because the displacement of rural populations in those Asian locations designated as EBI—primarily Taiwan, Hong Kong, Singapore, and South Korea (since Japan was there in the beginning)—could not be readily absorbed into jobs set up in the Export Processing Zones (EPZ), a large number of them ended up "right in the bowel of the global metropolis, the United States," where many people, mostly women, became heavily exploited low-wage workers in the apparel industry (garment factories, sweatshops). Hu-DeHart concentrates her analysis on the racialized exploitative system of this "reconstituted" female labor force through examination of the hierarchical structure of the subcontracting system at the core of the booming US garment industry, a system that "drives costs down to the lowest level of [the global commodity] chain" and "regularly violates both wage or child labor and safety and health laws." Hu-DeHart underscores "the fundamental class relation between this internationalized working class and transnational capital embodied in the idea and practice of the sweatshop" (Hu-DeHart 1999, 1–3, 6–9, 18), while underlining how such class tension is simultaneously gendered and racialized toward the American end of the contemporary transpacific flow.

Edna Bonacich comments specifically on the disappearance of class in recent academic discourses: "Although lip service is often paid to the importance of class, ... in practice class appears to have fallen into the background as a topic" of "identity," or "another basis of difference." She contends: "Class is not an identity, but a system of economic power and domination. Class relations are not relations of identity, but relations of dominance and resistance" (Bonacich 1995, 67). Sau-ling Wong, whose literary discussion is consistently grounded in ethnic studies, observes: "[Lisa] Lowe's model of identity and cultural transformation celebrating[sic], at least in part, extrapolated from the wide range of options available to a particular socio-economic class, yet the class element is typically rendered invisible" in her arguments (Wong 1995a, 15). David Li also reflects: "If the register of race, in all its colored connotations, evokes the historical unevenness within the constitution of the U.S. nation-state, the figure of class must be equally foregrounded to reveal the discrepancy within an Asian Pacific diaspora" (Li 2003, 622). E. San Juan further argues that postcolonial theory cannot "explain the plight of millions of 'oversea contract workers'—women domestics, 'hospitality girls,' and mail-order brides [who] comprise this large, horizontally mobile cohort—all over the world" or "understand the interpellation of bodies by the 'law of value' in the international stratification of labor" (San Juan 1998, 13). These diverse forms of race-, gender-, and sexuality-based social inequities, he suggests, are always derivative from and organized around the class antagonisms in the US commercial capitalist system. But "the disappearance of the national question" in current discourses on transnationality, which are shaped (at least in part) by the ludic visions conjured up from a "postcolonial semiotics of mixture and amalgamation," has effectively removed political critique from everyday experiences (San Juan 2003, 324).

A growing number of scholars interested in class concerns have fruitfully explored the coolie phenomenon in global contexts, an effort that has yielded significant results primarily in the realm of social or cultural studies (Hu-DeHart 1989; Jung 2006; Lai 1989). In a 2014 survey of this emerging area of inquiry, Eric Hayot emphasizes the analytical value of the concept "coolie," which, in his view, simultaneously denotes back-breaking work performed by racialized Chinese laborers under harsh conditions and connotes the larger processes of economy, politics, displacement, violence, and human affect that condition the migration of such indentured labor forces worldwide: in Cuba, Mexico, Peru, Brazil, California, Massachusetts, and Louisiana (Hayot 2014, 81, 89). In Asian American literary studies, Colleen Lye spearheads the interrogation of indentured Chinese labor smuggled to the West Coast United States during the late nineteenth century. She links the presence of this labor force in the American West to popular perceptions of the "Yellow Peril" among economically hard-pressed white workers, as well as to a burgeoning of naturalistic genres informed by a "degenerationist imagination" in American society (Lye 1995b, 51–2; Lye 2005, 7–8). Additional contributions to this line of study include Lisa Yun's 2002 article "Under the Hatches: American Coolie Ship and Nineteenth-Century Narratives of the Pacific Passage," in which she proposes several methodological innovations, especially by juxtaposing "coolie" to "slave," the "Pacific" to the "Atlantic," colonialism to global labor economies, and the bygone era of coolie traffic to present-day global trafficking of women, children, and illegal immigrants (Yun 2002, 56–7).[7] Caroline Yang's essay "Indispensable Labor: The Worker as a Category of Critique in Asian American Literature" is another notable effort to enrich this body of scholarship. In this study, she uses aspects of Maxine Hong Kingston's nonfiction *China Men* to foreground the coolie phenomenon as "one of the indispensable components in the development of capital and empire in the United States and worldwide" (Yang 2010). Like Yun's study, Yang's essay has opened up possibilities for transnational and comparative readings of Asian American literature that do not eschew narratives of economic exploitation, class subjugation, and political resistance.

Meanwhile, several Asian American critics work to fill the blind spots in Edward Said's critique of Orientalism—a foundational frame for the field's East–West analytic since the early 1980s. For example, Arif Dirlik points out that Said's project is not exempt from a general weakness manifested by other postcolonial intellectuals in that "their more radical ideas, chief among them the idea of class, are somewhat watered down in the course of their representation in the enunciation of postcolonialism" (Dirlik 1994, 338). In addition, E. San Juan notices "the absence of references" in Said's theory to "the Puerto Rican dilemma, the Hawaii sovereignty struggle," and "the current crisis in Africa, in East Timor, Myanmar, Peru, Nepal, Columbia, the Philippines, and other societies suffering from neocolonial structures" (San Juan 2006, 54). Victor Bascara problematizes Said's 1976 classic *Orientalism* for its detached symbolic approach to social issues, as well as "its emblematic invocations of pluralism, relativism, and valorization of previously denigrated categories of persons, places, and cultures" (Bascara 2006, xvii). Jinqi Ling contributes to such rehistoricizing efforts by using Karen Tei Yamashita's fictional portrayal of the Global South to derive an alternative model for literary referentiality, which he finds latent in David Harvey's 2005 theorization of the process of global capital's "accumulation by dispossession." He suggests:

> The crux of Harvey's argument is that in claiming new landscapes for facilitating its expansions, capital must always articulate its fluid and flexible movements across space into "physical structures," "geographical patterning," or land use authorized by the state in order for its value to be realized in substantial forms. Such a requirement for relative infrastructural fixity then produces temporal "drag" or "inertia," as well as physical "regionality," whose boundaries, though "fuzzy and porous," have "enough structured coherence to mark the geographical area off as somehow distinctive relative to all other areas," at least for a period of time—until it falls to other territorial

appropriations required by the competing and unpredictable accumulation force at play on various levels of capital's operation. (Ling 2012, 10)

Ling considers Harvey's model more effective than that offered by Ernesto Laclau and Chantal Mouffe, whose well-known concept of "nodal point[s]"— "objective points of contact"—can "find temporary stabilization of meaning and identity only in the discursive and relational struggles of language" (Harvey 2005, 100–39; Laclau and Mouffe 1985, 142; Ling 2012, 10).

The transnational shift in Asian American literary studies is undoubtedly the single most important development since the founding of the field. This shift seems also difficult to generalize in terms of how it is enacted, what it accomplishes, or when it matters, because the conceptual range and social mobility opened up in the process are interpreted quite differently by scholars with varying degrees of investments with the theory or representation of Asian diaspora, the market-driven opportunities that globality provides, or the intercultural appeals exercised in zones where actual border-crossing takes place. From this perspective, transnationalism can rarely be a unified critical program serving Asian American studies in the same way, but functions more as an aggregation of interests either conveniently grouped together or hegemonically spoken through—positionalities that remain to be differentiated and recontextualized in ongoing debates. Of the numerous challenges facing the field during this stage of its development, one seems rather persistent. That is, if transnational Asian American literary criticism is developed with an explicit purpose of reversing the nativist orientation in cultural nationalism, what do US-based scholars make of the objections voiced by their Asian Pacific counterparts to some of their own practices in that region? For these Asian Pacific scholars sense in such practices a familiar tendency toward US-centrism. Does this contradiction mean that there is a performative inconsistency between how transnationalism is promoted by Asian American critics as a general theory and the way such theory is applied as a kind of a geographically specific cultural mission? Can one assume that transnational Asian American literary studies, insofar as the most visible aspect of its operation is concerned, has yet to acknowledge its actual reliance on sensibilities derived from and meaningful only to the conditions of the United States? This chapter ends by reiterating several questions posed by Asian Pacific scholars to US-based transnational literary criticism as an unfinished Asian American project. These questions include: "How does … Asia help you question your normative perception and truth as Westerners of color in the global terrains?" (Nakamura, quote in Kurashige 2016, 383); "how could U.S.-based scholars of color carry out 'a more qual dialogue' with their Asia-Pacific colleagues?" (Takezawa 2016, 396–400); and whether "the largely domestic focus of ethnic studies" in the United States should be expanded "to include international perspectives" so that "the complex racial identities of non-white populations" can be better illustrated in a global context (Izumi 2016, 323).

Chapter 5 will delve into an important, though less often synthesized, recent development in the field: namely, Asian American critics' participation in debates over the extent to which literature can serve as effective commentary on Asian American histories and realities. Central to the survey in this chapter is a perspective on the mechanic of literary resistance as a textual engagement with the referential function of language.

CHAPTER 5
THE SOCIAL FUNCTION OF LITERATURE

In a 1996 essay titled "Reading Asian-American Poetry," the poet and critic Juliana Chang, expresses her concern about a gradual "turn away from poetry toward prose fiction" in mainstream Asian American literary criticism, a shift that, in her view, contributes to an implicit downgrading of the sociological role that poetry used to play as "an important vehicle for expressing the importance of race" during the 1960s and the 1970s (Chang 1996, 81–2). This perception of poetry's marginalization in the field is shared by a growing number of scholars who conduct poetic studies. For example, Steven Yao contends in his 2010 monograph, *Foreign Accents: Chinese American Verse from Exclusion to Postethnicity*, that "the most trenchant critiques of Asian American critical practices from within the field by scholars such as Susan Koshy, Jinqi Ling, Viet Nguyen, and Lisa Lowe" have routinely failed to address this "vastly disproportionate methodological skewing" because of the sole emphasis they place on the representational efficacy of prose fiction and its interpretation (Yao 2010, 5). The continuation of such a state of affairs, complains Timothy Yu, has unfairly placed Asian American poetry writing into "a curious position," where it is made at once "mature" and "marginal," "well-established" and "ephemeral," despite its ongoing contribution to the field's political diversity and artistic sophistication (Yu 2011, 818). Dorothy Wang adds to the dissent by emphasizing, somewhat polemically, that "this marginalization of Asian American poetry," though "a synecdochic reflection of the larger state of poetry in a capitalist society," reveals a "more profound and troubling fundamental misapprehension" in the Asian American reading community, one that "pits the sociological ... against the aesthetic in a false binary" (Wang 2015, 437).

The criticism voiced by these scholars helps raise important questions for framing the surveys and discussions in this chapter, while it also cautions, as does Dorothy Wang, against the danger of reducing serious investment with the social function of literature to the polar opposite of approaching literature as nothing but an experience of aesthetic enjoyment. One may ask, for example, whether the "sociological role" of literature can be assumed as a given in either poetry or prose fiction on solely empirical grounds, or if such role has to be borne out through text-specific enactment under given reading conditions. What would a text-specific enactment of the sociological role of literature entail on the part of the writer? What role does the reader play in this process? If investigation of the social function of literature does not involve treating literature as sociology, how do principles of composition (style of writing) or rationales for textual analysis (purpose of reading) influence the outcomes of an ideologically motivated poetic or narrative insertion of an Asian American point of view into the discourses constructed out of American social and cultural conventions? What ultimately matters to the concerns raised by Chang and further engaged by other critics, it seems, is something that lies inside the text itself, namely, the extent to which the speech performance of literature can be mobilized in the service of socially symbolic writing or reading practices. The formal premise established through the preliminary discussions here—a premise already assumed in Chang and others scholars' complaints about the differential treatment of poetry and prose fiction in the field—underlies the survey in this chapter because it has a direct bearing on what lies at the heart of the argument advanced by these critics: that is, genre deployments or genre expectations.

Essential to this formal premise of the social function of literature is a diachronic use of the sign (which prioritizes the cognitive or referential performance of speech), a linguistic feature that is notably repressed in poststructuralist-influenced ethnic American literary studies, including mainstream Asian American literary criticism. What this prevailing mode of literary investigation favors is the opposite of the referential function of language, namely, the indeterminate speech performances of unrelated signifiers, whose operating principle of nonequivalence and relationality tends to be seen as the best formula for critical visions or subversive strategies. The first subsection of this chapter will provide an overview of major theoretical positions about the internal structure of literary language, with a focus on the dialectal relationship between cognitive (or diachronic) and symbolic (or synchronic) speech performances. The formalistic assumptions of this chapter, it should be noted, overlap those adopted in Chapter 6, which addresses literary aesthetics more explicitly by raising a different set of questions.

Cognitive Uses of Language

Exploration of the internal dynamics of literary language began in the early twentieth century and has remained an intellectual preoccupation at sites far removed from Asian American literary studies. The initial attempts to define the nature of such dynamics were made by the Russian Formalists (Viktor Shklosky, Roman Jakobson, Yuri Tynyanov, and Boris Thomashefsky, among others), who were active in the years from before the October Revolution to the 1920s. According to Terry Eagleton, these formalists, who apply the formal logic of linguistics to the study of literature, see literary language as a kind of "deformed" ordinary speech in possession of its own laws. The literary work made up of such language thus becomes "a more or less arbitrary assemblage" of devices that intensify, condense, twist, telescope, draw out, or reverse ordinary language, while making it "strange" and "unfamiliar" to everyday reading experiences (Eagleton 1983, 3–4). Fredric Jameson detects a "profound historical and cultural divergence" between the literary doctrines of the Anglo-American New Criticism that had shaped literary studies in the United States from the 1930s to the 1960s, and those of Russian Formalism. The latter, he observes, is largely a reaction against the utilitarianism in the early twentieth-century Russian/Soviet official discourse on literature, by distinguishing the production of verse (poetry) from that of prose, without intending to dismiss the latter as part of a total linguistic system. New Criticism, on the other hand, not only "repudiated English Romanticism and its radical tradition" (as represented, for example, by William Blake), but also celebrated "Metaphysical and Cavalier poetry" as the only model for artistic excellence, hence ending up promoting a purely aesthetic doctrine that separates literary language from ordinary speech. New Criticism does attend to the internal dynamics of prose fiction, but only insofar as it meets the New Critical criteria for poetry writing. Jameson thus concludes: in their attitudes toward "history," "literary history," and "the internal literary diachrony which is narration and plot, the [Russian] Formalists may be seen to have a far more positive and dialectical attitude than the American New Critics" (Jameson 1972, 46–7, 49, 61).

Retrospectively, the divergent views toward history that Jameson highlights between Russian Formalism and New Criticism find their way to the architectonics of two linguistically based Western philosophical doctrines that have come to dominate the post-1960s literary studies in the United States: structuralism and poststructuralism. The former (represented by Jakobson, the early Roland Barthes, Gérard Genette, Algirdas Julien Greimas, Althusser, Julia Kristeva, and Tzvetan Todorov, among others) is partially open to the diachronic linguistic model established by the Russian Formalists; the latter (represented by Derrida, de Man, in Barthes's later work, Foucault, Deleuze, J. Hillis Miller, and Jonathan Culler, among others) is more attuned to the metaphysical role of literary language central to New Criticism. It is important to note that poststructuralism, both derivative from and hostile to structuralism, rejects the dialectical residue the latter retains and rules out any possibility of reclaiming the diachronic and referential function of language. Yet, because of its explicit critique of Western civilization and imperialism, poststructuralism has been a privileged conceptual tool in academy-based ethnic American literary studies during the past four decades.

This lengthy preamble about the internal structure of literary language is provided to underscore two challenges facing Asian American critics in their attempts to address the concerns raised by Chang and others at the beginning of this chapter. First, a formalistic study of the cognitive or referential dimension of language in literature, most developed in Russian Formalism, has not been a significant aspect of American (or Asian American) literary or critical practice since the 1980s or of today's theoretical fashions in the United States. Second, the Anglo-American New Criticism, though institutionally displaced and ideologically discredited since the 1970s, has renewed its ahistorical investment with synchronic relationality through the linguistic programs of structuralism and poststructuralism as the theoretical norms in today's Asian American literary studies. So, the question of the marginal status of poetry cannot be adequately addressed only on ethical grounds, without considering how the reader—especially the everyday reading subject—responds to variously coded or stylized Asian American poems written with different linguistic orientations and appealing to different audiences. It is worth mentioning in this context that New Criticism's rise is closely associated with the ascendancy of aesthetic modernism that Jameson characterizes as an "inward turn" of literature (Jameson 1979, 2), of which the early-twentieth-century literary avant-garde—Dadaism, Surrealism, Futurism, Cubism, and their formal principle of the collage and montage—is but a radical expression. This "inward turn" of the literary art, as a protest against cultural and linguistic conventions that modernist writers find oppressive, is distinctly marked by its quest for artistic autonomy on highly individualistic grounds, an undertaking that can be sustained only through modernist writers' insistence on the self-referential logic of all representations.

It is important to observe in this context that, since the 1970s, Asian American scholars have been using literary modernism as a basic frame of reference for staking out their positions about the social function of literature in two ways: one by appropriating usable aspects of its politics; the other by working against its aesthetics. The first approach, a relatively recent trend in the English Department-based critical practices, is exemplified in Timothy Yu's research; the second, rooted in the self-representational traditions of the ethnic community, can be found in George Uba's poetic practice and criticism. Yu makes a case for the sociological function of Asian American poetry by linking its activist phase of the 1960s and the 1970s to the literary avant-garde of Euro-American modernism. Drawing on an assertion made by Peter Bürger, he maintains that "the avant-garde imagines not an art that grows organically out of society but rather the reverse: a social life that is itself grounded in art … The avant-garde is thus a kind of echo of socially grounded, collectively produced and received art in an era when such groupings are no longer possible—an attempt to create a community by aesthetic means." From this perspective, he argues, "Asian American poetry of the 1970s represents a concerted attempt to perform precisely that task Bürger finds characteristic of the avant-garde: to organize a distinctively Asian American life praxis" on the basis of race relations (Bürger 1984, 59, 84, 91; Yu 2009, 6–7). Yu's characterization of Asian American poetic activism in these terms is thought provoking in two senses: it designates the avant-garde use of language as an ideal medium for registering socioeconomic relations fraught with race and class tensions; and it establishes the highly abstract modernism and its various anti-humanist permutations—the Beats among them—as a compelling initial site for conceiving a dialectical relationship between Asian American politics and aesthetics. Somehow downplayed in the connections made in such a way is the most eminent feature of modernist/avant-garde poetry, which is marked, as Shelley Wong points out, by its emphasis on linguistic difficulty, as well as its preference for impersonality, allusiveness, obscurity of reference, and indirection as the most valued poetry writing strategies (Wong 2001, 286).

Uba provides a different view of the conditions that surround the movement-inspired Asian American poetry production. He considers the "development of a pan-Asian, Third World consciousness" the most important ground for the birth of an Asian American critical consciousness about art-making, and the *Aiiieeeee!* editors' advocacy for Asian American "vernacular traditions" premised on "orality or aurality" an ethnic-specific moment, during which many Asian American poets "found themselves gaining voice" (Uba 2001, 312). Such an "imputation" of capacity to express, Uba suggests, was intertwined with the poets' urges "to 'unmask' poetry by removing it from the elitist academy (which had sealed meanings in the esoteric and the arcane, renounced plainness of speech, and conferred shamanistic status on university professors)." From this perspective, he insists that "the activist writers sought to deliver poetry to the People, who, apprehending its 'essentials,' would renew it in the spirit of emerging political freedom" (Uba 1992, 33). This is the context in which several Asian American poets closely associated with the social movement took an explicitly cognitive stance toward language use, aware that they were responding "initially to the harsh reality and then the haunting legacy of formal racial exclusion" (Yao 2010, 12). Such an understanding of the stakes of poetic activism strongly informs the movement poets' refusal to draw "undue attention" to the linguistic operation in the poems they wrote (Eagleton 1983, 6), as well as their implicit commitment to bringing into play the diachronic dimension of the poetic messages they delivered.

Hence, Mitsuye Yamada, well known for her "meditative" style and the intensity of her poetic reflections as an interior process, uses what she calls "a grass roots form" to fashion "open poems," "impromptu poems," or "blatant poems," so that she can integrate "the art of poetry with the activist's commitment to work for change in the outside world" (Jakoski 1988, 97, 99, 102, 104). In a similar vein, Janice Mirikitani's movement poetics eschews "unnecessary verbal complexity and 'difficulty'" so that her political philosophy can be unambiguously communicated, while her essentially oral or aural poetic practice (frequently augmented by music or other performative elements) can "prove important, entertaining, and accessible or else heavy-handed and didactic to different sets of readers" (Uba 2001, 318). This is the context in which Russell Leong, another movement poet, vividly describes what he calls the "practical side" of poetry, as follows: "Poems are portable. They are easily held, to a paper or between the brows. They do not need leather bindings, do not require a light projector, a picture frame, a wind or percussion instrument to carry their images or produce their sounds. Poetry is the form which, given the unity of speaker and listener, can quicken our emotions and color our perceptions. ... For our generation, poetry was the most broadly-based of crafts" (Leong 2011, 1).

The review here is not intended to prioritize a practical use of or response to poetic expression in binary terms. Instead, it points to the complexity of how poetic language can be used or appropriated depending on the purpose of its writing or the needs of its audience, with a recognition that both poems and prose fiction can be linguistically and syntactically difficult, as is the case with Myung Mi Kim's language poetry or Chuang Hua's 1968 surrealist novel *Crossings*. As Eagleton argues, it is "far from clear that we can discriminate neatly between 'practical' and 'non-practical' ways of relating ourselves to language" as the definition of literature is entirely "up to how somebody decides to read, or to determine the nature of what is written. There are certain kinds of writing—poems, plays, novels—which are fairly obviously intended to be 'non-pragmatic' in this sense, but this does not guarantee that they will actually be read in this way." Eagleton then asserts: "Some texts are born literary, some achieve literariness, and some have literariness thrust upon them" (Eagleton 1983, 8–9). From this perspective, the range of critical positions surveyed in this subsection of the chapter is relevant only insofar as they point to the internal dynamics of linguistic articulation toward its executive (cognitive or pragmatic) or emotional (synchronic or subliminal) orientation, their different effects on the audiences, and the possibility that there may be a certain brief, coincidental, or contingent matching between the authorial and auditory investments in the cognitive zone of expressions or perceptions—a possibility that is often mistaken for literature's own capacity to fulfill its social functions. This chapter will return to discussing several ambiguous aspects of literary production and reception within the purview of literature's sociology.

Community-Based Self-Representation

Although there is no denying the fact that poems may be written in ways that allow them to be read somewhat realistically in terms of literature's social effect, some Asian American scholars still believe that a basic distinction between a poetic mode of writing and that of an expositional bent is necessary. Such a view can be found in a comment made by the poet Meena Alexander during a 2006 interview. She muses: "I find it's satisfying, comforting to write essays. It's more solid [than poetry], you're speaking a language that seems more accessible. It may not be, but it seems to be. You're setting yourself in connection with other writers or looking at some theory of language. It seems to be more knitted into the fabric of a shared world, whereas a poem necessarily for its creation requires an enormous silence, apart" (Maxey and Alexander 2006, 22–3). The distinction made by Alexander between poetry and narrative is clearly occasioned by the spontaneous flow between her and the interviewer, but it also points to her interest in the kind of prose narratives composed for the explicit purpose of relaying common-sense meaning to everyday audiences. Understood in this light, Alexander's view on essay writing becomes suggestive of what Hazel Carby calls a "shared linguistic community" during the formation of an internally complex nineteenth-century African American women's discourse seeking recognition in the public domain (Carby 1987, 16–17). This community-based linguistic struggle for possession of a sharable language for women of color also finds a parallel in George Uba's concept of poetic "tribalism," by which he refers to

> a common way of negotiating identity, especially valuable as an ethnographic signifier of resistance to an oppressive, well-armed, and thoroughly entrenched dominant culture. It was a means of resisting the assimilationist ethic for so long spreading insidiously across the American ethnic landscape by focusing on and celebrating differences between whites and people of color, while acknowledging both similarities and differences among the latter as well. To some degree, much of contemporary Asian American poetry presupposes this activist base. (Uba 1992, 35)

The felt need for such literary "tribalism" is an important component of the 1974 argument made by the editors of *Aiiieeeee!*, who challenge the Anglo-American linguistic convention of the era seen as working to reinforce status quo. The editors specifically single out the "tyranny" of white language for attack, contending: "The critics were wrong in calling Toshio Mori's language 'bad English,' as William Saroyan did in his introduction to Mori's book *Yokohama, California*. … The [Asian American] critics were also wrong in ignoring or being too embarrassed by Okada's use of language and punctuation to deal with his book at all. The assumption that an ethnic minority writer thinks in, believes he writes in, or has ambition toward writing beautiful, correct, and well punctuated English sentences is an expression of white supremacy." The editors insist that the Asian American writer's "task is the opposite—to legitimize the language, style, and syntax of his people's experience, to codify the experiences common to his people into symbols, clichés, linguistic mannerisms, and a sense of humor that emerges from an organic familiarity with the experience" (Chin et al. 1974, xxxvii).

The editors' oppositional literary practice at the time—which led to their construction of an activist Asian American literary canon centering on the works of Carlos Bulosan, Louis Chu, and John Okada—was but one of the numerous expressions of the era's "cultural front," an umbrella term used to describe loosely connected political initiatives embraced by a wide range of communities and populations inspired by the spirit of the Third World Liberation Front struggles of the 1960s and the 1970s, including the radical political left (such as Black Panthers and Red Guards) and the counter-cultural rebels (such as the Hippies and the Beats) (Ling 2012, 177). During this period, aspects of Asian American creative production became an organic part of social activism. For example, the cultural workers in San Francisco Chinatown founded the Kearny Street Workshop (KSW) in 1972—the first Asian Pacific American multidisciplinary arts organization in the country—which offered classes, showcased student presentations, and hosted professionally curated and produced exhibitions, theatrical performances, reading events, and film screenings. As Laura Kang has shown in her 2002 monograph *Compositional Subjects*, Asian American women writers and artists were mobilized around community-oriented agendas either by forming social groups—such as Asian Women United of San Francisco, Organization of Asian Women in New York, Pacific Asian American Writers-West (PAAWWW), and Unbound Feet (a radical-feminist writing and performance collective)—or by establishing nonacademic publishing venues, such as *Gidra*, *Amerasia Journal*, and *Bridge*: An Asian American Perspective" (Kang 2002, 8–9).

Another aspect of engaged literary practice in the period involves Street Theatre (or the "social protest theatre"), through which Asian American artists combined politics with aesthetics in a more or less direct way. According to Lucy Burns, Asian American cultural workers "imagine different life-worlds in which their work founded possibilities for a life not yet realized and a reality not yet present. Cultural workers and artists thus played a central role within such movements where the imaginative labors of artists lay the groundwork for new worlds to come." Burns considers the musical trio A Grain of Sand and the theatrical work of *Sining Bayan* vivid embodiments of how "active gestures toward imagining other worlds" function "as a means to articulate social causes, to galvanize support, and to direct sympathizers toward campaigns of political resistance." A Grain of Sand, an Asian American popular folk music group emerging out of the

1960s, "adheres to the politics of empowering the common person, their presumed primary audience," and is well known for its 1973 album *A Grain of Sand: Songs for the Struggle by Asians in America*. *Sining Bayan*, on the other hand, is a protest theater against Ferdinand Marco's martial law regime in the Philippines, famous for its hosting "the artistic voice of the radical politics of the KDP/the *Katipunan ng mga Demokratiokong* in the United States from 1973 to 1981" (Burns 2015, 237–9, 240–8; Maeda 2009, 127–53). Such efforts, suggests Karen Shimakawa, led to the establishment of Asian American theater companies throughout the United States both in the 1970s and in the post-civil-rights era, such as the East West Players in Los Angeles, the Asian American Theater Workshop of San Francisco, the Northwest Asian American Theatre, New York's Pan-Asian Repertory, and Hawaii's Kumu Kahua theatre. These theater companies have played a unique institutional role in fostering and legitimizing Asian American cultural workers' attempts to forge productive links between staged performance and actually lived experience, and between academic setting and community ethos (Shimakawa 2001, 41, 55n3; Shimakawa 2002, 61–3). In this process, Asian American video or film organizations mushroomed in major cities, such as Visual Communications (Los Angeles), Asian CineVision (New York), the National Asian Telecommunications Association (San Francisco), King Street Media (Seattle), Asian American Resource Workshop (Boston), Asian American Arts and Media (Washington, DC), and New York City's Third World Newsreel, Women Make Movies, and the Downtown Community Television Center (Gong 2002, 101–10).

These are some of the backgrounds against which Elaine Kim coins the phrase "Defining Asian American realities through literature" (Kim 1990a), in recognition of the field's long-standing tradition of valuing the relevance of its creative expressions. Kim clarifies her sociological stance toward literature as follows: "Although I have used my understanding of Asian American social history to interpret the literature, I have focused on the evolution of Asian American consciousness and self-image as expressed in the literature." She further explains: "The problem of understanding Asian American literature within its sociohistorical and cultural contexts is important to me because when these contexts are unfamiliar, the literature is likely to be misunderstood and unappreciated" (Kim 1982, xi, xv). Kim's emphasis on the need to historicize Asian American literature is widely shared in the field, a consensus further evidenced by the routine inclusion of a pedagogical section in most Asian American studies anthologies published since the late 1970s, as well as by the availability of several book-length studies that are solely concerned with Asian American pedagogy for literary, cultural, or community studies. The latter efforts are represented, for example, in *Approaches to Teaching Kingston's The Woman Warrior* (edited by Shirley Lim, 1991); *Teaching Asian America: Diversity and the Problem of Community* (edited by Lane Hirabayashi, 1998); and *A Resource Guide to Asian American Literature* (edited by Sau-ling Wong and Stephen Sumida, 2001). Worth noting in this context are two literary monographs that give centrality to issues of social justice: James Lee's *Urban Triage: Race and Fictions of Multiculturalism* (2004); and Min Song's *Strange Future: Pessimism and the 1992 Los Angeles Riots* (2005). The former offers a powerful critique, through a multiethnic literary perspective, of the stark contrast between multiculturalism as a dominant corporate imaginary during the Reagan-Bush era and a high degree of socioeconomic stagnation and decay in racialized and underserved American urban spaces. The latter historicizes the 1992 Los Angeles riots by treating them as more than a social or communal tragedy, arguing that the riots, though directly affecting the Korean American community, "laid bare the many contradictions and pathologies quavering beneath America's skin-deep claims to civil society." Song maintains that these contradictions— rampant "economic opportunism," flagrant "state coercion," influx of "new and racially diverse immigrants," rising class-based interethnic tensions, and continued "diminishment of social services"—had been obscured before the "outburst of public violence" in Los Angeles because of the emergence of a neoconservative hegemon in the post-Cold War United States. Song's monograph, which focuses on Asian American writers' aesthetic responses to the anxieties and pessimism that reigned in the wake of the social unrest, is a compelling illustration of how literature can be used as a necessary tool for intervening in the realities confronting the Asian American artist (Song 2005, 3–4, 12).

Although the question of whether a writer bears responsibility for the community from which he or she speaks remains debatable, the poet Marilyn Chin believes that she has an obligation to be socially responsive as a woman writer of color, stating: "I believe that as a minority writer in this country, I must be an oppositional force. This is expected of me, no? To shake things up? My work is always classically poised on the basic level (a sound foundation): then, after that, it's my job to speak out. How many short brown girls in this world get to speak? So, while I have the page, I must rattle some cages" (Weisner and Chin 2012, 223). In a similar vein, Wendy Law-Yone, the "first Burmese diasporic author to write and publish fiction in English" (Ho 2014, 245), insists on getting at "the essence of buried truth" as a woman writer of color, emphasizing: "One of my ambitions is to write an unrestrained, unvarnished book completely flagrant and tasteless and silly. Because in some sense I think that would be not just liberating, it would also be true" (Law-Yone and Bow 2002, 190). From a readerly point of view, the need of unpacking what is implicit in a seemingly straightforward Asian American narrative can be challenging in that such a need is often premised on a recognition of the performative potential in the cognitive function of language. Illustrating the kind of intellectual labor that may be involved in realizing such a goal is Robert Lee's interpretation of the letters that Mary Kimito—a *nisei* woman stranded in Japan for seven years as a result of the outbreak of the Second World War—sent to two of her female friends, one in California and the other, like herself, also a *nisei* stranded in Japan. Lee observes:

> Reading letters written as private communication demands a reorientation to the particular use of language. Letters script a relationship. They contain subtexts of cues whose intention is to elicit a specific emotional response. Familiarity between correspondents allows written language to drift closer to spoken language as the writer imagines the presence of her reader and imagines the letter itself as a performance. In this sense, letters have a ritualistic quality that is not immediately accessible to the public reader. Often, the letter writer deploys a personal vocabulary, words whose encoded meaning are shared by the correspondents and whose use underlines the relationship between them. In order to decode this language, the public reader is compelled to enter into that relationship. (Lee 1995, 5)

Lee's nuanced reading of Kimito's epistolary narratives is affectively and intellectually rewarding because he approaches these letters as mediated rhetorical constructions, while it takes seriously the dialectical shift between the synchronic and diachronic speech performances in the given text by consciously foregrounding what is not said or not written.

Controversies

Despite the amount of attention accorded to the internal complexity of literary language, as well as a heightened awareness of the need to historicize literature as a rhetorical construction, controversies erupt over two concerns in the ethnic communities. First is a perceived tendency among aspiring Asian American writers to omit unflattering ethnic details from their works under the pressures of mainstream publishing industry; second is whether the content of Asian American literature disrupts or affirms persistent Asian racial stereotypes in American culture, which are seen as tied to Asian Americans' existential conditions. The first concern is often manifested in negative reactions to commercially successful Asian American writers from an ethnic subgroup undergoing self-empowerment, as is the case with the publication of Jade Snow Wong's *Fifth Chinese Daughter* (1954), Maxine Hong Kingston's *The Woman Warrior* (1976), or Le Ly Hayslip's *When Heaven and Earth Changed Places* (1989). These writers are chastised for allowing their works to be published under terms that compromise the artistic integrity of their writings or the political interests of their communities. For example, Wong is criticized for agreeing to the publisher's purge of the less polite aspects of her book prior to its publication;[1] Kingston for her failure to resist the publisher's imposition of the autobiographical genre on her fictive portrayal;[2] and Hayslip for her reticence about her Anglo-American cowriter's editorial manipulation of the original tale she tells in Vietnamese.[3]

The second concern is reflected in polarized responses to artistically sophisticated but thematically ambiguous Asian American texts: such as David Henry Hwang's *M. Butterfly* (1986), Amy Tan's *The Joy Luck Club* (1989), Bharati Mukherjee's *Jasmine* (1989), and Lois-Ann Yamanaka's *Blu's Hanging* (1998). The charges brought against Hwang, Tan, and Mukherjee are based on perceptions that these texts deliberately use exotic or mythic accounts derived from Asian lore to cater for their institutional acceptance at the expense of the communities they represent.[4] The controversy over Yamanaka's *Blu's Hanging* arises from the novel's depiction of a local Filipino laborer's tendency toward sexual violence in the context of structured interracial tensions and power imbalance resulting from centuries of colonial impositions on the islands and its populations (see Chapter 2 for a further review of this controversy).

Sometimes, the opinions voiced about how best to represent Asian American community to mainstream American culture take rather arbitrary forms, as shown in the positions taken by the editors of *The Big Aiiieeeee!* (1991). In a long introductory essay for this volume, Frank Chin makes a rigid distinction between what he considers "the real and the fake" use of Asian materials in Asian American literary writings. Taking Kingston, Tan, and Hwang to task, he calls them "the first writers of any race, and certainly the first writers of Asian ancestry, to so boldly fake the literature and lore in history." He asserts that "to legitimize their faking, they have to fake all Asian American history and literature" (Chin 1991, 3). Chin's diatribe has received a rebuttal from the poet Garrett Hongo, who argues in strong defense of the writer's creative freedom. He states:

[Chin's positions] seem chained to traits of bitterness and anger in a kind of political activist model of the Asian American writer that they have made paradigmatic, indeed, *universal.* They have alleged that literary recognition is itself a sign of a given writer's personal assimilation of an insidious bourgeois culture and a corruption of that which is the "authentic" literary culture of Asian America— something which stands defiantly and belligerently apart from the world of mainstream American letters. They have engaged in the ideological practice of judging the cultural pertinence of a given poetic work by employing a litmus test of ethnic authenticity. ... This practice, to me, is nothing more than fascism, intellectual bigotry, and ethnic fundamentalism of the worst kind. (Hongo 1994, 4)

Reflecting on the uncompromising disputes among Asian American literary scholars over the questions of representation and interpretation, Jinqi Ling detects a deeper tension between Chin's attempt to enforce a narrowly defined writerly responsibility under conditions where freedom of speech is assumed, and Hongo's implicit claims on creative autonomy or artistic license when he operates under the constraints of America's Eurocentric cultural environments. He therefore retheorizes the question of literary resistance as follows:

It is never easy to distinguish ideologically transformative texts from ideologically reinforcing ones, for judgements of a text's meaning are formed not only out of its immediate reading environment but also out of its retrospective use by subsequent interpretive communities. In this sense, there are no explicitly "oppositional" or inherently "conservative" texts but only texts that function in such ways in specific contexts. As critics we need to look into the use to which such texts have been put under specific circumstances and to explain why they generate the responses they do. (Ling 1998, 18)

Partially drawing on Ling's critique of ahistorical privileging of instant agency and equally ahistorical claims on absolute creative freedom, Viet

Thanh Nguyen develops a somewhat different argument in his 2002 monograph *Race and Resistance: Literature and Politics in Asian America*, by extending Ling's problematization of the positions of Chin and his critics to a questioning of the critical mission of the entire field of Asian American literary studies (Nguyen 2002, 179n42). He argues, without naming the actual target of his criticism, that scholars in the field are prematurely "predisposed to read for resistance, to either look for and place value upon those works that embody this type of politics or emphasize the propensity toward opposition that may be found in ambivalent texts" (Nguyen 2002, i). Elsewhere, Nguyen observes: "What the literature frequently records is not so much a project of resistance on the part of people of color, but the story of those who survived and escaped the conditions of oppression" (Nguyen 2000, 138). From this perspective, he contends that the protest literature privileged by the Asian American movement plays right into the hands of America's endlessly expansive multicultural state apparatus, while critics prone to read literature oppositionally can accomplish nothing other than socially detached performances (Nguyen 2002, 3–32).

Nguyen's critique draws tangentially on Pierre Bourdieu's notion that humanistic knowledge is a form of symbolic capital that intellectuals have accumulated in the serve of the modern French bourgeois institution from which they in turn seek economic rewards, an argument that he considers fully applicable to describing the conditions and practices of Asian American literary criticism (Nguyen 2002, 5). Yet, due to a degree of abstraction at the core of his argument, Nguyen's legitimate distrust of the binary opposition between accommodation and resistance seems to tilt in only one direction, that is, it gets close to rejecting the very idea of literary resistance. This tendency in Viet Thanh Nguyen's argument then makes Phuong Nguyen, a reviewer of his 2002 monograph, wonder if he indeed wants to pursue that line of argument. Phuong Nguyen observes:

Nguyen cannot fully come to grips with the ramifications of his radical critique. If he can prove ... that the Asian American literary canon, a canon premised on resistance to and critique of racism, can be reread for signs of flexible strategies, does he then concede that the canon can be radically rethought? While flexible strategies allow Vietnamese Americans, a more accommodationist group, to occupy the center of Asian America, how comfortable would Nguyen be with a reconfigured canon whose greats are Amy Tan, Eric Liu, and Dinesh D'Souza? Is there no room in Nguyen's analysis to recognize that some flexible strategies are more resistant than others? Nguyen does not answer these questions. (Nguyen [2004] 2005, 109–10)

Phuong Nguyen's skepticism about the applicability of Viet Thanh Nguyen's anti-essentialist critique as a general guide finds only sporadic echoes in the field.[5] More pronounced are voices that affirm or substantiate his argument, especially among scholars attracted to the visions of a post-racial Asian American literary criticism.

For example, Min Song poses the following question: "should reading, writing, and the study of literature be political acts?" To make his point, Song proposes an alternative reading strategy in place of what he considers "an aggressive interrogation of the text, a searching for ideological incongruity and contradictions." He calls the recommended interpretive strategy a "deep reading" of text for enjoyment and pleasure free of the constraints of ideological presuppositions and without "rubbing against the grain of what is written on the page" (Song 2013, 4, 16–17). Amy Tang's 2016 monograph *Repetition and Race: Asian American Literature after Multiculturalism* is premised on aspects of Nguyen's diagnosis of the resistance problematic. She suggests that US racial minorities and their politics of dissent are "firmly inscribed within" and inescapably managed by the American neoliberal institution. This situation, she maintains, sustains the accommodation/resistance binary through Asian American subject's ritualistic evocation of the dualism of trauma and rebellion as an inherent "formal logic" of Asian American literary visions, a discourse animated by an endless supply of inclusion/subjugation, visibility/marginalization, contestation/complicity, or model citizen/subversive agent binaries (Tang 2016, 1, 3–4, 11–13). To demonstrate the illusory nature of literary resistance, Christopher Lee further suggests that the seeming cohesion in visions of oppositional possibilities entertained by the idealized Asian American intellectual can be justified only through his willful blindness to the subjective nature of his own epistemology, which, in Lee's view, always "exceeds the parameters of rational knowledge," hence "alluring" or "compelling" to him as nothing but an aesthetic semblance (Lee 2012, 3–4, 13, 22).

Debating Resistance

One form of "idealized" literary/cultural resistance that Nguyen disapproves of in his critique of the said binary, but without engaging it deeply in his study, is the politics of resistance espoused by Lisa Lowe (Nguyen 2002, 153–4), which has strongly influenced Asian American cultural studies since the early 1990s. This underdeveloped aspect of Nguyen's argument receives close attention from several scholars who participated in an earlier phase of the Asian American debate over the question of literary resistance. For example, Tim Libretti observes, in his review of the interventionary method that Lowe proposes for canon revision, that "Lowe's post-structuralist solution for resisting canonization in Asian American literature is merely to catalogue the diverse constituencies of Asian American literature and by marking these differences to militate against a homogeneous construction of Asian American identity. The result, however, is yet another celebration of diversity without an exploration of the contradictions these differences represent" (Libretti 1996, 158). John Hutnyk, a cultural critic in England, is similarly skeptical about the effectiveness of Lowe's oppositional approach used in her 1996 monograph *Immigrant Acts: On Asian American Cultural Politics*. He observes: "Lowe seems to locate oppositional practice—action and theory—outside the realm of material and political struggle. … [It] seems that her analysis overdetermines the cultural in ways that are possibly reactionary responses to a rigid economism inherited from the more overtly orthodox reifications of Marxism. If this bogey were not considered so threatening, then the privilege of culture may be less absolute" (Hutnyk [1999] 2000, 44, 53). Tomo Hattori voices strong reservations about the nature of the resistance that Lowe formulates in *Immigrant Acts*, pointing out that such resistance—which renders Asians' exclusion by and distance from US national apparatus and culture into "a positive site of emergence"—misrepresents the reality and consequence of their "failed integration." He argues: "This Panglossian tactic of calling one's prison one's home and one's exile one's opportunity is a perfect expression of the adaptive and complicit logic of model minority discourse," which, he asserts, makes Lowe's "immigrant acts" an ironic exemplar of the "jouis-sense of Asian American resistance" (Hattori 1999, 232, 242).

Sustaining the oppositional visions that Lowe cherishes and the critics find wanting, it should be mentioned, is the macrological ambition of a cultural studies approach to literature in general, that is, its drive to uncover the patterns that underlie broadly conceived processes of art-making seen as unambiguously serving the interests of commercial capitalism. A distinguishing feature of this mode of literary studies, according to Russell Berman, is that it tends to "disprivilege traditionalist discussion of the particular meaning of a work of art or the intentional substance of a philosophical inquiry. It will instead attempt to describe the normative status ascribed to cultural activity in order to demonstrate the resonance between the particular work and its institutional context; for the critical significance of a work is likely to depend on the degree to which it can call the conventionality of its setting into question" (Berman 1989, 155). Although it is entirely legitimate for the Asian American critic to prioritize larger setting of literary production over the specificity of literary form and content, one problem that prevents his approach from becoming truly effective is that, as Peter Feng suggests, it "tends to de-emphasize historical contexts of another sort: generic conventions and other aesthetic traditions" (Feng 2000, 761). Hence, Wenying Xu complains that contemporary Asian American scholarship often treats literary texts as nothing but "testing grounds" for "political positions," thereby producing literary criticism that "imposes theory and politics upon literature, or colonizes literature" (Xu 2008, 16). More at stake here is that the marginalization of generic and aesthetic conventions of literature in cultural studies inevitably leads to a neglect of how resistance is enacted in specific textual situations, as well as underestimation of the complexity of counterhegemonic work generally, which, as Hazel Carby reminds, can "never [be] finally and utterly won" but must be "continually worked on and reconstructed" with patience and an open mind (Carby 1987, 17).

Whether one reads literature pragmatically, leisurely, or for its pure fictionality is, in the end, wholly a matter of personal choice. This is where a perspective articulated by Patricia E. Chu seems provocatively refreshing. She calls attention to

> the common belief that social inequality is at least in part attributable to the dominant majority's lack of knowledge about—and therefore lack of sympathy for—various minorities and their experiences. And this belief comes with a corollary: that writing, reading, teaching about, and writing about ethnic literature is a liberatory political act because ethnic literature challenges dominant ideologies about supposed lesser capacities of minority groups that cause them to be less socially valued. ... [As such,] the argument for the political value of ethnic American texts ... is grounded in the idea that ethnic peoples' material realities are affected by state policy determined by citizens who can be influenced by narrative. (Chu 2011, 530)

Xiaojing Zhou concretizes this perspective from an explicitly aesthetic point of view. She observes that "critics tend to evaluate individual texts and authors according to a predominant formula" in terms of "whether texts demonstrate complicity with or resistance to hegemonic ideologies of assimilation." She considers that this approach overlooks "the ways in which Asian American authors have resisted, subverted, and reshaped hegemonic European American literary genres," as well as how "such interventions demonstrate a much more dynamic and complex relationship between Asian American and traditional European American literature." Zhou then argues: "The agency of Asian American literature must be located in and realized through textual strategies, which include the formal structure of a text, whereby the articulation of conformity or resistance, and activities of preservation or transformation, are made possible" (Zhou 2005, 4–5).

Viewed from this perspective, the usefulness of unsettling the art/politics dichotomy in Asian American debates lies not in abandoning critical consciousness, and hence suspending the politics of resistance, but rather in the critics' refusal to essentialize or antagonize approaches that do not speak to their own agendas or fall outside their own epistemic comfort zones. This chapter ends with a perspective provided by Murray Krieger, a post-New Critical formalist who champions literary resistance as a necessary textual feature of aesthetic productions. He suggests that

> there is indeed an ideological imperative that we are learning to live with; but literature, as always, has found its own subtle way to respond to it, the way of a strangely compliant resistance. It is this resistance that marks literature's special and lasting contribution to our culture, though it is the compliance that allows its contribution to appear guileless. It is up to the critic to look past the compliance, and to remember his obligation to dwell upon the resistance as a special feature of literature. In doing so he also serves us as a socio-historical commentator who is indispensable in leading us beyond the constraints of the cultural discourse that otherwise imprisons us all. (Krieger 1993, 82)

To sum up, literary resistance to social power can hardly translate to an opposite of accommodation, which, as Krieger suggests, may simply be an act of resistance in disguise. Nor can the question of resistance be truly avoided in any serious investigation of literature, for the potential of resistance is already structured in the twin linguistic orientation of speech act, its dialectical performativity contingent upon the reader's willingness to activate such a process by consciously foregrounding the cognitive function of language, which remains undervalued in recent Asian American literary criticism. Ultimately, it is the reader—and the reader alone—who can decide whether a rhetorical construction or a narrative detail in a text should be taken as it is or it can be mobilized to accomplish the task of reorienting a discourse that he/she enters into away from official knowledge or established value systems. Understood in this way, literary resistance—an act of conscious occupation and revision of the aesthetic modalities of America's late capitalist culture—is not only deeply historical, but also inherently formalistic. It is without a doubt that such a view of literary resistance does not make the social function of literature less symbolic or less gestural, but it does tell itself apart from the utilitarianism of vulgar Marxism (whose didactic tendency seems inadvertently revived through versions of cultural studies applied in the field), or from an overtly ideological rendering of the merits or defects of literature through the ethical lens of poststructuralism, which does not always treat creative writing in its own terms. What Asian American critics may want to guard against—short of theoretical options for conceptualizing resistance in non-reductive terms under the circumstances—is an impulse of retreating to apolitical appreciation of literature on individualistic grounds.

CHAPTER 6
AESTHETIC FORM

Since the beginning of the twenty-first century, Asian American literary criticism has witnessed a significant surge of interest in aesthetic form, as part of a general shift in literary studies away from what some scholars describe as "the apparent exhaustion of cultural studies" (Beaumont 2015, 6; Hegeman 2012, 2–3). What the new formalists react against is the tendency in cultural studies to privilege the forces or processes that surround literary production over the specificity of literary form and substance, a tendency that originates from the latter's penchant for expanding the meaning and function of "text" in ways that connotes a whole range of nonartistic or nonfigurative experiences. Frequently, however, the interpretive tools utilized by scholars pressing for an aesthetic return are still rooted in the assumptions and protocols of cultural studies, which, as a central intellectual formation of the humanities in the United States during the past three decades, has remained almost the only usable paradigm for scholars who attempt to revive formal studies of literature. This dilemma seems evident in Jessica Hagedorn's 1999 characterization of Asian American aesthetics. She muses: "Is there an Asian American aesthetic? Perhaps one exists insofar as influences that extend from the mother country (place of birth) and merge/clash with the influences of a pop culture that is universally perceived as 'American' (i.e., North American). Some of these pop culture clichés include fashion and hence, dictate our self-image (jeans/black leather jackets/baseball caps), music (rock 'n' roll, black rap), which dictates the rhythms in our speech; TV ('The Cosby Show'), our notions of the model 'minority.'" She then asserts: "As Asian Americans, as writers and people of color in a world still dominated by Western thinking, it is vital that we straddle both cultures (East/West) and maintain our diversity and integrity" (Hagedorn 1999, 176–7). Noteworthy in Hagedorn's definition of Asian American aesthetics is her exclusive attention to the disruptive effect of a postmodern style of hybridity, an emphasis that has left little room for her to consider the roles of narrative or poetic form more basic to the aesthetic procedures that she is best at enacting.

Keith Lawrence and Floyd Cheung's coedited 2005 volume *Recovered Legacies: Authority and Identity in Early Asian American Literature* is another notable attempt to recenter, as they declare, "what might be termed, in the broadest sense, a 'formalist' approach" to Asian American texts. Yet, before they make clear what such an approach entails, the editors shift their attention to the audience of their book, assuring them that the formalist readings in store will be properly grounded in a variety of other approaches that would serve to "balance and contextualize 'close readings' ... without de-emphasizing or displacing the literary analysis itself" (Lawrence and Cheung 2005, 8–9). Despite the care taken to rationalize a formalistic rereading of early Asian American literature, Lawrence and Cheung remain vague about what they mean by aesthetic form. One may ask, for example, whether "close reading" of texts is the same as formalism or it is but a New Critical reading routine established under the initial assumption that the text is a linguistically self-sufficient entity devoid of biographical or historical intrusions. In addition, do the textualized discursive procedures of other analytical approaches they name—such as New Historicism, feminism, neo-Marxism, and neo-Freudianism, and postcolonial criticism—function in exactly the same way as the referential conditions of literary representation or those of literary response?

Such a tension between conscious deployment of formal methods and unconscious reliance on cultural studies logic seems also present in David Palumbo-Liu's 2008 article "The Occupation of Form: (Re) theorizing Literary History," in which he uses the concept of "form" as a connecting mechanism (or a "placeholder") for a wide range of practices and processes, such as historical analysis, spatial politics, transnational dynamics, receptive conditions, high theory, psychology, and classroom pedagogy (Palumbo-Liu 2008, 815, 833). Mark Chiang raises concerns about the myriad functions that form is made to serve in Palumbo-Liu's formulation, wondering whether there is "any basis for conceiving of an alternativeness to form outside the field of literary studies" in such a way; or "what are the material and institutional conditions that sustain the possibility of a recognition of and attention to form from its circulation among various transnational publics." Chiang then asks the crucial question: "what exactly do we mean by Form" (Chiang 2008, 836–7).

Form after New Criticism

The vagueness with which Asian American critics evoke "form" or "aesthetics" in the examples cited above affirms a point made in Chapter 5, that is, formalist studies of Asian American literature in the twenty-first century is faced with the difficulty of having too few choices in terms of available/usable paradigms. A quick summary of this perspective would bring to the foreground three institutional constraints on recent attempts to revive formalism in literary studies: the irredeemable nature of New Criticism as a once-dominant formalistic approach to literature, the undervalued status of Russian formalism in current American theoretical fashions, and the omnipresent influence of structuralism and poststructuralism well known not for their aesthetic investment, but rather their anti-foundational critique of all traditions. These circumstances then often make "form" a kind of misnomer for what is actually being practiced under the category in the recent revival of aesthetic studies, including that in Asian American literary criticism. One way to understand the ambiguous nature of the formalistic return is by taking a closer look at the relationship between the three formal options mentioned above, especially that between New Criticism and structuralism—two formalistic doctrines most adhered to in the United States during much of the twentieth century.

According to Edward Said, the sole purpose of the existence of New Criticism is to search for "a technical language with no other possible use than to describe the text's functions" (Said 1983, 144–5). From this perspective, New Criticism's fall from its pedestal since the 1970s seems inevitable because of its apparent Arnoldian bias toward culture, its historical amnesia, its anachronism with the ethos of the social movement, and its unsustainable indulgence in a polishing of the gem. Russian Formalism, though open to investigation of the cognitive dimension of literary language and hence to non-elitist aesthetics, has not been a vibrant constituency in American literary education. Under the academic climate in the United States, structuralism, with its internal distinction between a syntagmatic (diachronic or temporal) and a paradigmatic (synchronic or spatial) shifts in speech performance, is closer to Russian Formalism in its makeup, but such dynamics in structuralism, as shown in the discussions of Chapter 5, almost always veer toward the latter language situation. In retrospect, it may be appropriate to say that structuralist criticism, starting off as a leftist aesthetic reaction to the failure of the French social movement of the 1960s, has been somewhat successful in renewing the radical politics of the era, but only by shifting activism from the street to the textual labyrinth and, along with its poststructuralist descendant, by transforming literary studies into a theory-driven undertaking that favors the play of scrambled linguistic signs. It is therefore not surprising that, when Asian American literary critics are ready to make formal claims in the twenty-first century, a mission that involves a reckoning with the cognitive function of literary language, they find little intellectual grounding available to them for making it happen. For scholars dedicated to ethnic literary study (including Asian American literary criticism), the challenge seems to lie especially in how to reintroduce aesthetic or formal categories without assuming that such categories have a European essence, although literary aesthetics has been and can still be used to serve ahistorical or conservative agendas.

Tzvetan Todorov, a key figure in French structuralism, observes: "Beginning in the mid-sixties, the renewal of poetics in France was carried out in the name of the same two requirements: that criticism be internal and it be systematic" (Todorov 1987, 92). By this remark, he highlights two basic assumptions of structuralism as a formalistic approach to literature: 1) its belief that the meaning of each literary image is solely a matter of its relationship to other literary images, hence its designation of literary action as one of impersonation and the goal of literary investigation as that of producing endless difference; and 2) its vested interest in identifying all-encompassing linguistic patterns able to explain the meaning-making of literature as a general process rather than demonstrating what individual literary utterances mean or do within the contexts of their voicing, hence its tendency to suspend literary judgment and all forms of text-based political motivation or symbolic resistance (Eagleton 1983, 94–6, 112–13). In its determined drive for objectivity and comprehensiveness, structuralism thus not only rids literary studies of its New Critical complacency and parochialism, but also rules out any consideration of aesthetic pleasure, historical process, or the need for socially based subjectivity.

This ahistorical orientation in structuralism is taken to a whole new level in poststructuralism, whose operating principles are centrally concerned with identifying antitheses and contradictions, as well as exposing the effects of their paradoxical workings. Yet, because of an ethical emphasis at the core of its methods, poststructuralism often lapses into positions against its most cherished beliefs, that is, it essentializes the critical agendas of its own ideology by establishing, as Eagleton points out, "rigid boundaries" for what it deems unacceptable—coherence, stability, center, final signifieds, unitary speaking agents, and so on (Eagleton 1983, 133)—hence ironically relegitimizing the binary logic that it adamantly opposes. This is the context in which, Michèle Barrett, a cultural critic in Britain, considers "the dominant influence of the concept of ideology" that animates the anti-humanist programs of structuralism and poststructuralism a major obstacle to "serious consideration of aesthetic questions" in contemporary literary studies (Barrett 1988, 697–9). Barrett's assumption is that only by reviving the dialectical interplay between the synchronic and diachronic movements in language can the aesthetic question be effectively reintroduced.

In Asian American literary criticism, Lisa Lowe has been admirably deft and resourceful in using a cultural studies method to fashion oppositional politics across a wide range of issues or concerns. For example, her emphasis on the heterogeneity of Asian American culture as "an alternative site" that gives visibility to "fractured" histories and allows "the unlike varieties of silence [to] emerge into articulacy" has effectively challenged the uniformity of a cultural nationalist historiography (Lowe 1991, 28; Lowe 1998b, 10). Along the line, her remapping of Asian America's internal complexity and its equally complex associations with other identities, practices, and processes, as Stephen Yao puts it, has "put Asian American Studies as a whole on a closer par with other, more established fields of minority or ethnic studies, most notably African American and Latino studies, by offering an encompassing theoretical framework for the discussion of Asian American culture" (Yao 2010, 17–18). At the same time, Lowe is characteristically reticent about how the aesthetic function of Asian American literature might fit in with the complex visions she articulates, except for noting that "Asian American literature *resists* the formal abstraction of aestheticization" (Lowe 1995a, 54), or that "the question of aesthetic representation is always also a debate about political representation" (Lowe 1998b, 6).

Yao traces this underdeveloped aspect of Lowe's theoretical work to its poststructuralist roots, especially the idea of "hybridity" central to her critical program. He observes that

established conceptions of "hybridity" entirely lack the analytical capacity to distinguish between, let alone assess the political significance of, *formal* differences between texts within a field of cultural production such as Asian American verse, where matters of stylistic presentation carry at least as much signifying weight as the actual subjects or theme of representation. ... For Asian American texts, merely noting the presence of multiple cultural elements or languages and declaring them "hybrid" … falls far short. Rather, in order to address more fully the political and/or social meaning of such works, we must examine what strategies and to what ends these different cultural strands and languages are brought together to represent Asian American ethnic identity or experience. (Yao 2010, 20–1)

Lowe's largely ideological take on Asian American literature, however, is not the only reason for the field's lack of vigor in formalistic investigation of texts. Another contributing factor to this lack is the lasting effect of the culture wars of the 1990s, which works to discourage positive responses to the call for an aesthetic return among Asian American scholars. These culture wars were triggered by a right-wing attack on aspects of the humanities in American academy, specifically those concerning curricular reform, affirmative action, canon revision, gender and sexuality studies, and multiethnic literary education. Central to this right-wing hysteria is the argument that "the denunciation of Eurocentrism" in the literary profession constituted a *de facto* rejection of "an entire system for producing knowledge" about the "essential 'human' values" in American higher education (Pecora 1995, 201–3, 205). To reclaim such traditional grounds of Western civilization, conservative cultural critics E. D. Hirsch and Allan Bloom, among others, championed the ideas of Core Knowledge and Great Books, while they worked to revive classical visions, values, and traditions. Under these circumstances, scholars dedicated to ethnic literary studies felt the need for a more rigorous self-representation of what is under attack, rather than the imperative to explore the intricacy of literary aesthetics.

This is a context in which Elaine Kim reminds readers of Asian American literature that "boundary crossing must not be merely an aesthetic and intellectual exercise; we must beware lest our texts cross boundaries that a majority of our people still cannot" (Kim 1992, xiv). Grace Hong also warns against the danger of engaging in a "politics of respectability"—in reference to close engagement with literary traditions—which, in her view, may inadvertently further the humanistic reach of the neoliberal offensives (Hong 2015, 23). Rajini Srikanth states more straightforwardly: "It is my conviction that reading this literature is more than just an act of aesthetic or narrative pleasure. Rather, it must be a *just* act—doing justice to the contexts from which the writing emerges and challenges one's imagination to encounter the texts with courage, humility, and daring" (Srikanth 2004, 1). The combination of these and other factors then gives rise to what Paul

Bové finds to be a common perception among practitioners of cultural studies that careful examination of literature is not only conservative but also "hopelessly outdated" in its "reactionary effort to re-establish literature's old ideological privilege and academic position" (Bové 1995, 3).

Hence, James Lee takes issue with Jinqi Ling's formalistic reading of Emi, a politically ambivalent female character in John Okada's 1957 novel *No-No Boy*, as a figuration for authorial negotiation between the Cold War American nationalism, a conservative publishing industry, and the divided Japanese American community wrought by the racial logic that led to the internment, incarceration, and draft process during the Second World War (Ling 1998, 45–8). Lee argues: "The risk of turning Emi into an archetype, whether a figure of resolution or ironic limit, is that we tend not to look at her eyes as we listen to what she says. … We must hear both the words and muffled cry that we can see in Emi's eyes" (Lee 2006, 80). Mathew Elliott finds such a somewhat positivistic approach to literary portrayal also at work in Lee's discussion of the creative career of Hisaye Yamamoto, whose omission of the activist aspects of her post-internment life in her autobiographical accounts is read as a mirror-reflection of the author's "flight from the tense political atmosphere she encounters as a writer" in the 1950s (Elliott 2009, 52, 54–5). Elsewhere, Lee argues that there is a "dire and urgent need" for critics in the field to "read and act beyond the protocols of institution and discipline," to "move beyond finding oppositional modes within literature itself," and to respond to the "disciplinary crisis" with "intellectual honesty and institutional limits" (Lee 2004, xxiii–xxiv). Lee's legitimate emphasis on the moral obligations of literary studies echoes Elaine Kim's passionate call for "defining Asian American realities through literature" as a core mission of the field since the 1970s. Yet, as Stephen Sumida also reminds in his review of Kim's sociologically oriented 1982 monograph *Asian American Literature: An Introduction to The Writings and Their Social Contexts*, such awareness of the interconnection between literary representation and social power should not translate to precluding literary studies from engaging such textual features as "symbols, images, forms, tones, plots, or characterizations," which mark this discourse as fundamentally different from those constructed out of non-imaginative or non-rhetorical premises or intents (Sumida 1984, 105–6).

Sumida's emphasis on the need to grasp Asian American literature in its own logic or contexts of production presents the occasion for reintroducing the question of aesthetic form, which, as shown in the survey of Chapter 5 through the lens of Russian Formalism, is but the flipside of literary resistance. The discussion below thus highlights two aspects of such formally motivated literary resistance as a way of arriving at several working definitions of aesthetic form, vis-à-vis those easily reduceable to nonliterary or nonartistic discourses or arguments. First is that the most promising aesthetic modalities in literature tend to be those associated with genre deployments or genre innovations. Second is that literary resistance occurs mainly in the textual realm, in which the shifts between cognitive and intuitive speech performances manifest symptoms of literature's gaining its social accents in the form of symbols or figurations.

Within this frame of reference, Michèle Barrett describes literary aesthetics as originating in the writer's or the reader's response to their "sensory" experiences marked by "tension," "abundance," "extravagance," or excess (Barrett 1988, 697–8). Edward Said believes that aesthetics should "at a very profound level" be "distinguished from the quotidian experiences of existence that we all have" (Said 2004, 63). Drawing on the work of Jan Mukarovsky (a member of the Prague School of Linguistics), Raymond Williams asserts: "Art is not a special kind of object but one in which the aesthetic function, usually mixed with other functions, is *dominant*" (Williams 1977, 152–3). Tony Bennett, a British cultural critic, considers class- or gender-oriented "genre expectations" the key "formal mechanisms" for soliciting and organizing readerly responses in aesthetic terms (Bennett 1993, 72–3). Along the line, Mikhail Bakhtin and Pavel Medvedev forcefully maintain: "Genre is the typical totality of the artistic utterance" and, as such, poetics "should ... begin with genre," given that each genre is understood as in possession of "definite principles of selection, definite forms of seeing or conceptualizing reality, and a definite scope and depth of penetration" (Bakhtin and Medvedev [1928] 1978, 130, 131). Taken together, these working definitions of aesthetic form seem applicable to Asian American literary studies: they do not dismiss the social function of literature (in which pragmatic reading takes priority and the cognitive dimension of language is actively pursued). At the same time, as Derek Attridge suggests, a recognition of formalized literary features such as "sound-patterns, rhythm, syntactic variation, metaphorical elaboration, narrative construction" would allow texts to be investigated as "performative responses" to concrete sociohistorical conditions of artistic production (Attridge 1994, 247). Literature can thus be grasped without undue emphases on its ideology or its ethics—which always impinges on readers' consciousness through their textualized forms—a condition of reception that in turn requires acknowledgment of the different logics or dynamics of literary artistry as closely associated the imaginative and the fictitious.

Legacies and Practices

Such an understanding of the role of aesthetic form would not appeal to Pierre Bourdieu, who is more interested in identifying how "cultural capital" accumulates through university-anchored disciplines of humanistic studies and how academic certification of the technical forms of aesthetic knowledge gives art a kind of legitimacy, autonomy, or authority similar to the way social relations are ceaselessly produced and reproduced under consumerist capitalism. This process of cultural capital's accumulation, he argues, makes literary studies an implicit ideological instrument in the service of maintaining the class distinction and hierarchy in modern French society, hence inherently problematic as an intellectual investment.[1] Mark Chiang considers Bourdieu's argument the right paradigm for analyzing the 1998 controversy and protests over the Association of Asian American Studies Fiction Award bestowed on Yamanaka's novel *Blu's Hanging*, a turn of events that, for him, is symptomatic not only of Asian American intellectuals' complicity with the corporate value of American multiculturalism, but also of the failings of the entire field. Thus, following Bourdieu, he emphasizes the institutional ills of the Asian American literary profession: the increasingly autonomous status of its discourse, its quiet conversion of the movement-based political ideals to symbolic capital, and the "unacknowledged interests" of academy-based Asian American scholars who place textuality and aestheticism above social inequity and disfranchisement (Chiang 2009, 1–21). Skepticism abounds, however, outside Asian American studies regarding the soundness of Bourdieu's argument when used as a general theory for analyzing the tensions between art and politics. For example, Martin Jay detects a woeful lack in Bourdieu's knowledge about the complexity of artistic production in relation to the role it plays for social change (Jay 1993, 3, 108); Michael Denning criticizes him for overlooking the "social contradictions at the heart of middlebrow culture" (Denning 1997, 392–3); Dominick LaCapra finds his "indiscriminately" conceived notion of cultural capital unfairly discounting the participation of women, the working class, and ethnic minorities in the construction and critical revision of the Western canon (LaCapra 1989, 139–40); John McGowan points out the delusionary nature of his defining a critical space against bourgeois culture as an "ossified" institutional order (McGowan 1991, 238); and Fredric Jameson calls attention to his tendency toward anti-intellectualism (Jameson 1991, 139, 255).

Despite the currency of Bourdieu's theory of cultural capital in recent Asian American debates, aesthetic inquiry has been fruitfully conducted both during and subsequent to the formative years of Asian American literary studies. For example, in *Carlos Bulosan and the Imagination of Class Struggle* (1972)—the first solo-authored monograph in the field—E. San Juan carries out formally motivated textual analyses in the tradition of what Eagleton would call "the Marxist sublime," with an emphasis on the role of a "dual form" of revolutionary desires and the sensuality of creative labor during the birth of Filipino American subjectivity from the 1930s to the 1940s (Eagleton 1990, 196–7). The editors of *Aiiieeeee!*, though frequently criticized for their political dogma, are among the first Asian American scholars to attach importance to rhetorical styles, narrative points of view, linguistic innovation, and orality in Asian American creative writing (Chin et al. 1974, xxxv–xl). These early efforts to tackle Asian American literature by attending to its aesthetic performativity became a notable trend in the years to follow, which is represented, for example, by Patricia Lin Blinde's exploration of the techniques of genre collage and hybrid narration in *The Woman Warrior* (1980); Kathleen Loh Swee Yin and Kristoffer Paulson's analysis of the female protagonist's double voicing in *Fifth Chinese Daughter* (1982); Stephen Sumida's scrutiny of narrative gap, subtext, limited omniscience, and mock-heroic tradition in depictions of generational conflict (Sumida 1984; 1986); King-Kok Cheung's reading for authorial suspension, muted plot, and strategic reticence in the writings by women of color (Cheung 1988); Marilyn Alquizola's examination of the dialectic between manifest and latent motifs in the *bildungsroman* form used in *America Is in the Heart* (1991); and, more recently, Joseph Jeon's theorization of the "surplus novel"—a term that he derives from a pair of enigmatic displays dedicated to Theresa Cha at an exhibition—as the material form emblematic for the experimental temper of Cha's 1982 text (Jeon 2012, xvi, xiv).

Since the beginning of the twenty-first century, there has been a burgeoning of book-length studies devoted to the formal aspects of Asian American literary writings, a development anticipated by Jinqi Ling's 1998 monograph *Narrating Nationalisms: Ideology and Form in Asian American Literature.* Prominent titles in this expanding body of scholarship include: Rocío Davis and Sue-Im Lee's coedited book *Literary Gestures: The Aesthetic in Asian*

American Writing (2005); Xiaojing Zhou's *The Ethics and Poetics of Alterity in Asian American Poetry* (2006); Josephine Nock-Hee Park's *Apparitions of Asia: Modernist Form and Asian American Poetics* (2008); Timothy Yu's *Race and the Avant-Garde: Experimental and Asian American Poetry since 1965* (2009); Steven Yao's *Foreign Accents: Chinese American Verse from Exclusion to Postethnicity* (2010); Betsy Huang's *Contesting Genres in Contemporary Asian American Fiction* (2010); Pamela Thoma's *Asian American Women's Popular Literature: Feminizing Genres and Neoliberal Belonging* (2013); and Dorothy Wang's *Thinking Its Presence: Form, Race, and Racial Subjectivity in Contemporary Asian American Poetry* (2014). A notable feature of this list, which is by no means complete,[2] is that a majority of the works enumerated reflects the achievements made in poetry studies. This comes as no surprise in view of a general lack of interest in examining the interiority of Asian American narratives by scholars practicing cultural studies, as well as the fact that the recent aesthetic return took shape within circles of poetic production and poetic criticism, a field in which scholars are more confronted with and hence more sensitive to the workings of literary language.

Asian American critics participate enthusiastically in discourses on the representational politics that animates high modernism, including the avant-garde, through employment of two basic interpretive strategies. First is engaging modernism by looking into its moments of Asiatic fascination or orientalist fetish as constitutive elements of modernist aesthetics. Second is forging a connection between the avant-garde as a mode of radical artistic experimentalism and Asian American social activism enacted as a form of literary revolution. The first approach is reflected in Anne Cheng's study of what she calls "ornamentalism," by which she critiques orientalism by showing how the Asiatic figure becomes a fetishized "ornament"—inarticulate, primitive, uncivilized, and excessive—on which the coherence of high modernism's preference for aesthetic simplicity, cleanliness, minimalism, and abstraction depends (Cheng 2014, 315). Josephine Nock-Hee Park adopts a similar approach to her reading of Myung Mi Kim's poems, with a focus on the latter's "strategic" disruption of the orientalist lineage started in Ezra Pound's poetic imaginary. She argues: "Kim's work returns to Pound's Image, reimagining this modernist poetic renewal" that was begun with "fantasies of the ideogram" and ended up in "orientalist hallucinations" (Park 2008, 235). Timothy Yu's examination of Jose Garcia Villa's brief rise to literary prominence in the United States from the 1940s to 1950s is explicitly premised on a critique of orientalism. He argues: "American modernism could only adapt to the phenomenon of a Filipino modernist writer by placing him squarely within the Anglo-American literary tradition, while filtering his racial difference through an orientalism already present in modernist ideology. The presence of that orientalism also meant that there was a particular space available for Villa to occupy. In this sense, race became a curious kind of asset in his US canonization" (Yu 2004, 42). The second interpretive strategy can be found at work mainly in Yu's 2009 monograph *Race and the Avant-Garde and Asian American Poetry since 1965* (see Chapter 5 for a further discussion of this topic), and, to lesser extent, in the poetic studies conducted by Nock-Hee Park (2008, 91–121) and Joseph Jeon (2012, xxv–xxx).

There seems to be a tension between these Asian American approaches to literary modernism, however. On the one hand, critics appear to engage this elitist Euro-American literary tradition by working against its aesthetics—seen as intertwined with orientalist desires and technologies—through a critical race perspective familiar to ethnic studies. On the other hand, critics seem also working to retrieve aspects of modernist aesthetics by making a connection between Asian American artistic experimentalism in the movement era and the radical artistic revolution staged by the avant-garde as an ethical attack on Western civilization and commercial capitalism. This performative contradiction in the Asian American modernism studies then leads Brian Kim Stefans to observe that scholars in the field are somehow "forced into a consideration of the Western literary tradition ... in a peculiar way because of a vague sense of membership in a racially defined community" (Stefans 2002, 72). The point made by Stefans is clearly not that demystification of orientalism through the lens of critical race theory is unimportant to modernism studies. Rather, he seems to suggest that Asian American critics are yet to fully and rigorously engage the internally diverse aesthetic programs of modernism in their critical efforts, without assimilating them entirely into the categories of Asian American studies. Beyond the cautionary note registered by Stefans, scholars tapping into the revolutionary potentials of modernism are likewise faced with a similar challenge: that is, the need to look seriously into the socialist-inflected formalistic philosophies and writing techniques used by a long line of surrealist and futuristic figures, such as Comte de Lautréamont, André Breton, Paul Valéry, Filippo Tommaso Marinetti, Vladimir Mayakovsky, and Natalia Goncharova, among others, and to specify how exactly the Asian American movement poetry either converges with or departs from the aesthetic assumption and practices of the Euro-American avant-garde.

In his 1996 monograph *The Philippine Temptation: Dialectic of Philippines-U.S. Literary Relations*, E. San Juan dwells on (without evoking orientalism) the significance of the modernist writings of Jose Garcia Villa, the Filipino immigrant writer operating within the US poetic circles since the 1930s. He considers Villa's poems belonging to a region of "allegorical constructions of a subject-position for the decolonizing artist," whose "aestheticism registered the advent of a heterodox, transgressive creativity," and "a substitute sense of wholeness, ecstasy, and fulfilment realized in the pastiche of mimicry and verbal mock play." It is through this "inveterate avant-gardism" that, San Juan argues, Villa provocatively "demarcates a space for the subject of enunciation not just to be represented but to speak and challenge the laws of hegemonic representation" (San Juan 1996, 172, 199, 203–4). Commenting on aesthetic modernism's capacity to sponsor diverse forms of alterity, Derek Attridge emphasizes the critical potential of its politically motivated formal innovations, observing that in its "foregrounding of language and other discursive and generic codes," modernism performs "a major role in producing (and simultaneously occluding) the other." He further suggests that "it is in language—language aware of its ideological effects, alert to its own capacity to impose silence as it speaks—that the force of the other can be most strongly represented" through modernist art (Attridge 1994, 253).

Reinventing Realist Genres

Realism, an aesthetic category intricately connected to the rise of modernism in the early twentieth century and to the dominance of postmodernism and poststructuralism since the early 1980s, is a crucial, though underexamined, aspect of formal studies in recent Asian American critical discourse. The downgraded status of realism, according to Eagleton, can be traced to the work of the later Roland Barthes, who believes that the "most intriguing texts" for criticism are no longer "those which can be *read*, but those which are 'writable' (*inscriptible*)—texts which encourage the critic to carve them up, transpose them into different discourses, produce his or her semi-arbitrary play of meaning athwart the work itself." From this perspective, the "realist representational sign ... is for Barthes essentially unhealthy" (Eagleton 1983, 136–8). In Asian American literary studies, this poststructuralist tendency to devalue realism often goes hand in hand with impulses to equate realist representation with its most superficial or reductive versions. Lisa Lowe's 1995 reading of Theresa Cha's experimental work *Dictée* (1982), in which she opposes this text to the realist literary tradition of the field, seems to exemplify this trend. Lowe contends:

Dictée resists the core values of aesthetic realism—correspondence, mimesis, and equivalence—and approaches these notions as contradictions. Rather than constructing a narrative of unities and symmetries, with consistencies of character, sequence, and plot, it emphasizes instead an aesthetic of fragmented recitation and episodic nonidentity—dramatizes, in effect, an aesthetic of infidelity. Repetition itself is taken to its parodic extreme, and disengaged as the privileged mode of imitation and realism. (Lowe 1995c, 37)

Patricia P. Chu similarly suggests, in another context, that "the realist novel solicits our identification with an implied subject who is both normally unmarked by race, gender, and class and defined by the selective exclusion of particularizing traits. By erasing the operation of excluding its others, this system of reference exaggerates the universality of a perspective that, when returned to its proper framework, defines by a process of exclusion and division" (Chu 2000, 14). Along the line, Viet Thanh Nguyen provides an overtly ideological characterization of the *bildungsroman*, the prototype of Georg Lukács's interwar conception of critical realism, as part of his larger critique of the agendas of Asian American cultural nationalism. He argues: "The *bildungsroman*, while narrating the public inclusion of its subjects, also enacts violent exclusion against those who do not match the profile of its ideal subjects (white, heterosexual, male, and eventually propertied). A significant strand of American literature adapts the European *bildungsroman* by presenting narratives that trace the successful struggle of characters who achieve this public identity and its prerogatives: the formal or informal rights to property, political participation, and patriarchal domination of women" (Nguyen 2000, 132).

Colleen Lye contests this tendency in the field by pointing out that "the 1990s vogue for stylistically modernist Asian American works as bespeaking a kind of aesthetic formalism that is the flip side of a sociologically transparent reading of realism; the celebration of the avant-gardism of newer formalisms depends upon ceding the treatment of older literature by and large to sociologists (professional or not), whose naïve readings of realist narrative contemporary critics have mistaken for the naivete of the literature itself" (Lye 2008b, 549). This is precisely a perceptual/cognitive confusion that Jinqi Ling attempts to clarify in his rereading of Louis Chu's 1961 realist novel *Eat a Bowl of Tea*, in order to show realism to be a "historically constituted aesthetic phenomenon." He emphasizes: "The kind of social engagement that marks the power of Chu's realist novel is not its tendency to produce correspondence, condensation, or typification, but rather its ability to expose the inadequate modernist representation of American society in the period … , to bring to light its own split historical referent and then to call for further narrative supplementation of the reconstituted intertextual dynamics revealed by the novel's conjectural—but only conjectural—realist 'elucidation of difference' " (Ling 1998, 23, 77). Commenting on how the performativity of realist literature may be brought into play through conscious readerly engagement with the uneven conditions of the genre's deployment, he further suggests that

> patterns of repetitive similarity deducible from the [realist] novel are not necessarily innate to the latter's realist bent, but rather often determined by particular ways of seeing or reading … because readers have different degrees of familiarity with and access to its contexts, use different modes of interpretation, and occupy different cognitive domains of the novel's shifting horizon of expectations. Understood in this way, the repetitive everyday events described in the Asian American realist novel should also be seen as inherently varied in scale and irregular in duration as a result of their association with multiple temporalities that condition reading experiences, as well as the unsteady pulses produced by different forms and degrees of Asians' participation in modernity, the resultant disjunctions and upheavals always lurking beneath the given textual symptoms. (Ling 2015, 199)

A premise frequently assumed in negative assessments of realism in the field is that realist literature legitimizes its portrayal through its proponents' indulgence in mimetic illusions, a characterization of the nature of realism that, according to Karheinz Stierle, reflects but "an elementary form of reception" of the genre (Stierle 1980, 84). In recent years, Asian American critics have done significant work to complicate this aspect of Asian American formalistic studies, especially through engaging the performative potential of realism in two ways: epistemological or ideological reformulation of its literary functions; and examination of the workings of its formal mechanics under specific reading or writing environments. The first is exemplified in Pin-Chia Feng's argument about how racially or class-inflected female memories can contribute to a reconstitution of the internal structure of the *bildungsroman* form (Feng 1998, 15); Helena Grice's interpretation of a triangulated "history-memory-trauma matrix" at work in Asian American women's autobiography, memoir, or personal journal (Grice 2002, 81–2);

Rocío Davis's identification of ways in which the *bildungsroman* form can both "limn particular forms of belonging and knowledge," and "challenge textual authority and prescriptive paradigms" (Davis 2006, 162); and Betsy Huang's designation of immigration fiction, crime fiction, and science fiction "as the loci where some of the most compelling disruption and reinvention of well-worn generic formulas are taking place" (Huang 2010, 5). The second strategy can be recognized in Alicia Otano's study of the ironic tension between a given "child perspective" in the *bildungsroman* form and an implied agent (the author) that enhances such a perspective through linguistic, sensory, or perceptival innovations (Otano 2004, 31); David Shih's analysis of the "insufficiently mimetic" character of Winnifred Eaton's 1914 autobiography *Me, A Book*, in the context of the genre's routinely "formulaic reduction of the complexity of the human condition" to which Eaton's persona in the book—Pearl—is subjected (Shih 2005, 42–5); and Oscar Campomanes and Todd Gernes's demonstration of how the "epistolary mode" of writing central to Carlos Bulosan's search for "proper techniques of expression and communication" can be made "aesthetically and spiritually useful" to readers similarly placed in an "epistolary situation" (Campomanes and Gernes 1988, 16–19).

A formally motivated approach to realism is a prominent feature of the scholarship of Dominika Ferens, who promotes the literariness of the Eaton sisters' early twentieth-century writings from the intersection of presumed ethnographical authority, formal pressures of journalistic literature, and the unmarked boundaries of biracial aesthetics of self-representation (Ferens 2002, 1–18); of Traise Yamamoto's theorization of Miné Okubo's extensive use of visual lexicon and "physical and cognitive information" in the author's emotionally fraught narratives of the camp life during the Second World War (Yamamoto 2015, 173–4); of Cathy Schlund-Vials's advancing a "refugee aesthetics" that centers on reinvented witness forms consisting of elegy, textile art, oral literature, and mixed genre anthology (Schlund-Vials 2015, 489–91); and of Jeffrey Cabusao's analysis of how Bulosan's engagement with the late-nineteenth-century Euro-American convention of naturalism leads to his invention of a new mode of critical realism attuned to an emerging subaltern consciousness among the Filipino immigrants in the United States. He suggests that Bolusan uses the former genre's "deterministic logic to dramatize" the hostile forces (or the outward influences) that shape the existential dilemmas of the characters he portrays in *America Is in the Heart*—such as personal, familial, and communal "disintegration"—thus anticipating the novel's narrative shift from depicting its characters' passive survival to their joyful participation in collective struggle. This process, Cabusao argues, can best be captured only through engagement of the performativity of critical realism (Cabusao 2011, 134; Cabusao 2014, 35).

During Asian American critics' rethinking of the meaning and function of realism, Sharon Chon turns her critical gaze to the difficult relationship between race and its symbolic representation in literature, arguing that the question of visibility be theorized anew through reengagement with the social dimension of Asian Americans' racial formation, vis-à-vis the post-structuralist tendency to reduce the ontological to nothing but a naïve positivistic given (Chon 2018, 9–12). Philosophically speaking, equation of the visual with the representational is bound up with the Cartesian *cogito* central to the eighteenth-century Western modernity; such equation is also the epistemological basis on which classical realism is defined and then discredited in modernism and postmodernism. Yet, as scholars conducting critical techno-orientalism studies have shown (a topic that will be addressed in Chapter 8), racialized construction of Asian images in American popular literature reveals a persistent operation of scientific racism as a viewing apparatus, as well as the ongoing relevance of visibility as an active concern in artistic representation. From this perspective, science—which is basic to realist epistemology—should be a site to engage with or contest for, rather than one to underestimate or dismiss (Ling 2014, 498–9).

Poetic and Theatrical Studies

George Uba's 2001 survey of Asian American poetry remains an indispensable frame of reference for making sense of the extensive scholarship on poetic production in the field. In that survey, Uba designates the following formal innovations as the distinguishing features of Asian American poetry writing, especially during the formative years of its practice. They include "daring fusion of Western and non-Western poetic elements"; deliberate enhancement of the effects of "oral and aural" spontaneity (often augmented by music or performance); reliance on spatial discontinuity, grammatical dissonance, or verbal difficulty; and experimentation with nonlinguistic and purely bodily rhythms or visual means of representation (Uba 2001, 318–19). Since the beginning of the twenty-first century, a growing number of poetry studies in the field have been focused on the artistry of individual writers or groups. For example, Robert Grotjohn probes into Mitsuye Yamada's "aesthetic revision" of the trope of "desert," a stock imagery in Japanese American camp poetry, by demonstrating how the author transforms the rhetorical function of this trope from its largely denotative reference to arid lands associated with the physicality of the camp to its connotative embodiment of the spirit of "outcast harmony" on the part of the internees—inner qualities often symbolized by the images of snakes, spiders, lizards, rats, and scorpions (Grotjohn 2003, 251–2). Steven Yao contributes to an evolving post-ethnic aesthetics in the field by identifying several writing techniques—such as "cross-fertilization," "mimicry," "grafting," "transplantation," and "mutation"—as pivotal in reorienting Asian American poetic production from its initial emphasis on subjectivity-driven "lyric[s] of testimony" to that on languages of "ethnic abstraction" (Yao 2010, 4–5, 15, 23–7). Along the line, Timothy Yu foregrounds introspection, "a burrowing into language," and a downplaying of Asian American themes as some of the defining features of such a move toward "postconfessional" lyrics (Yu 2011, 819, 821–2).

In this process, Asian American scholars have developed a strong interest in comparative poetics. For example, Shelley Wong uses the Chinese concept of *tibishi*—a place-based and temporally specific inscription of traumatic feeling onto mediums available to the writer under conditions of imprisonment—to organize her discussion of the Angel Island poems. She points out that the contemporary reader, often mistaking these poems as nothing but "artifact," tends to unwittingly participate in discourses that obscure the fact that the inscriptions found on the walls of the detention barracks are more associated with a historical "event" (Wong 2015, 74–83). Josephine Nock-Hee Park recognizes a parallel between Myung Mi Kim's poem *Dura* and Theresa Cha's experimental work *Dictée*, as well as the authors' shared interest in using the long poem format and the bicultural concept of "duration" that is imbued with multiple contextual overtones (Park 2008, 235–56). Dorothy Wang delves into the representational potential of hybrid speech acts that she finds at work in many Asian American poems, observing that writers of these poems often combine a use of "deictic pronouns" (whose references must be fixed throughout their usages) with that of "shifters" (whose meanings differ from one situation to another) in order to convey poetic sensibilities that are at once "lyrical and abstract," grounded and metaphysical, for maximum aesthetic or political effects (Wang 2015, 445). In her discussion of the "diptych form" (which resembles "the hinge spinning the two panels of a painted diptych") favored by John Yau, a poet known for the experimental temper of his artistry, Wang considers its juxtaposition of two ways of being and seeing—that is, the historical and the personal, the past and the present, or the mythic and the prosaic—especially challenging to its non-Asian American readers in terms of the ontological questions it evokes (Wang 2002, 137, 150).

Since the late 1990s, Asian American critics have made fruitful efforts to engage the formal aspects of the theatrical productions in the field, although the scale of such engagement remains somewhat tentative. Notable contributions along the line include Josephine Lee's examination of how "theatrical realism" practiced by Asian American playwrights both challenges and reconstitutes its viewing communities by "involving the positioning of the spectator" on stage through "a particular level of detail in the theatre set, props, and acting style"—a strategy that she finds exemplified in Frank Chin's 1974 play *The Year of the Dragon* (Lee 1997, 34–6). Karen Shimakawa looks into the fraught space between theatrical performance and its reception, observing that "theatre is a medium that arguably depends on both the functioning and dysfunctioning of (racial/national) identity," a contradictory dynamic "both less and more embodied than others—less, in the sense of the ephemerality of a given performance; and more, in that it requires the presentation of live bodies for its full exposition" (Shimakawa 2001, 44, 46). For Lucy Burns, the performative value of theatrical art (in her case, the Filipino American stage)—given the spectator's awareness of "the gall, the guts, and the sheer effort needed to put on such a display"— resides ultimately in the genre's potential to find affective resonance in those possessing intimate knowledge about the "everyday life" of the subaltern. This provisional linkage between acting and viewing, Burns suggests, would allow for appreciation for the performed ethnic body—one simultaneous defiant and ambivalent—because of its active mediation by colonial history and cultural imperialism (Burns 2013, 2, 6–7, 9). In an extended discussion of the multiethnic American theater emerging out of the 1960s, Angela Pao explores a range of nontraditional dramatic genres—comedy, anti-realist drama, modernist drama, and the Broadway Musical—in terms of how their casting techniques and routines, as a mode of what she calls "interior positioning" for staging effects, both shape and are being shaped by considerations of race and ethnicity, hence ideologically transformative in practices of generic deployments and spectatorial expectations in the United States since the 1960s (Pao 2010, 1–22).

The survey of Chapter 5 ends with the assertion that the social function of literature can be best demonstrated not through the reader's equation of literary meaning with her/his own political beliefs, but rather through her/his conscious interpretive enhancement of the performative potential of the cognitive dimension of literary language. From this perspective, aesthetic form merits attention only insofar as it can evoke the social and historical forces at work underneath the immediacy of textualization, which, as the formalized surface of an artistically recreated world, may best be approached, before all else, in formalistic terms to do full justice to literature as a rhetorical construction. At stake here is how to rationalize a formal quest in the actual practice of literary criticism. Part of the answer to this question is provided by Xiaojing Zhou, who argues that a formal method can be productively applied (by which she refers to poetry writing) through ideologically motivated aesthetic innovations. In this process, she suggests, language becomes "inflected with 'alien' sounds or 'foreign' accents" that disrupt received literary values or conventions (Zhou 2006, 2, 5). What Zhou describes is a contribution made by the writer, who consciously revises the linguistic norms of given genre conventions in order to expand their horizons of expectations. More important, it seems, is the role played by the reader who has the potential to exert a greater influence on the outcomes of an insertion of a minoritarian point of view into sedimented attitudes or habitual thinking, for the consumption phase of literary production is mainly centered on acts of interpretation, including those aimed to discern, elucidate, and extend the oppositional possibilities lurking beneath a finished literary product. What needs to occur during the shift from writing to reading as the chief site for socially symbolic work on literature is a realignment of the order between ideology and form in Zhou's formula. That is, the ideologically motivated formal innovation engaged in by the writer be given way to formally motivated reading for ideology on the part of the critic.[3] Such an understanding of a formalistic approach to literature under the current academic climate would require certain awareness of the limitations of structuralist and post-structuralist methods—in which the referential role of language has been displaced by a hermeneutic of misreading (often troped on the figure of catachresis)—and a degree of receptivity to alternative theoretical models (such as Russian Formalism) as a prerequisite for dialogizing Zhou's writerly based Asian American poetics.

Chapter 7 shifts the focus of its survey to a different concern, that is, how the field has evolved and renewed itself institutionally since the late 1980s, by paying attention to several aspects of its practices as an academic discipline: its efforts to build and reshape its reading communities, to periodize its creative productions, to address the methodological tensions in its pedagogic and critical discourses, and, since the advent of the new millennium, to engage in post-identity politics.

CHAPTER 7
PROTOCOLS AND THE POLITICS OF INSTITUTIONALIZATION

This chapter examines several aspects of Asian American institutional practices since the 1980s. Such practices include, among others, efforts to enlist audiences for the field's evolving discourse on its creative or critical production, to rationalize its teaching and research activities by way of periodization, to negotiate the methodological tensions that arise from its engagement with multiple trends or influences, and to fashion strategies for its self-renewal in shifting contexts. Within the scope of this examination, a number of questions have repeatedly come to the fore and become guiding principles for the discussions to follow. For example, what were the initial indicators of the field's professionalization and how have they changed over time? What are the gains and losses during the field's acceptance into the cultural establishment since the late 1980s? How do scholars negotiate the tension between their aspirations to transform the field in purely intellectual terms and the practical constraints on how the field performs as a community-based cultural formation? What are some of the conditions that give rise to a post-racial politics among scholars who came of age in the twenty-first century and how would such a shift in political commitment impact the Asian American literary profession that remains peripheral in the larger realm of American culture? These aspects of the field's professional work, as shown in the surveys and discussions of the preceding chapters, are intricately linked to its internal debates over the theory and practice of its work, which has been continually shaped by the dominant, the residual, and the emergent forces that surround its evolution.

Reading Formations

It is a general agreement among Asian American scholars that King-Kok Cheung and Stan Yogi's 1988 coedited *Asian American Literature:*

An Annotated Bibliography constitutes a major milestone in the field's professionalization. Sau-ling Wong, for example, considers its presentation of Asian American creative writing as a discourse flourishing in mixed genres studies (poetry, autobiography, prose, travelogues, nonfiction, and drama, among others) a strategic rearticulation of the meaning of "literariness" from a minoritarian perspective, a move that effectively dislodges the term from its belletristic emphasis in traditionally conceived English department (Wong 2001, 235–6).[1] In addition, this annotated bibliography is explicitly heterogeneous in its coverage: it includes the works by Asian writers in Canada, of non-permanent-resident status in the United States, and of mixed descents, as well as the translated works originally written or published in different Asian languages (Cheung and Yogi 1988, v–vi). Shirley Lim thus praises the editors of the annotated bibliography for giving the body of writings they have assembled "a contemporary breadth of references" and for their forward-looking acknowledgment of the contributions of Asian immigrant writers—Vietnamese, South Asians, and Southeast Asians, among them—who are either underrepresented or entirely absent in *Aiiieeeee!* and *The Big Aiiieeeee!* (Lim 1993b, 576). By all accounts, this annotated bibliography has admirably fulfilled its promise of producing "the most comprehensive reference guide to Asian American literature possible to date" (Cheung and Yogi 1988, vi) and, as Stephen Yao observes, its content can be readily articulated into the critical concerns of the field in the twenty-first century (Yao 2010, 272n12).

Shirley Lim and Amy Ling's 1992 coedited volume *Reading the Literature of Asian America*—the first collection of essays on literary criticism in the field—represents, in the words of its editors, "a pioneering feat" that "underlines both the newness of the concept of an Asian American literature and, paradoxically, its crucial belatedness" (Lim and Ling 1992, 5). Similar to what Cheung and Yogi aim to accomplish through their annotated bibliography, this collection of essays is committed to pluralizing the gains of the cultural nationalist period (by including in it, for example, the previously little examined Asian Pacific islander American literary output), rather than entirely displace the canon established by *Aiiieeeee!* with something else. This feature of the book is reflected in its double thematic emphasis. On the one hand, contributors of the volume foreground the "multiple and shifting" identities that characterize the new modes of Asian American critical work (Lim and Ling 1992, 4). On the other hand, they also affirm the continuing relevance of the legacies of cultural nationalism by recognizing that "it was immensely difficult for Asian Americans to find venues for their writings" in the 1970s and that "insisting on a unitary identity seemed the only means of opposing and defending oneself against marginalization" (Kim 1992, xii). Meanwhile, this volume resonates with Cheung and Yogi's annotated bibliography in two specific ways: it pays close attention to mixed genres studies, while it also presents the progress made in Asian American critical production since the early 1980s with a legitimate sense of optimism. This sentiment is voiced in the preface of Cheung and Yogi's annotated bibliography that ends with the remark, "let us rejoice that Asian American literature is flourishing and hope that our effort will further stimulate scholarship in this expanding field" (Cheung and Yogi 1988, vi). In the 1992 edited volume, Elaine Kim, a contributing author, similarly reflects: "At the moment, we are experiencing the start of a golden age of Asian American cultural production" (Kim 1992, xi).

David Palumbo-Liu, a reviewer of Lim and Ling's collection of essays, feels less certain about the state of the field celebrated by Kim and others. Instead, he raises questions about the critical methods employed by several authors included in this volume, problematizing especially "two new cultural passwords, *postcolonial* and *postmodern*," that he considers used carelessly without adequate attention to their applicability to Asian American texts. He contends: "Theory may prove its analytical strength by excavating theretofore hidden 'truths' of an ethnic literary text, and ethnic literary critics may champion the legitimacy of ethnic literature by finding in it the confirmation of theory, but both may do so precisely by ignoring significant contradictions that inhere in these texts. Such contradictions should be acknowledged." From this standpoint, he cautions:

Scholars of ethnic literature today should pause over its new centrality in postmodern culture. If the movement toward the wholesale embrace of these discourses entails as well the abandonment of the very material histories that have shaped ethnicity in importantly different ways, then one should at least directly address that elision and argue for its legitimacy. In tracking ethnic literary studies from the margin to the new center, one should ask whether that movement has not been accompanied by a particular critical reformulation of the texts and consider the significance of that reconstruction. (Palumbo-Liu 1995a, 161, 167–8)

What Palumbo-Liu fears is that Asian American literature may have become theoretically tokenized during its acceptance into the American literary mainstream, a possibility that, he also worries, has received little consideration in the way Lim and Ling launch their 1992 essay collection as but a success story (Lim 1992a, 13–14). These concerns seem to be the motivating forces behind the publication of his 1995 edited volume *The Ethnic Canon: Histories, Institutions, and Interventions*—a multiethnic assemblage of opinions about the pros and cons of the ethnic American scholar's working within the cultural establishment. Of the Asian American critics included in this collection of essays (Lisa Lowe, Sau-ling Wong, E. San Juan, Colleen Lye, and Palumbo-Liu himself), the positions taken by Palumbo-Liu and Lowe are symptomatic of an emerging tension in Asian American cultural studies that would intensify in the years to follow. Palumbo-Liu, recognizing the "neutralizing operations" of canonization, emphasizes the strategic importance of the "angles" of the ethnic text's "entry" or "insertion" into the established cultural apparatus, which, in his view, would allow a critical multicultural project to develop among "the fissures, tensions, sometimes contradictory demands of multiple cultures, rather than (only) celebrating[sic] the plurality of cultures by passing through them appreciatively" (Palumbo-Liu 1995b, 2–3, 5). Lowe, on the other hand, sees Asian American literary studies as an "inherently contestatory" site by virtue of its presence in the expanded canon because, she argues, "the non-equivalent determinations of race, class, and gender" disrupt the uniformity, autonomy, and developmentalism of Western and nationalist narratives (Lowe 1995a, 49, 51; Palumbo-Liu 1995b, 19). Despite an obvious overlap between the positionalities they assume respectively, what remains to be clarified is how to "theorize points of opposition and resistance" in ways that can be embraced by "a truly critical multicultural criticism" (Palumbo-Liu 1995b, 15), without resorting to ungrounded quests for conceptual tensions or differences.

Within a span of six years since 1995, three more collections of essays were published, which, in one way or another, continued with the existing trend of positioning the field beyond cultural nationalism, while acknowledging the negotiated nature of such a transitional process. Of the three volumes, Elaine Kim and Norma Alarcon's 1995 coedited *Writing Self, Writing Nation* represents a most radical break from the agendas of the cultural nationalist period through its establishment of Theresa Cha's 1982 experimental text *Dictée* as the model for an emerging Asian American diasporic subjectivity. King-Kok Cheung's 1997 edited *An Interethnic Companion to Asian American Literature*, on the other hand, emphasizes the "interethnic cohesion" of the field in transition despite her awareness of the contested relationship between a continuing hold of a cultural nationalist ideology on aspects of the field's practice and the irresistible nature of the field's post-national shift (Cheung 1997, 1–4). Within this context, Sau-Ling Wong and Stephen Sumida's 2001 coedited *A Resource Guide to Asian American Literature* may be seen as the last concerted effort in the field to maintain a productive tie between an Asian American diasporic imaginary and the legacy of cultural nationalism. Central to the editors' efforts along the line is their rearticulation of the meaning of "Asian American," a term that, they argue, does not connote "reified identity," but rather functions as a "dialogic" signifier open to registering the heterogeneity of Asian American realities implicitly anticipated by the foundational work done during the cultural nationalist period (Sumida and Wong 2001, 3–5).

The first two decades of the twenty-first century have witnessed a continued high yield of Asian American critical productivity, a proliferation of theoretical models, and ongoing intellectual innovations across a wide range of interests. Embodying the field's transformation during this period are several collective efforts that engage with the concerns energizing the field since the mid-1990s. Such efforts include, among others, Kandice Chuh and Karen Shimakawa's coedited *Orientations: Mapping Studies in the Asian Diaspora* (2001); Rocío G. Davis and Sämi Ludwig's coedited *Asian American Literature in the International Context: Readings on Fiction, Poetry, Performance* (2002); Keith Lawrence and Floyd Cheung's coedited *Recovered Legacies: Authority and Identity in Early Asian American Literature* (2005); Shirley Lim, John Blair Gamber, Stephen Sohn, and Gina Valentino's collectively edited *Transnational Asian American Literature: Sites and Transits* (2006); and David Roh, Betsy Huang, and Greta Niu's edited *Techno-Orientalism: Imagining Asia in Speculative Fiction, History, Media* (2015). Testifying to the cumulative gains in this phase of the Asian American critical practice are two volumes specifically designed to synthesize, update, and showcase the range and diversity of the field's latest work. Rachel Lee's 2014 edited volume *The Routledge Companion to Asian American and Pacific Islander Literature* uses key words to highlight the multiple lines of expertise and unfolding strengths of individual or collective work, while underscoring the potential of post-identity, post-humanist, and multi-disciplinary inquiries. Rajini Srikanth and Min Song's 2015 coedited volume *The Cambridge History of Asian American Literature* provides a most comprehensive mapping to date of the field's major trends, emerging intersections, recent accomplishments, and growing intellectual sophistication, with a usefully synthetic view of the range and depth of Asian American literary history, as well as the defining moments of its evolution.

Periodization

Periodization of literary history is always complicated because scholars use different methods of classification and different criteria of analysis in making sense of the relationship between the past and present of such history. Especially challenging to Asian American literary critics in this process is that the field they attempt to rationalize is well known for its multiple and asynchronous origins and traditions, as well as its constantly changing priorities due to its emphasis on the rights for new constituents. According to Colleen Lye, the periodizing methods adopted by a majority of scholars in the field are those formulated along two historical trajectories: that of the political history of the 1969 San Francisco State Third World Liberation Front Strike, a moment that marks the birth of an Asian American political consciousness; and that of the legal history of the 1965 Immigration Act, which ushered in a new demographic era for an unprecedented growth of Asian American communities. Acknowledging the tremendous service that such a historiographical approach has done to the field since the late 1980s, Lye also underlines its tendency to limit the range of questions scholars are able to raise, especially regarding how the increasingly diversifying Asian American cultural productions today can still meaningfully relate to the field's political insurgent 1970s (Lye 2008b, 550–1).

As shown in the preceding discussions of this chapter, anthologized scholarly opinions since the early 1990s are not only established through a continued reliance on these historical cutoff years extrinsic to literature, but also prioritizing, with a certain degree of unanimity, the political benefit of distancing contemporary Asian American critical discourse from that of the cultural nationalist period. Such a perception of a temporal break between the field's past and its present seems to underlie Keith Lawrence and Floyd Cheung's Introduction to their 2005 coedited volume *Recovered Legacies*, an admirable attempt to reengage with the "rich, diverse, and complicated writings of Asian American literary pioneers" from 1880 to 1965. But the editors have simultaneously sidestepped cultural nationalism—a linchpin connecting the historical period that their volume delves into and the contemporary Asian American creative and critical practices—by deflecting the issue of contextualization they prominently raise to the realm of textual authority as a "self-contained structure and content" of the literature they revisit (Lawrence and Cheung 2005, 1–2). In so defining the purpose of their study, the editors inadvertently minimize the periodizing/historicizing mission central to their project, while reinscribing the agendas of presentism common in recent Asian American literary and cultural studies, despite their declaration to the contrary.

During this process, such historiographical/legal dividers have also become conceptual instruments for scholars to reimagine the field's future in two basic ways: first, by articulating it into a postcolonial imaginary; and second, by redescribing it through the identity politics of post-1965 Asian American generationalism. The former approach, still tentative in Lisa Lowe's "wedding of Antonio Gramsci and Homi Bhabha" in her 1991 article (Lowe 1991, 29–32; Lye 2008a, 551), became somewhat programmatic in Viet Thanh Nguyen and Tina Chen's guest-edited 2000 special issue of *Jouvert* on "Postcolonial Asian America." The editors contend: "Postcolonial identities … offer challenges to Asian America in terms of questioning the stability of racial identity to be an effective tool of mobilization and change. American identity is challenged in another, perhaps more surprising way through the histories of colonization themselves." Reversing Kingston's cultural nationalist rhetoric of "claiming America," they suggest that a postcolonial perspective foregrounds the contradictory concerns of homeland, diaspora, and global capitalism, which "create the conditions of migrancy and resettlement for many postcolonial populations" (Nguyen and Chen 2000, 2).

This postcolonial rearticulation of Asian American literary studies, though reciprocated by Kandice Chuh and Karen Shimakawa in their 2001 coedited collection of essays, is met with skepticism from several scholars who participate in this aspect of the Asian American debates. For example, Malini Schueller points out that the trope of migrancy works to privilege only Third World diasporas operating at First World metropolitan centers, emphasizing that the editors, though seeing their positionality as "inherently destabilizing and disruptive of modernity" as members of such diasporic communities, have overlooked the basic fact that "the most massive movements of population since decolonization have occurred among these decolonized nations [themselves]: Bangladesh to India, Afghanistan to Pakistan, Rwanda to Zaire." From this perspective, Schueller voices strong reservations about the applicability of the "postcolonial" as a blanket term for future Asian American literary studies (Schueller 2004, 171–4).

From an Asian North American point of view, Iyko Day also argues that the phenomenon of "racialization in capitalism emerges from the particular contours of settler colonialism in North America whose conditions are distinct from the geopolitical context" from which the postcolonial arguments are made. She suggests that "the formal end of British and Dutch imperial rule and colonial administration in the late 1940s initiated a complex process of decolonization that was encoded into the 'post-' of postcolonialism. Settler colonialism, on the other hand, is effectively immune to the process of decolonization." Day stresses in particular: "The corresponding features of Asian racialization in settler colonies capture the moving spirit of settler colonialism: a formation that is transnational but distinctively national, similar but definitely not the same, repetitive but without a predictable rhythm, structural but highly susceptible to change, everywhere but hard to isolate" (Day 2016, 16–18). Jenny Sharpe, a postcolonial theorist working in the intersection between postcolonial and feminist/ethnic studies, considers it unwise to lump Asian American social conditions and experiences with postcoloniality, emphasizing that "when used as a descriptive term for the United States, *postcolonial* does not name its past as a white settler colony or its emergence as a neo-colonial power; rather, it designates the presence of racial minorities and Third World immigrants." Sharpe especially calls attention to Spivak's hesitance to associate US postcoloniality with migrancy, reflecting that the only case in point is Robert Blauner's internal colonialism analogy for African Americans, native Americans, and Asian Americans so far as urban ghettos and internment camps are concerned. The weakness of such an analogy, she suggests, lies in its drawing too sharp a distinction between voluntary (assimilation-oriented) and involuntary (refugee-centered) movements of populations, and hence "neglecting racism in immigration" (Sharpe 1995, 191, 193).

The second way of using the historical/legal break to reimagine Asian American literary studies is foregrounding the role of "the post-1965 Asian American immigrant subject," the cultural agent theorized by Lisa Lowe and charged with the mission of disidentifying from the "racial essentialism" of *Aiiieeeee!*'s cultural nationalist ideology, which subtends the field's founding visions and much of its ongoing creative and critical practice (Lowe 1996, 103–4; Lowe 2001, 267–8, 273). Lowe's call for departure from the tradition of Asian American studies through a generational lens has been a source of inspiration for quite a few Asian American scholars, who find it not only theoretically justifiable but also morally imperative to go against the basic assumptions of the field as a minoritarian academic discipline. For example, Leslie Bow rewrites traditional Western literature's tendency to misrepresent women as the perpetrator of perfidy into an Asian American feminist strategy of "betrayal," one that, she suggests, can be used to undermine the cultural nationalist emphasis on "collective identification, subjectivity, and belonging" (Bow 2001, 3). Kandice Chuh likewise calls for "putting aside the use of the signifier 'Asian America'" as well as its legal designator of "citizenship," arguing that the field's "bonding" with "the cultural and material imperialism of this nation" must be snapped (Chuh 2001, 277–8). Employing the methods of psychoanalysis and clinical studies, David Eng and Shihee Han advance a politics of "mourning" by which they intend to register the American-born or American-reared Asians' sense of being caught between a double bind: their alienation from the ethnic immigrant community that remains not fully American and their inability to participate in mainstream American culture and society through equal assimilation. Although Eng and Han also gesture toward an alternative form of community building by evoking the politics of mourning, they are generally vague about how exactly it can translate to a collective ethos in social and material senses (Eng and Han 2003, 344–5, 367).[2]

Several scholars choose to straddle the legal (1965) or historical (1969) divide that most periodizing efforts rely on, by focusing on the Cold War as a major frame of reference for tracing the origins or key developments of Asian American literature. For example, E. San Juan has worked extensively to uncover the Cold War conditions against which Carlos Bulosan enacts his literary activism, as a labor movement activist and an alleged "communist" agitator facing FBI investigation and deportation in the 1950s (Alquizola 1991, 202–3; San Juan 1996, 155–7). Paul Nadal looks into the history of American exportation of New Critical doctrines to the Philippines, which began in the 1930s and culminated in the early years of the Cold War. Identifying the Rockefeller-funded 1958 National Writer's Conference held in Baguio as a defining moment that witnesses the convergence of several transpacific discourses emanating from the United States (that of containment of communist and anti-colonial movements in the Third World, that of nationalist revival in the US-backed Philippines, and that of global reach of an ahistorical Anglo-American literary formalism), he underscores the ideological purpose that New Criticism was made to serve in the Eisenhower era (Nadal 2021, 562–8). In their respective analyses of American culture and popular imagination during the Cold War, Caroline Chung Simpson and Heidi Kim call attention to the generic "battles" frequently waged in the American publishing or entertainment industry, which was constantly pressured by its mainstream consumers to omit Asian characters in literary, TV, or film productions (Kim 2016; Simpson 2002).

Jodi Kim's 2010 monograph *Ends of Empire: Asian American Critique and the Cold War* is by far the most sustained effort to use the Cold War as a main reference point for comprehending the nature of Asian American creative writing during the post-Second-World-War decades. Focusing on the histories and consequences of American military involvements in the domestic politics of several Asian countries (such as China, Japan, Korea, and Vietnam), she maintains that the massive destruction, widespread human tragedy, and tremendous loss of innocent lives that result from such interventions best illustrates the logic and substance of the American Cold War foreign policy. On the basis of this observation, she argues that much of the contemporary Asian American literary or cultural imaginary, which bears the traces of "the U.S. Cold War's violent displacements" and "the conditions of possibility for the post-World War II formation of Asian America," need to be understood in such contexts (Kim 2010, 6).

Susan Koshy makes a notable attempt to periodize the field by linking its post-1980s practices to mainstream American literary history, suggesting that, since that time, the production of the Asian American novel (the topic of her discussion in the article referenced here) "coincides" with the larger US literary history's "transition from the modern to the postmodern" (Koshy 2011, 1046–7). This view of the field's post-1980s development, though shared by other critics who see a similar shift from the humanist to the post-humanist in literary studies generally, is somewhat debatable when examined in light of an unresolved definitional "war" in the field regarding the placement of Theresa Cha's experimental work *Dictée* in American literary history. For example, a significant number of analyses of this text have been conducted under the rubric of modernism (Cheng 2000, 139–68; Lew 2001; Park 2008, 122–46; Stefans 1994; Yu 2009, 100–37), whereas the modelling of a non-essentialist Asian American subjectivity is routinely predicated on treating *Dictée* as a quintessential postmodern or poststructuralist narrative (Chuh 2001, 281–6; Kang 1995; Kim 1995; Lowe 1995; Wong 1995, 103–6). In this process, there is an occasional loss of distinctions between modernism as a formal investment in the autotelic function of language and modernity as a set of Western social-cultural premises or conditions, or between postmodernism as the quantifying logic of late capitalist culture and postmodernism as a self-designated periphery consciously embraced by those who see themselves as modernity's other. Alternatively, some Asian American critics—such as Daniel Kim, Timothy Yu, and Joseph Jeon, among others—turn their gaze to the activist years of the 1960s and the 1970s in order to find a renewable literary referent for contemporary Asian American creative practice that is not only politically engaged but also aesthetically flexible. As a consequence, the periodizing efforts made by the majority of Asian American critics seem more in tension, rather than in resonance, with mainstream literary history's shift from modernism to postmodernism, as suggested by Koshy.

A periodizing approach that uses literary realism as its rationale is proposed by Jed Esty and Colleen Lye in their 2012 essay on "peripheral realism." According to the authors, redeployment of this realist genre as a way to periodize ethnic literary productions may do more justice to the "variegated terrain" and "converging trajectories" from which ethnic literature makes its appearance in the Western metropolis, while it also helps bridge a widening gap between reality, cognition, and self-representation in emerging fields that undergo rapid growth and transformation under the influence of poststructuralism (Esty and Lye 2012, 269, 272, 278, 287). In the larger realm of American literary studies, T. V. Reed's 2021 *The Bloomsbury Introduction to Postmodern Realist Fiction* represents a more substantive move, both conceptually and in terms of the mechanics of literature, toward forging productive links between post-humanist theoretical visions, subaltern aesthetics, asynchronous conditions of articulation, and the need to update the referential technologies for inorganic literary representations (Reed 2021, 1–69).

Methodological Challenge

In her 1996 monograph *Immigrant Acts: On Asian American Cultural Politics*, Lisa Lowe writes: "Interdisciplinary studies disrupt the narrative of traditional disciplines that have historically subordinated the concerns of non-Western, racial and ethnic minority peoples, and women, insofar as they hold the potential to transform disciplinary divisions that guarantee the self-evidence of these narratives" (Lowe 1996, 40). Along the line, she further suggests in a subsequent study: "Asian American history narrates the breakdown of the explanatory power of the abstract divisions of society into the political, the economic, and the cultural. Thus, studies of the 'Asian American' engage with the traditional disciplines of history, literature and the arts, and the fields of social sciences, and, in the process, requires a revision of the objects and methods in these fields" (Lowe 1998a, 41). Lowe's emphasis on how the social conditions of Asian American existences are shaped by Western knowledge, as well as the possibility that changing the way knowledge is produced or disseminated may lead to a total transformation of such conditions in a material sense, has generated enthusiastic responses among Asian American critics who aspire to revamp

American society in the exclusive domain of superstructure. For example, Laura Kang maintains that disciplinary revision of the field "necessitates an attentiveness to how the current formation of knowledges under the banner of the various identity-based disciplinary 'studies' are bound by certain disciplinary protocols as well as possibly complicit with disciplinary power's penchant for surveillance, documentation, and categorization." As a countermeasure, she proposes the idea of "trenchant interdisciplinarity," by which she refers to disciplinarity that is at once "agonistic" and "situated" in relation to prevailing forms of knowledge and their reproductions, as well as to the differential historical status accorded to those knowledge formations and epistemological frameworks (Kang 2002, 19–22). What such an interdisciplinary Asian American subject seeks to accomplish is not only destabilization of received epistemology but also a canceling out of the ontological basis for the knowing Asian American subject within the United States modernity. Hence, Kandice Chuh argues that the logic organizing Asian American studies research has so far been that of "the imperialism of American ideology" and that, by "claiming ownership of U.S. national identity, Asian Americanists must also claim responsibility for the cultural materialism of this nation" (Chuh 2001, 278).

Victor Bascara voices a divergent view by emphasizing the ongoing relevance of the concept of "Asian American" fashioned out of the movement era, as well as what he considers the unfinished Asian American mission of "claiming America" as envisaged by Maxine Hong Kingston in 1980. For him, the latter concept still "holds out the possibility of the self-determination that begins at naming," while it also allows for effective social or intellectual interventions either "through earnest appeals to the state for ... reparations or access to resources, or as an ironic performance designed to demonstrate the state's inability to redress wrongs" (Bascara 2006, xxvi–xxvii). Sau-ling Wong contends forcefully that "if claiming America becomes a minor task for Asian American cultural criticism and the espousal of denationalization becomes wholesale, certain segments of the Asian American population may be left without a viable discursive space." She suggests: "It would be far more useful to embrace *modes* rather than *phases* of Asian American subjectivity: an indigenizing mode can coexist and alternate with a diasporic or transnational mode, but the latter is not to be lauded as a culmination of the former, a stage more advanced or more capacious." Wong's position, articulated in her 1995 essay "Denationalization Reconsidered," is in line with a dialogic model of coexistence of and alternation between the "indigenous" and the "transnational" investments (terms that she sometimes makes exchangeable with "domestic" for the former and "diasporic" for the latter) that she proposes in the same essay. Unequivocal about her belief in community-based struggles through textual coalition, Wong endorses transnational studies—which she has participated in pioneering in the field—only insofar as the latter can be used to better understand and help transform the circumstances surrounding the domestic concerns because of the continuing institutional prejudices (especially in terms of race and class inequalities) still facing Asian Americans (Wong 1995a, 16–17).

As indicated in the various discussions in the foregoing chapters of this study, the disciplinary or methodological challenge posed for recent Asian American literary studies often centers on concerns about the day-to-day operation of the profession: that is, how to reconcile the tension between an overabundance of the particularistic and frequently conflictual positionalities in the field under the overarching ideal of heterogeneity, and the field's practical need to represent itself with a degree of unity and consistence in the larger realm of American culture and society. Susan Koshy sheds light on some of these entangled questions by pointing out the limitations of the field's habitual conflation of emerging group identities as a sociopolitical concern with its canon formation as a literary event. She observes that "the pace of production of critical and theoretical statements about the writing has lagged well behind the prolific production of anthologies of Asian American literature. This is, in part, because significant scholarly energy has been directed toward editing and introducing the works of individual or groups of Asian American authors" mainly through "biographical summary or thematic observations." One result of this approach to legitimizing the expanding institution and constituency of Asian American literary studies, she warns, is that the anthologized opinions can easily assume a "canon-forming power" that guides the interpretation of this literature (Koshy 1996, 324–5).

Methodologically, the tension between the semiotically valenced sociology of cultural studies and the applied requirement basic to ethnic studies approaches—a tension, as Stuart Halls observes, rooted in the uneven theoretical development in academy-based Western humanistic and social science discourses since the mid-1970s—may boil down to a fundamental question, that is, whether the linguistic logic and performative procedure in the former can fully describe or sufficiently explain the empirically verifiable concerns or experiences that the latter is designed to tackle. For example, the 1986 edition of Michael Omi and Howard Winant's *Racial Formation* contains a long inventory of how racism affects people of color in the United States of the pre-1965 era in matters of "employment, housing, social program design, and the disbursement of local, state, and federal funds" (Omi and Winant [1986] 1994, 3–4). The sociological facts that Omi and Winant present on the basis of data collecting and data analysis obviously belong to a domain of knowledge both unfamiliar to and perhaps often misunderstood by Asian American humanists. Thus, Omi and Winant remind their detractors that "radical pragmatism" will remain essential to sociology for its capacity to "fully situate" racial formation "in the context of structural racism." They point out: "Understanding intersectionality requires a strong recognition that self-reflective action shapes the production and transformation of individual and collective identities. Self-activity happens as we choose our battles in the contradictory conditions of the post-civil-rights and, yes, post-second-wave-feminism periods that we are in" (Omi and Winant 2008, 1566, 1569). Yen Lê Espiritu, who is both open to and adept at applying postmodern insights to her socially grounded research, makes clear her preference for situating Asian American studies "both intellectually and institutionally within Ethnic Studies," with which, she emphasizes, "it shares a political commitment to link epistemological critique with the struggle for social change." She insists that "rather than celebrating particular identities or focusing on personal alienation and personal affirmation, we need to engage instead in sustained and systematic studies of social power, social institutions, and socially sanctioned forms of knowledge—especially the complex roles played by race, as well as gender, class, and sexuality"—through comparative and intersectional research both nationally and on a global scale (Espiritu 2005, 195–6).

Post-identity Subjects

The pursuit of a post-ethnic or post-racial politics in recent Asian American literary studies seems to reflect the emergence of a new structure of feelings that has made itself felt in the profession since the beginning of the twenty-first century. Generally speaking, scholars embarking on these quests seem responding to at least two kinds of circumstances: the undiminished racial ideology and racial practice in American society despite the gains of the civil rights struggles, and a growing sense of frustration among these scholars as to the relevance of Asian American theory and politics fashioned out of the institutional apparatuses of American capitalist modernity. The anxiety and discontent that give shape to such a structure of feelings are plainly manifest in Kandice Chuh's calls for "conceiving Asian American studies as a *subjectless discourse.*" She states:

> "Asian American" is/names racism and resistance, citizenship and its denial, subjectivity and subjection—at once the becoming and undoing—and, as such, is a designation of the *(im)possibility of justice*, where "justice" refers to a state as yet unexperienced and unrepresentable, one that can connotatively be implied. Arguably, the overarching purpose of Asian American studies has been and continues to be pursuit of this (im) possibility, the pursuit of an as yet unrealized state of justice of tracing, arguing, critiquing, and by alternatively imagining the conditions that inscribe its (im)possibility. (Chuh 2003, 5, 9)

From this perspective, Chuh believes that "subjectlessness" plays the role of "undermining the knowability of 'knowledge'" and "the authority of the 'knowing' subject, whose grounds for action are consequently called into question." She contends: "Here, subjectivity is conceived as an unstable construct of repressive/constructive orders of knowledge. Neither 'subject' nor 'knowledge' has within this framework immanent authority/validity/ stability" (Chuh 2003, 5, 9). Leslie Bow proposes a concept of "racial interstitiality," by which she presses for "a spatial and temporal understanding of [Asian Americans'] status transition" in the American deep south beyond a black-white dichotomy. Key to her counterstrategy is "turning one's gaze toward the space of the in-between to envision alternative connections and affiliations" through "multiple axes of differentiation." She considers such a "symbolic spatial placement" of Asian Americans as "liminal personae" an act of "interpretive necessity": that is, the "intermediacy" of their ontological status thus established is able to resist any socially or legally regulated identity or any possibility of racial, gender, class, or sexual hierarchy (Bow 2010, 5, 11–12, 16).

Along with such theoretical efforts to dislodge Asian American subjects from their "rationally" conceived categories of being, critics in the field are increasingly vocal about their disenchantment with community-based traditions of self-representation that prioritize explicit Asian American content in literary descriptions. Such traditions, these critics argue, have reductively circumscribed the way Asian American literature is written or read in a culture that habitually treats Asians stereotypically. Hence, Stephen Sohn urges Asian American writers to work on the "construction of narrative perspectives" that do not "overlap with ethnoracial backgrounds" or "mirror their own ethnoracial ancestries" but "move increasingly toward those that seem to have little to do with Asian American racial formation." Only in this way, Sohn suggests, can Asian American literary works cease to "promote a form of racial authenticity" (Sohn 2014, 7, 14, 19, 22). Laura Kang engages this concern by focusing on the role of knowledge production, arguing that, although "the marginalized can 'claim a voice' or 'come into visibility' as a distinct subject under the most insidious compulsions," yet, in constantly "affirming familiar truths or giving rise to new certainties," such efforts are "more often bound up with, not liberated from, disciplinary regimes of codification and documentation" (Kang 2002, 19). This is the context in which Yoonmee Chang makes a defining move by advocating for a "postracial aesthetic" for the field: she intends Asian American literature to become a "literature written by Asian American writers that does not contain Asian American characters or address Asian American experience." Chang asserts that "this rejection frees the author from the ostensible shackles of ethnic particularity and difference to examine transcendent universal themes, like 'love and honor and pity.' For Asian American authors, the postracial more specifically frees them from writing Orientalist caricatures and reductive ethnographies—from the 'Chinatown' book" (Chang 2010, 201–2).

The evolution of a post-identity politics in the field, as shown in the survey of Chapter 5, is inextricably connected to a perceived accommodation/ resistance dichotomy at work in the criticism conducted by Asian American scholars. Viet Thanh Nguyen, who comments extensively on this binary, suggests a post-racial alternative to Asian American subject formation by tapping into Louis Althusser's idea of "bad subjects" whose behaviors deviate from those of "the vast majority of (good) subjects," although neither group, according to Althusser's formulation, can rise above its confinement to interpellation, a mechanism of pervasive ideological influences imposed on all subjects by the bourgeois state apparatus (Nguyen 2002, 179n39). Juxtaposing Althusser's speculation that bad subjects can "resist the interpellative power of dominant ideology" to the ongoing Asian American critiques of the model minority paradox, Nguyen reflects that, if "model minority discourse tends to idealize the model minority, the discourse of bad subjects responds by tending to idealize the bad subject, ignoring the contractions and excesses that make the bad subject amenable to discipline by dominant society. Thus, Asian American intellectuals often implicitly posit model minority discourse and the discourse of the bad subject as a binary." He then recommends: "Asian Americans can frequently occupy both situations simultaneously" or "alternate between them, as realized perhaps most graphically in the role of the panethnic entrepreneur" (Nguyen 2002, 144–5). Min Song, similarly concerned about the constraining nature of racially based Asian American oppositional politics, stakes out his post-identity argument somewhat differently. He asks, "if this literature is no longer one focused self-consciously on politics, then does it also make sense to keep using a term like Asian American to describe it? This term, after all, names a racially based political project that began as politico-economic critique and aspirations for alternative social formations, and may therefore appear from another vantage point to be a hindrance to the making of aesthetic projects." From this perspective, he contends that "the term [Asian American] seems to put people into a neat box. It is no surprise, therefore, that many writers might not only refuse the conventions that seem to boundary Asian American literature, but might also refuse to be called an Asian American altogether. It is a label that is affixed haphazardly onto one's person. It lacks flow, beauty, familiar self-identification" (Song 2013, 5–7, 11–12).

The post-identity arguments discussed in the preceding survey are thoughtful and wide ranging: from that recommending strategies for transgression to that calling attention to the limits of ethnic narrative points of view, and from that expressing desires for assimilation on the basis of professional successes to insistence on the rights of creative freedom and deserved artistic license.[3] If these positions can still be seen as shaped by critics' desires to transform the public sphere that interfaces with their individual acts of creation or interpretation, other forms of post-racial quests seem to have turned entirely inwardly, to realms not only free of the confounding effects of binary oppositions but also devoid of any meaningful action. A case in point is Anne Cheng's monograph *The Melancholy of Race*, in which she suggests that "we need to understand subjective agency as a convoluted, ongoing, generative, and at times self-contradicting negotiation with pain." Such subjective negotiation with pain, Cheng clarifies, entails staying clear of "a vocabulary of victimization with its accompanying vicious cycles of blame, guilt, and denigration," as well as refuting "the pure distinction between subject and object, oppressor and oppressed, agency and agentless." From this angle, she further suggests that "intrasubjectivity exists as a form of intersubjectivity and intersubjectivity often speaks in the voice of intrasubjectivity: a mutually supportive system" (Cheng 2000, 15, 28, 124, 202). To a certain degree, Cheng's conception of Asian American agency as a psychic effect of relationality is similar to Amy Tang's theorization of the "productivity" of Asian American subject's "stuckness" amidst overwhelming differences or of the possibility of "converting political impasse into critique"—a hypothesis that can be rationalized only through the logic of aleatory detour or linguistic errancy as an experience of pure discursivity (Tang 2016, 3–4, 11–13).

Christine So shifts the grounds of post-identity debates by approaching the question of Asian American subject formation beyond arguments for a post-Asiatic Asian American literature (which is informed, as it were, by a precritical idealism about race relations not yet complicated by the perspectives of Fanon, Blauner, Said, or Omi/Winnant) and outside the post-humanist formulas of intertextuality. She states: "I would argue that it is equally important—especially in this era of global capitalism, mass commodification and consumerism, and widespread cooptation and institutionalization of all forms of resistance—to explore more fully Asian American culture's production of not only differences but also sameness, nativization, assimilation, and belonging." For So, such an alternative does not connote "reiteration and mimicry" of dominant American values, but rather aims to show how "anxiety and slippages" would manifest themselves when "Asian Americans make an appearance in the American imaginary," or in the way "Asian Americanness" is circulated or reproduced through privileged circuits of American culture and ideology (So 2007, 8). The prime symptom of the "anxiety" or "slippages" that she identifies is the paradox of "assimilation," a classical Asian American dilemma examined in Chapter 3 and, in the context of the survey here, continually informing the post-identity arguments endorsed by an increasing number of Asian American critics. So suggests that, as an unavoidable terrain through which Asian Americans come to terms with their selfhood, this paradox may be tackled in two different ways. One is to take it as an opportunity to enhance "difference" (or to argue for the undesirability, if not impossibility, of collective Asian American action). The other is to seize on it as an occasion for revisiting "sameness" (or to follow through the community's unfinished project of becoming Asian American) as the central plank of a protracted communal struggle for self-empowerment or self-realization.

The option recommended by So recalls the premise of Asian American agency theorized in the introduction of this study. Conceptualized as a form of social-semantic construct, this agency emerges from the competing demands voiced from a shared zone of subaltern affect, while it also develops, as shown in the surveys of this study so far, through the interplay between or among Asian American critics' heterogeneous responses to the capitalist routines in which they are fully, though concretely, embedded as racialized US subjects. Assumed in this formulation of Asian American agency is that the negative effect of racialization on the Asian American psyche may not be done away with through textual strategies of self-parody or self-deconstruction. On the contrary, overreliance on such strategies not only obscures the question of Asian assimilation as but an aspect of the American neoliberal democratic ideology constitutive of what David Li calls the "national contradiction" of the United States (Li 1998, 12), but also reduces the critical force of a post-identity argument to little more than an expression of individualistic ethos, which is easily assimilable to the self-possessive logic of America's commercial capitalism.

Chapter 8 of this book will focus on several emerging areas of research in recent Asian American literary studies that reflect the rich potential of interdisciplinary work. Showcased in this chapter are critical analyses of the relationship between literature and food, militarization, refugee sensibilities, ecology, techno-orientalism, and digital humanities.

CHAPTER 8
EMERGING INTERESTS

The first two decades of the twenty-first century have seen Asian American literary criticism make significant strides toward developing research projects in the intersections between or among ethnic studies, literary criticism, high theory, and areas of inquiry that used to fall beyond the immediate interests of either the humanistic or social science investigations. Such efforts have profoundly changed the way Asian American literary studies is conducted, while they have opened up a whole realm of conceptual or cognitive possibilities for innovative teaching and research. In this process, Asian American scholars have acquainted themselves with a range of new cultural idioms, taxonomy, and analytical or interpretive etiquettes—intellectual tools that allow them to address both familiar and emerging concerns with fresh insights and original findings. What the cumulative results of these efforts translate to, ultimately, is revival of interests in subliterary genres, popular cultural forms, and paraliterary practices traditionally marginal to academy-based literary studies. Although it might be premature to predict that such developments necessarily represent the future shape and direction of the field, the horizon of Asian American expectations has been expanded to such an extent that the business of literary studies can no longer be conducted as usual, especially regarding questions of what literature can mean or what it can do in the twenty-first century. It is therefore logical to assume that cross-fertilization between or among different epistemic forms or disciplinary approaches has already become a new intellectual frontier for cutting-edge Asian American creative and critical productions.

Food Studies

Evocation of foodways or alimentary images has been a familiar, though less often synthesized, aspect of Asian American literary practice since the inception of the field. An early effort to pursue this line of study can be found in Sau-ling Wong's 1993 monograph *Reading Asian American*

Literature: From Necessity to Extravagance, in which she discusses the pros and cons of Frank Chin's invention of the concept of "food pornography" in his 1974 play *The Year of the Dragon*. Chin intends to use this term to satirize the ethnic community's apathy toward its own members' aspirations for literary creativity in the pre-civil-rights era, an attitude that Chin considers exemplified in the ethnic mindset of "making a living by exploiting the 'exotic' aspects of one's ethnic foodways." Wong recognizes the importance of Chin's critique of this "survival strategy" adopted by many Asians at the time, which, according to Chin, ironically "translates to reifying perceived cultural differences by exaggerating one's otherness in order to gain a foothold in a white-dominated social system." At the same time, she also voices reservations about Chin's "impassioned, almost savage, rhetoric," which, she considers leaving "little room for a nuanced view of cultural presentation" of how Asian food can serve as an enabling rhetorical instrument for commenting on Asian American realities and experiences (Wong 1993, 55–66).

Wenying Xu's 2008 monograph *Eating Identities: Reading Food in Asian American Literature* is a notable attempt to update and expand the premise and scope of food studies initiated by Wong. One of the contributions of Xu's book is that she places food studies alongside questions of cultural hegemony, race/class relations, and Asian American subject formation. She emphasizes that food "socializes our taste buds and metabolisms, which in turn stand in the frontline of demarcating the border between them and us." Such "demarcation," she argues, "is never simply a line drawn between good and bad cuisines or even clean and filthy food. It always informs the construction of a moral judgment of a particular social group." Based on these observations, Xu maintains that food consumption plays a key role in Asian Americans' subject formation in two ways: it functions as a vehicle through which Asian foodways are represented and appropriated by mainstream American culture as a process of racialization; and it also serves "as an index to a material history" of Asians' survival, struggle, and hybridization in the face of the great odds against them (Xu 2008, 2, 5, 8).

Xu's rethinking of the role of food studies in Asian American literary criticism anticipates more diversified scholarly productivity in this evolving area of inquiry. For example, Robert Ku uses the occasion of San Francisco's fifty-year anniversary celebration of the Kikkoman soy sauce company's founding in the city—a leading soy sauce producer in the world—to comment on the historical amnesia that underlies its 2007 official account of the event. Several emblematic years are key to Ku's rehistoricizing effort: 1886, when Kikkoman was first brought to Hawaii and then to California by Japanese immigrants; 1948, when Kikkoman began a semichemical soy sauce production in Japan; 1973, when the company's first US-based production facility was established in Walworth, Wisconsin; and 2003, when Kikkoman Foundation pledged a million-dollar gift to the University of Wisconsin-Madison to establish the Kikkoman Laboratory of Microbial Fermentation. Based on this chronology, Ku argues that the 2007 San Francisco celebration of the occasion overlooks the entire Japanese immigration history, while it downplays the company's post-Second-World-War market strategy for establishing its global dominance by shifting from the traditionally slow-fermented soy sauce to a nonbrewed chemical one (Ku 2013). Heidi Kim uses food study to reassess the role of the mess hall in Japanese American internment camps during the Second World War, a site around which limited familial activities centering on food sharing and food consumption took place. In foregrounding the camp mess hall in such a way, Kim critiques the immediately postwar tendency in American publishing industry to euphemize the disintegration of the Japanese American family into a Cold War discourse that extols the virtues of tradition, domesticity, and assimilationism. Within this frame of analysis, Kim delineates two mess hall scenarios as alternatives: first is its function as a survival strategy adopted by the internees suffering from a loss of family cohesion and disintegration of the ethnic community; second is its provision of an opportunity for covert networking among the internees agitating for camp activism (Kim 2013, 125–6).

Several practitioners of food studies approach the topics of their investigation with an explicit diasporic or transnational emphasis. For example, Mark Padoongpatt looks into an obscure aspect of the American imperial operation in Asia-Pacific during the early years of the Cold War, when cooking was utilized by the military-industrial complex to advance US agendas in the region. He particularly comments on how American food companies promoted Pacific cuisine and culinary practice to white suburban housewives, as part of a coordinated effort to stir up nationalist fervor in support of American involvement in the Pacific theater as key site for Cold War military confrontations with the Soviet bloc (Padoonpatt 2013, 187–8). Denise Cruz rereads Monique Truong's 2003 novel *The Book of Salt* by situating it within a different transnational dynamic: the colonial relationship between France and Vietnam in the pre-Second-World-War period. Focusing on the novel's depiction of a queer male Vietnamese chef, who fled the French-occupied Saigon during the first decades of the twentieth century and ended up cooking for Gertrude Stein and her partner Alice B. Toklas in their Parisian apartment, Cruz interprets the servant-master relationship as an authorial ploy devised for "reversing the usual directionality" of "the Western appetite for an Asian other," by letting the Vietnamese chef take pleasure in the knowledge that the West not only desires but also depends on him as a subversive Asian alterity (Cruz 2013, 355–6). In this process, Anita Mannur, author of *Culinary Fictions: Food in South Asian Diasporic Culture*, voices reservations about placing too much weight on the racial assumptions of Western attitudes toward Asian cooking or food preparation in discourses on Asian American culinary diaspora, arguing that such a link may turn out ideologically confining to both food studies as a textualized engagement with Orientalism and Asian American subject formation as a social experience overdetermined by the ideologies of the American modernity and nationalism. What Mannur suggests in this argument is that a severance of food studies from its habitual attachment to critical race theory (which she endorses in other contexts) may free Asian American identities from being perpetually exoticized as objects of US cultural imperialism. The alternative she prefers is using the ambiguity that inheres in Asians' racial or ethnic identity formations as a way of interrogating and deconstructing "American taste mechanisms" from a truly diasporic perspective that distances food studies from the site of Asian racialization in the US context (Mannur 2010, 173, 177). Illustrating the possibilities of such an alternative approach to transnational food studies is Mannur's reading of the "South Asian Diasporic Queer Kitchen" featured in South Asian diasporic texts and films, by which she shows that the home space, though traditionally tied to "an unyielding form of heteronormativity," is "always already a homosocial space that allows for articulations of same-sex intimacy through and against the strictures" of Western modernity and its constitutive categories (Mannur 2013, 393).

In a different context of the Asian American debates, Jennifer Ho urges for a differentiation between ethnicity (which she associates with US citizenship and national belonging) and race (which she considers activist and collectivist by implication) in Asian American food studies, insisting that race is an indispensable primary site for productive investigations of Asian American culinary practice as an integral part of the Asian American critique of US commercial capitalism. She argues:

> Asian American eating and acting become forms of resisting Asian American stereotypes that demean, belittle, and objectify Asian

Americans, stereotypes that usually are trafficked through foodways. To eat and to act Asian American is [therefore] to acknowledge the ways in which Asians in America have been subjected to institutional forms of white supremacy and the complicated history of racialization that has pitted them against other minority groups. (Ho 2013, 305–6)

The contrastive meanings and functions accorded to race as a basic frame of reference in Mannur and Ho's food studies evoke an ongoing methodological tension in the field, that is, an emphasis on the ontological dimension of race (often seen as embodied in economic and class relations) as a necessary context for grasping the race issue in its entirety, and a perception of race as mainly an ideological construct or a textualized rendition of Asian American identity more associated with symbolic procedures.[1] Like Mannur, Min Song, Stephen Sohn, and Yoonmee Chang are similarly vocal about the undesirability of placing too much emphasis on racialization in Asian American creative or critical practices. At the same time, critics like Sau-ling Wong, Colleen Lye, and Iyko Day continue to see representations of the Asiatic body in the US context as a chief site for maintaining a critical edge for research in the field, in echo with the spirit of Ho's argument.

Militarization, Critical Refugee Studies, and Ecocriticism

The second emerging area of interest in recent Asian American literary criticism takes shape in the overlapping concerns of several evolving discourses: that on militarization, that on critical refugee studies, and that on ecocriticism. In the introduction to their 2001 coedited volume *Perilous Memories: The Asia-Pacific War(s)*, Takashi Fujitani, Geoffrey White, and Lisa Yoneyama provide a conceptual framework for war-related trauma studies by dwelling on the relationship between military conflict, the wounded body, and memory work. They suggest that war memory and its imagined reproduction are comprised of several interrelated dimensions. First, the stakes of memory production lie in its emphasis on "the structures of power and desire," as well as its connection to historical representations and a political use of catastrophic events (such as violence, mass destruction, sexual atrocity, and military oppression). Second, recollections of war take place through different temporalities and are infused with different political purposes, with the voices of the victimized and the spaces of invisibility or silence intertwined with those of the victimizing, the apologetic, and the dominant. Third, memories can be distorted, disavowed, or effaced through hegemonic representations. From these perspectives, Fujitani, White, and Yoneyama consider it important to investigate the different technologies devised either to recuperate from trauma or to produce forgetfulness. They especially emphasize the pressing need for data collecting as a key step toward a "critical re-membering" of forgotten or repressed histories (Fujitani, White, and Yoneyama 2001, 2, 4–5). Within this conceptual framework, several Asian American scholars focus on militarization as "a particularly vexed and significant key word and locus of critique"—to use Jodi Kim's apt characterization (Kim 2014, 154)—in order to show the extent to which its gendered and racialized processes either "constitute the conditions of possibility for ongoing forms of militarization," or function as "an extension of colonialism" and imperialism (Najita 2006, 14; Shigematsu and Camacho 2010, xv).

Reflecting on the complexity of Asian American literary representations of the war in Vietnam, Anh Thang Dao-Shah and Isabelle Thuy Pelaud observe: "To frame diasporic Vietnamese literature in relation to this war is not the same as to assert that these representations constitute the full story of what has occurred in the past, … or to claim that the war is the only event determining the experience of diasporic Vietnamese. Instead, by foregrounding Vietnamese writers of diaspora and their works we attempt to make clear that memory is always a space of contest and struggle, in which who tells the story matters." Dao-Shah and Pelaud remind readers that war is featured differently in works written in Vietnamese and in the language of the host country. Thus, the body of Vietnamese American literature they examine is specific both in terms of the generation it represents and the kind of memories it promotes or downplays (Dao-Shah and Pelaud 2015, 469, 471). Along the way, Viet Thanh Nguyen offers a particularly insightful view of the contested nature of war's representation in the larger realm of transnational politics:

> The Vietnamese ethnic enclaves in the US had not put the war behind them. Veterans still wore uniforms and marched at public events. The South Vietnamese national anthem was still sung and the flag was still waved. Everyone was on the lookout for Communist infiltrators, and signs of subversion were sometimes met with violence. Domestic abuse and home invasions where Vietnamese gangs attacked Vietnamese homes were commonplace. The violence that had supposedly ended erupted once more in the refugee community, caused by those

traumatized by the war or by those who had no other opportunities because of the war. The conclusion was clear: to be a refugee was to be a survivor of war as much as a combat veteran. (Nguyen 2013, 144, 146)

Cathy Schlund-Vials, who has introduced the term "refugee aesthetics" to the field in honor of the perspective of those surviving and writing about the war experience, further argues that Southeast Asian American writers of Cambodian, Laotian, and Hmong backgrounds, in narrating the state-sanctioned atrocity and violent history they directly went through, have made visible "the expansive contours and enduring legacies" of the American war in Southeast Asia, while legitimizing a unique Asian American "artistic mode marked by human rights testimonial, commemorative remembrance, and juridical activism" (Schlund-Vials 2015, 486, 489).

An important aspect of war-related trauma studies is concerned with the brutality experienced by survivors of the Korean War, and exemplified in two book-length treatments of the topic published in 2010: Jodi Kim's *Ends of Empire*; and Mark Jerng's *Claiming Others: Transracial Adoption and National Belonging*. Kim has contributed to this line of inquiry by introducing two useful terms: "militarized interconnectedness" and "militarized kinship." By the first, she refers to militarized prostitution in South Korea as a result of the significant presence of American troops since the end of the Korean War, as well as the "militarized logic" frequently evoked by apologists for the war to justify "the sexual and intimate relations between camptown prostitutes and their American GI clients" (Kim 2014, 155–6, 158). Vividly illustrating the traumatic results of this form of dehumanization inflicted on Korean women are two Asian American novels: Heinz Insu Fenkl's 1997 *Memories of My Ghost Brother* and Nora Okjia Keller's 2002 novel *Fox Girl*. The former, told from the point of view of a mix-raced boy (Insu), recounts the widespread poverty and prostitution in postwar Korea, especially his Korean mother's decision to give up her other son for adoption so that she could marry his American GI father stationed near Inchon, her hometown (Lee 2008a, 317). The latter describes the social ostracization and permeating despair faced by three mix-raced Korean teenagers abandoned by their American GI fathers during the same period. *Fox Girl* is a sequel to Keller's 1997 fiction *Comfort Woman*, a reconstruction of how young Korean women were coerced into the Japanese military as sex objects for soldiers during the 1930s and the 1940s (Lee 2003). Both fictional accounts serve to highlight an argument made by Jodi Kim: that is, there is a long history of colonial and imperial subjugation and sexual violence imposed on and endured by Korean women.

The second term that Kim introduces to militarization studies is concerned with the practice of a "large-scale and long-standing export of children" displaced by war, as well as that of transnational adoption of children from Asian countries either experiencing militarization or impacted by military conflict (Kim 2014, 159). Mark Jerng provides a useful overview of Asian adoptee studies in a 2014 essay, in which he calls attention to Jo Rankin's 1997 edited book *Seeds from a Silent Tree: An Anthology by Korean Adoptees* as a foundational text for this emerging area of Asian American research. Comprised of poetry, fiction, and personal narratives written by thirty Korean adoptees, this anthology is marked by a sense of profound ambiguity on the part of the contributors, who have grown up in America while being confronted with a realization of the vast "distance separating them from the terrains of two national cultures, those of both the United States and Korea" (C. Choy and G. Choy 2003, 277). In making "visible the conjunctions of love, rescue, and militarism," Jerng observes, this anthology emphatically highlights the interrelated workings of "sentimental humanism" and "liberal logics" in mainstream American attitudes toward the question of "child removal," which, he argues, are ultimately responsible for either a silencing or a forgetting of certain war-related trauma, or for decontextualized representations of damaged Asian life forms in the service of other agendas (Jerng 2014, 22–4). From this perspective, the volume may be recognized for its role of laying the ground for recent critiques of the problematics of Western neoliberalism in critical refugee studies.

Thu-Huong Nguyên-Vo provides a useful working definition of the concept of neoliberalism in the context of the American war in Vietnam and its aftermath, by underscoring American media's tendency to "universalize power relations in the American empire" through "appropriating particularistic markings of race and histories while gutting out the contents of these histories." A paradoxical result of such appropriations of trauma, she points out, is that it, on the one hand, "mimes acts of remembering by way of amnesiac memory" and, on the other, "reduces the complexity of the Vietnamese American community to a symbol of anti-communism," as "a resentful atavism to a lost war rather than anything of import for our common present and future" (Nguyên-Vo 2005, 158). Along the line, Cathy Schlund-Vials forcefully argues, in reference to Cambodian American experience, that "the Cambodian Syndrome in part encompasses the paradoxical non-admission of U.S. culpability before, during, and after the Democratic Kampuchean era." That is, American official approaches to the war in Southeast Asia, though cognizant of the Killing Fields as genocide, are "tactically forgetful of the U.S. role in the making of the Khmer Rouge," hence naturalizing "incomplete frames of forgetting" and "schemes of strategic remembering" (Schlund-Vials 2012, 13–14).

One contradiction that arises from this type of neoliberal representation of war, as Lisa Yoneyama observes, is that

> the U.S. offers both violence and liberation as debts to the liberated. This asymmetry in the economy of liberation, one that marks the liberated as eternally indebted to the liberators, bears profound significance for the (un)redressability of U.S. military violence. It implies that the injured and violated bodies of the liberated do not require redress, for their liberation has already served as payment/reparation that supposedly precedes the U.S. violence inflicted upon them. (Yoneyama 2005, 142)

Such neoliberal attitudes toward Asian life forms affected by war, according to Yen Lê Espiritu, have the predictable effect of "collapsing capitalism into freedom and democracy that discursively distances 'the free world' from the 'enemies of freedom': and it is this alleged distance that justifies continued U.S. military interventions in the service of defending and bestowing freedom." She thus urges scholars: "To take seriously the 'space between'" and ask different theoretical and political questions about death and the dead, such as "When does death begin? How to count the dead? Whose death matters? Who owns the dead? What about the living dead, who live as a shadow, already a ghost, never allowed to be fully present? And what about those who are kept alive but always 'in a permanent condition of 'being in pain?'" (Espiritu 2005, xv, xix).

Grace Hong's 2015 study *Death Beyond Disavowal: The Impossible Politics of Difference* delves into the history of racial violence and its myriad manifestations of trauma and embodiments of infliction, in contrast to approaches to social justice that only pay attention to certain situations of inequity to the neglect of other forms or modes of suffering or subjugation, and hence affirm, rather than undermine, the conditions of racial violence. The neoliberal underside of such approaches to social justice, Hong contends, is an unwary pursuit of "a politics of recognition" in institutionally sanctified multiculturalist terms, for such pursuit typically reproduces the categories, agendas, and ideologies of Western modernity. From this standpoint, she argues against understanding death in purely biological terms, which she considers tantamount to accepting a "premature death" of other life forms

(Hong 2015, 4–6, 10–12). In line with Hong's emphasis on the need for a relational "political and ethical rejoinder" to neoliberal representation of life and trauma, James Lee considers the rise of disability writing—frequently by way of somatography and autopathography—signaling "a shift toward taking seriously not only the need and desire to write about diseased and disabled bodies, but indeed to take seriously a strange idea that ill and disabled bodies might *desire*, and that this desire need not be only the desire to be healthy and not disabled." Noting the relative dearth of auto/soma/pathography in current Asian American creative and critical practices, Lee urges scholars in the field to move beyond the "possessive investment in normatively desirable bodies" sanctified by the notion of "ableism" in received medical regimes, and to contemplate the possibility of "unromantic" Asian American agency that does not aim at restitution, as a way of recognizing underprivileged embodiments of social and psychological atrocities (Lee 2014, 451, 453–4, 455).

Rachel Lee's 2014b monograph *The Exquisite Corpse of Asian America: Biopolitics, Biosociality, and Posthuman Ecologies* deals explicitly with "the terrain of biology and ecology—of health, diet, and environment as they affect *the reproduction and vitality of the population*" (italics in original). Recognizing the centrality of the process of racialization routinely undergone by Asian Americans as US social and legal subjects, Lee considers it imperative to "theorize in a sustained manner Asian American cultural representation for what it tells us about biopolitics, modern modes of governmentality, and the somaticization of social and political traumas." Among the conceptual and practical issues Lee examines in her study are Asians' criminalization as enemy aliens and spies, social and psychic wounding through harmful stereotyping, the lasting effects of warfare and necropolitical tactics (troop mobilization, civilian death tolls, and orphaning of children, among them), medical scapegoating or regulation, educational segregation, and "Zoe-ification" (Lee 2014a, 68–9, 72; Lee 2014b). Reflecting on the implications of scholarship on disability for Asian American studies from a critical race studies perspective, Cathy Schlund-Vials and Cynthia Wu have articulated a connection that seems strategic to the field's future growth as an engaged and ethnic-specific undertaking. They suggest: "Disability studies—which eschews long-standing medicalized diagnoses of difference in favor of politically inflected, socio-cultural critiques of normative embodiment—coheres with and extends the ways in which Asian American studies has historically taken as a first premise the problematic representation of bodies racially and ethnically deemed outside the nation" (Schlund-Vials and Wu 2015, 202).

Speculative Literature

Speculative literature is a type of writing that has elicited enthusiastic responses from Asian American scholars since the beginning of the twenty-first century. A major incentive behind such investment with this subliterary category is these scholars' ongoing concern about how to counter the negative Asian images perpetuated through the representational apparatuses of Western orientalism in ways that can sufficiently challenge, if not entirely invalidate its assumptions. Early attempts to tackle such concerns can be identified in the *Aiiieeeee!* editors' dissection of the operational rationale and mechanism of Asian stereotypes in American culture in the pre-civil-rights era (Chin et al. 1974, vii–xv); as well as in William Wu's 1982 monograph— *The Yellow Peril: Chinese Americans in American Fiction, 1850–1940*—a cultural analysis of the ideological roots of negative literary depictions of Asian characters in pre-Second-World-War Anglo-American writings. Since the early 1990s, there has been a revival of interests in this line of study among scholars of diverse backgrounds: such as James Moy's critique of the "Sinophobic" tradition in American theatrical practice (1993); Sheng-Mei Ma's analysis of the cultural constraints on constructing a truly effective counter-orientalist discourse in Eurocentric environments (2000); Colleen Lye's theorization of the shaping of an Asiatic racial form coproduced through East–West human or cultural exchanges in contexts of a rising US imperialism (2005); and Edlie Wong's probe into the "Chinese Invasion Fiction" genre that harkens back to nineteenth-century Western popular literary traditions (2014). Recent Asian American interest in speculative literature coincides with growing Western anxieties about the rise to prominence of certain Asian Pacific economic entities since the mid-1980s, a sentiment that often finds its expression through the lens of such newly available high technologies as cybernetics, biological alteration, digital form, or artificial intelligence. It is therefore not surprising that the inaugural moment of the speculative turn in the field occurred through its engagement with the science-fiction genre (see the 2008 special issue of *MELUS* on "Alien/Asians"), a tentative move that led to the 2015 publication of a more comprehensive essay collection titled *Techno-Orientalism: Imagining Asia in Speculative Fiction, History, and Media.*

The term "techno-orientalism," according to the editors of this volume (David Roh, Betsy Huang, and Greta Niu), denotes "the phenomenon of imagining Asia and Asians in hypo- or hyper-technological terms." Within this context, they further suggest:

Techno-Orientalist imaginations are infused with the language and codes of the technological and the futuristic. These developed alongside industrial advances in the West and have become part of the West's project of securing dominance as architects of the future, a project that requires configurations of the East as the very technology with which to shape it. Techno-Orientalist speculations of an Asianized future have become ever more prevalent in the wake of neoliberal trade policies that enabled a greater flow of information and capital between the East and West. (Roh, Huang, and Niu 2015, 1–4)

The editors of the volume designate Japan and China as the principal targets of techno-orientalism because both figure in its imaginary as threats to the economic hegemony of Western commercial capitalism. The difference between these two countries, they maintain, is that Japan is seen as competing with the West for dominance in technological innovation, while China is perceived as challenging the West in areas of labor supply and productivity. The editors consider digital media a chief medium by which Western perceptions of Asia in techno-orientalist terms become heightened, for it is through this viewing instrument that Asia is often reduced to either a "manufacturing base" (a producer), a "source of technological innovation" (a designer), or a "conduit for cultural export" (an affluent consumer) (Roh, Huang, and Niu 2015, 3, 14). Reflecting on the subversive potential of developing a counter-techno-orientalist discourse from a uniquely Asian American perspective, Victor Bascara muses: "What was once a sleek system for civilizing the world is revealed as a clunky ethnocentrism of the so-called West needing an incorporable alterity to be its frontier, materially and ideologically" (Bascara 2015, 53). That is, in making visible the schizophrenic workings of techno-orientalist representations, a sophisticated Asian American speculative critique of the topic would make the collusively futuristic Asia constructed through such imaginary vulnerable to critical dissections.

Cathy Schlund-Vials and Cynthia Wu designate the nativist fear of racial mixing in the United States from the mid- to late nineteenth century as an early example of techno-orientalism, a form of cultural racism often rationalized through the Western pseudoscience of eugenics for diagnosing "'advantageous' heritable [human] characteristics" on the basis on race. This early version of techno-orientalism, they emphasize, had a direct impact on Asian immigration to the United States and was responsible for the passing of a series of exclusionist policies toward Asia and its populations in the

United States (Schlund-Vials and Wu 2015, 198–9).[2] In a recent study of the changing Western assumptions and politics about the Asiatic body, Jinny Huh has noticed an ironic reversal of the ethno-orientalist directionality, that is, today "Asian genetics and bodies are in high demand" in both ART (Assisted Reproductive Technology) developed by Western medical researchers and child adoption pursued in Western parenting practice. Huh specially calls attention to a "fertility treatment process" on which Western parenting increasingly relies in selecting "not only a child's skin/hair/eye color but also gender, athletic abilities, weight, height, and susceptibility to certain diseases" (Huh 2015, 104–6). Wendy Chun contributes to the discussion of this aspect of ethno-orientalism by raising different questions. First, she suggests that the notion of "the breedability" of human species or the human race as technologically "manipulatable" shows the regimes of eugenics to be but one of the "technologies of difference" in late capitalism. Second, she argues that "breeding populations, if they do exist, are never simply natural, but rather result from a complex negotiation between culture, society, and biology."

Chun is therefore also interested in exploring "the extent to which high-tech Orientalism might be the ground from which some other future can be created; the ground from which dreams can be made to fly, flower, in freaky, queer unexpected ways." She observes: "High-tech Orientalism promises intimate knowledge, sexual concourse with the 'other,' which it reduces to data, to a standing resource. This will-to-knowledge structures the plot of many cyberpunk novels, as well as the reader's relation to the text; the reader is always 'learning,' always trying to understand these narratives that confuse the reader." This is the context in which Chun raises the following questions: "Can the abject … be a place for critical mimesis— can we critically assume the role of the abject in order to call into question the larger system of representation and its closure? That is, can Asian/Asian Americans as robots, as data, be a critical mimesis itself—a way for all to embrace their inner robots?" Chun's exhibit is the Hapa filmmaker Greg Pak's feature film *Robot Stories*, which, in her view, "asserts Asian Americans as human by emphasizing their alleged similarities and their opposition to robots *and* at the same time deconstructs the opposition between human and robots." In other words, Chun explains, "his stories play with the stereotypes of Asian Americans as relentless, robotic workers, as looking all the same (can't tell them apart), as dragon ladies, in order to create a livable future—literally a future in which Asian Americans and African Americans live as the non-abject" (Chun 2012, 44–5, 49, 51–2). In a discussion of robots featured in science fiction beyond Asian American studies, Seo-Young Chu envisions "situations where robots become identifiable—often painfully so—as human subjects worthy of sympathy." She speculates: "By creating situations in which the ontological status of humanoid artefacts seems almost to surpass our own [by way of two lyric figures: personification and apostrophe], science fiction opens up a luminous space in which the moral entitlements of sentient robots become not only legible and intelligible but also impossible to deny." She asks rhetorically: "What kinds of moral claims might such a creature have on us? Should a sentient robot be entitled, example, to free thought, conscience, and speech?" From this perspective, Chu thinks it conceivable to put forward ideas like "robot ethics," "robot rights," and "robot advocacy" (Chu 2010, 214–16, 226).

Scholars pursuing the study of speculative literature respond particularly enthusiastically to two aspects of its representational techniques: its generic innovation and its spatiotemporal politics. Representative of the first trend is Pamela Thoma's analysis of the detective, fantasy, and mystery novels written by Asian American women (such as Sonia Singh, Michelle Yu, Susan Choi, Suki Kim, and Sujata Massey), with an emphasis on the importance of teasing out their ethnicized formal features and gendered contextual overtones (Thoma 2013, 4–5). Reflecting on the critical potential of Asian American spy fiction, Betsy Huang expresses her belief in the following way: "The fusion of the spy thriller genre into immigrant fiction … gave the latter a fresh angle and a new set of tropes with which to tell a familiar story." She asks: "Is *Native Speaker* an immigrant novel as the book's back cover claims it to be, or is it a spy novel? What does it mean for readers and critics of Asian American fiction and for spy fiction if it is both?" Huang considers the value of such "genre-mixing" residing in its "simultaneous emphasis and de-emphasis of genre categories," suggesting that by "casting the Asian American as a spy, [Chang-rae] Lee has put a door in the wall between the genres of immigrant fiction and spy fiction." She then poses further questions: "Would the target audience for each genre … be prompted to read more fiction from the other side of the wall? And how might such perforations of genre boundaries generate new representational models for the familiar themes of immigration, assimilation, and subject formation in Asian American literature?" (Huang 2010, 1–2). The second aspect of recent work on speculative literature in the field is centered on the issue of temporality. Warren Liu articulates the technicality of "two key resisters" to Western time from an Asian American perspective, that is, "how temporality … (and not simply the 'objects' that measure it) might be understood as a technology by itself; and how, given such an understanding of temporality, specific techno-orientalist tropes … [might] be understood as themselves premised on a naturalization of a technologically-mediated ordering that equates the temporal with racial difference" (Liu 2015, 66). From this standpoint, Victor Bascara suggests that "utopian/dystopian texts are test balloons for measuring possible destinies for the present," which he considers often shown as a future envisioned as either "orderly liberation of the oppressed" or as "benighted for a chaotic hegemony of inequality and exploitation" (Bascara 2015, 52). The former possibility was explored in Liu's reading of William Gibson and Bruce Sterling's science fiction *The Difference Engine* in terms of how its protagonist's "obsessive focus on time opens up an interpretive frame that foregrounds the multiple ways images of (and references to) time and temporality feature in the text" (Liu 2015, 67–8). The latter was broached by Ruth Hsu who reads Karen Tei Yamashita's novelistic rendering of the US national temporality of the postmodern Los Angeles described in *Tropic of Orange* as an apocalyptic cartography of pure chaos (Hsu 2006; Hsu 2018).

In this process, Asian American critics approach the genre of speculative literature with very different assumptions about its functions. For example, Stephen Sohn suggests: "We can say that Asian American speculative fiction requires a critical practice that reorients our eyes toward the ways that issues of racial difference are obliquely encoded into narratives that include supernatural beings, otherworldly entities, or futuristic technologies." He therefore emphasizes "the ways that speculative fictions function analogically," under the conviction that the "plasticity and slippage" of their narratives make the fictional world constructed simultaneously transferable and applicable to the reader's world made up of multiple analogies (Sohn 2014, 172–3). Betsy Huang suggests, on the other hand, that "science fiction offers Asian American writers a unique way to engage in subversive political and ideological critique not by contravening genre conventions, but by using them to rewrite the rules of the genre. Creative uses of the novum instigate the processes of cognitive estrangement and dissonance that unmask entrenched ideological assumptions about familiar self and uncanny Other" (Huang 2010, 101). Using a broadly defined notion of the "speculative" to frame her emphasis on a "cultural production of futurity" promised by speculative genres, Aimee Bahng brings the insights of science fiction by writers of color into alignment with a very different kind of dynamics, namely, the speculative economics that have wreaked havoc on global markets (Bahng 2017, 2–3). Jinqi Ling considers speculative literature's capacity to reengage the vexing but undertheorized ontological question of referent more at stake for contemporary Asian American literary studies. He suggests that "speculative fiction complicates, rather than abandons, the referential reason explicit in the extrapolative function of science fiction. Its emphasis on the reflexive creative mind calls forth heterological epistemology that both disrupts and reaffirms counterintuitive performances, its open-ended literary construction of the external world explainable mainly through rationally conceived discursive procedures, hence meaningful only within the realm of representation" (Ling 2014, 498, 505–6).

Digital Humanities and New Media

Eileen Gardner and Ronald G. Musto, specialists in Renaissance literature studies, have identified a set of distinctions for examining the emerging intersection between the humanities and digital media—an interdisciplinary crossing that provides a range of new techniques for accessing, preserving, aggregating/disaggregating, and interpreting literary or cultural resource and scholarship. First, they recognize a tension in the role assigned to digital media by humanists and that assigned to it by computer scientists. The former tends to view the digital humanities "as a methodology that brings the tools and power of computing to bear on the traditional work of the humanities," whereas the latter treats the digital humanities mainly "as the study of how electronic form affects the disciplines in which it is used and what these disciplines have to contribute to our knowledge of computing." Simultaneously departing from the traditionally based philosophical and linguistic understanding of humanistic studies and maintaining a distance from the computational humanities as a field no longer invested in humanistic concerns, Gardner and Musto emphasize the importance of understanding the humanities in terms of its "deep historical roots and outlooks," as well as the need of "harnessing the computing power" and extending the reach of the digital humanities as a way to facilitate, improve, and expand how humanists work (Gardner and Musto 2015, 3–5). Their interpretations of the relationship between the humanistic and the digital seem applicable to Asian American literary studies in general, a field that, as shown in the surveys of the preceding chapters, is both empowered and constrained by the question of race, whose meaning and function can be radically reimagined or reformulated through digitally mediated work on the humanities.

Lisa Nakamura, a major theorist of the relationship between new media and race studies in the United States, makes unique contributions to Asian American studies. In her 2008 monograph *Digitizing Race: Visual Cultures of the Internet*, she suggests that digital culture has shifted in a fundamental way the traditional emphasis on race in ethnic studies from its being the subject of study to its being the object of study. Proceeding from this hypothesis, she presents readers of her book with the following scenario: "If we are starting to understand what the *subject* of interactivity might look like or might be formed, or what or who the *object* is, we might want to take a close look at our internet-saturated world, where the interface becomes the star, and just like other sorts of stars, it works to compel racialized identification; interfaces are prime loci for digital racial formation" (Nakamura 2008, 15). The implication of encountering and understanding race through digital information, she further observes, is that race "has itself become a digital medium, a distinctive set of informatic codes, network-mediated narratives, maps, images, and visualizations that index identity" (Nakamura and Chow-White 2012, 5). What such a recognition of the interfacing between race and technology ultimately leads to, according to Wendy Chun, is an opening up of "the possibility that, although the idea and the experience of race have been used for racial ends, the best way to fight racism might not be to deny the existence of race, but to make race do different things." Chun considers the challenge posed to Asian American scholars by digital race studies residing especially in how we can "theoretically and historically better understand the forces of race and technology and their relation to racism," as well as how "we can better respond to contemporary changes in the relationships between human and machine, human and animal, media and environment, mediation and embodiment, nature and culture, visibility and invisibility, privacy and publicity" (Chun 2012, 39, 56–7).

The interventionary potential of engaging in racial politics through the promise of digital media is the central concern of Konrad Ng's recent essay, titled "Asian American New Media as Literature for the Digital Age." Commenting on how Asian American activism can benefit online and offline activism, he observes:

Digital technology is more than a platform of increased communication: it is an opportunity for social and political intervention. In the field of communication technologies, Asian Americans have been traditionally unrepresented across the analog spectrum of print, film, and television, or have been obscured by stereotypes that range from seemingly harmless to blatantly racist. In the digital age, Asian Americans have opportunities to compose counternarratives about race, identity, and the Asian American experience; Asian American digital media, then, is a literature of activism and social justice. (Ng 2015, 552–3)

To illustrate how offline experience both informs and reshapes online representations of the ethnic community, Ng showcases the activist digital work conducted by the Asian American blogger Phil Yu and the online activism of the Asian American filmmaker Justin Lin. The former, founder of the <angryasianman.com> website that aggregates a broad range of topics and news events, is widely recognized for his successful management of "the longest-running Asian American blog" dedicated to confronting stereotypes and empowering the Asian American community. The latter, director of a 2002 crime-drama film *Better Luck Tomorrow* that satirizes the stereotype of Asian Americans as a high-achieving model minority, successfully promotes the film's anticipated Sundance debut through online fundraising. Ng considers Lin's success in fundraising success for his film epitomizing "a digital age convergence of the roles of cultural producer and consumer" in ways that go "far beyond 'breaking out' as most independent filmmakers aspire to do" (Ng 2015, 555–6).

Despite the seemingly infinite promise that digital race study holds for Asian American studies, scholars working on informatics do not overlook the ongoing structural constraints on race relations under US commercial capitalism, which continually frustrate Asian Americans in their daily experiences. Tara Fickle's 2019 monograph *The Race Card: From Gaming Technologies to Model Minorities* addresses precisely the problematics arising from such computer-mediated interactivity and its text-begetting luddism. The focus of her study is the "invidious" workings of "approximation" of race relations naturalized through the allegedly "colorblind" reality mobile game Pokémon Go, which entertains a wide spectrum of American populations since its initial release in 2016. She observes that

there is hardly an aspect of the digital game industry in which race— functioning intersectionally with gender, sexuality, class, and other categories—does not play a crucial role. It shapes the form and content of on-screen representations, online player interactions (e.g., on Xbox Live), and game modifications; the dynamics of professional game tournaments, fan communities and player-generated artifacts; the outsourced labor of global production and the privileged position of leisurely consumption; and the historical positioning of video games as the province of white heterosexual masculinity. (Fickle 2019, 1, 4)

Fickle's exposure of racialized Asian American everyday life obscured by the technologies of computer gaming finds a parallel in Karen Tei Yamashita's juxtaposition (in *Tropic of Orange*) of her description of the structured urban inequality of East Los Angeles to her parody of internet-mediated hyperreality embraced by Emi Murakami, a young media professional participating in the live TV coverage of the novel's imagined inner city revolt triggered by the irresolvable crisis of its homeless populations. Emi's dependence on the web links and feedback loops of cybernetic instantaneity for news gathering, according to the novel, initially blinds her to the gravity of the situation, as well as the violent potential of the government's response to the riots. The climax of this episode of the novel revolves around Emi's death, caused by a stray bullet fired by the police exchanging fire with the homeless, which is described in the manner of a failing computer performance. By this metaphorical scene, Yamashita emphasizes the continuing relevance of communally based struggles indispensable to rectifying America's urban inequality, which is ultimately responsible for creating the racial and class antagonisms in Los Angeles (Ling 2012, 138–9).

In his discussion of the current state of new media studies, Bryan Kim Stefans calls attention to the growing impact of "algorithm" as a by-product of the interactive dynamics of cyberspace culture. He defines "algorithm" as a process that involves a sequence of determinate computer procedures that is required to complete a digitally mediated task—a quantifying process that, in his view, has come to "permeate every aspect of life" since the beginning of the new century. The primary function of algorithm, he suggests, is that it "serves to break up material singularities … into discrete bits of information that get separated, shuffled, and reassembled elsewhere" either immediately or at a later time. Reflecting on the challenge that algorithm poses for Asian American studies, Stefans speculates: "[While] theorists of Asian American literature and art would want to maintain that there is a distinct field of activity tied to cultural differences, power interactions, social oppressions, and political representations, digital theorists would see culture as a series of anonymous, largely invisible microprocesses that are themselves ignorant of the particular needs or demands of the individual never mind the collective" (Stefans 2014, 440). To a certain degree, Stefans's consideration of the pros and cons of algorithmic culture compels a recognition of certain inevitable outcomes that computational thinking or computer-mediated informatics yields, chief among them being decontextualization and dehistoricization. These problematic aspects of new media then serve as an emphatic reminder of its limited usability. They also suggest the ongoing relevance of Colleen Lye's conception of "Asiatic racial form" as an irreducible social-semantic category that would continue to set agenda for Asian American debates over vital issues of the field, such as those concerning subject formation or the purpose of its intellectual work, in its shifting contexts and affiliations.

CONCLUSION
ANTI-ESSENTIALIST CRITIQUE AND THE ASIAN AMERICAN LITERARY PROFESSION

This study has offered a perspective on the history and practice of Asian American literary criticism since the 1970s, with a focus on its multiple interests, major debates, and individual scholars' investments with or contributions to the discourses in which they participate. It goes without saying that the Asian American literary studies we look at today is a far cry from how it was envisioned in the 1970s, especially by those who came up with the idea of "Asian American literature" and set the terms for its initial configuration and subsequent developments. It seems also plainly evident that the cumulative efforts to build, justify, and institutionalize Asian American literary studies have yielded abundantly gratifying results. Thus, the editors of a 2006 collection of essays titled *Transnational Asian American Literature* proudly observe: "Contemporary Asian American criticism is traversed by theories associated with postmodernism, poststructuralism, psychoanalysis, and discourse on globalization, diaspora, transnationalism, and postcolonialism. Critical modes and strategies in place during the first and second phases have been modified and rearticulated. Today we find studies on form and genre, pioneering works on queer sexuality, and metacritical texts that examine Asian American literary criticism as its own subfield" (Lim, Gamber, Sohn, and Valentino 2006, 8–9). In a 2010 review of the field, Christopher Lee reports additionally: "With the emergence of a critical mass of scholarship on Asian American literature and culture, historically situated interpretations of texts have undeniably been the dominant mode of reading. Moreover, the rise of ethnic studies, New Historicism, postcolonial studies, feminism, globalization studies, and other related fields has done much to dismantle the notion that knowledge can be ahistorical and apolitical" (Lee 2010, 26). Reflecting on the recent successes of the post-1965 generation of Asian American writers, Min Song calls attention to "the maturation of the children of Asian immigrants of professional background who made a significant impact on public consciousness in the 1980s for their many impressive academic achievements and who began to enter colleges and universities in numbers disproportionate to their population in the 1990s." He notes in particular: "This was the same decade we began to see these 'children' move into professions that their parents would not or perhaps could not have chosen. One career path some chose [such as that by Chang-Rae Lee, Jhumpa Lahiri, Han Ong, Ruth Ozeki, Susan Choi, and Julie Otska] was to become creative writers" (Song 2015, 12).

Conspicuously noticeable amid such optimistic views of the field's advancement, as shown in the surveys and discussions so far, is a permeating sense of frustration about its accompanying problems, especially among those attaching importance to maintaining the field's operation as an ethnic-specific US minoritarian formation. The latter approach to the current state of Asian American literary studies is typified in the stance taken by Sau-ling Wong, who repeatedly warns about the negative implications of the field's rush to reinvent itself according to postmodern or poststructuralist visions. Such an impulse, in Wong's view, may end up loosening Asian American literary studies from its social and communal ties, thereby suspending a whole range of unresolved Asian American issues that require continued on-site engagement (Wong 1995a). Susan Koshy, though not in agreement with Wong's critique of the field through reliance on the language and analytical frames of the cultural nationalist period, is similarly concerned about the ramifications of a hasty expansion of the parameters and constituencies of Asian American work, fearing that such a tendency may inadvertently jeopardize the field's integrity or even its existence as an academic discipline. She complains that the rubric of " 'Asian American' has ... become a term so hospitable that half of the world's population can squeeze in under its banner. Generous and catholic, yes—but the mix is also jarring and too eclectic" (Koshy 1996, 332). Colleen Lye shares Koshy's concern with an ironic reflex: "If in the early days of legitimation 'Asian American literature' had to confront a skepticism that there might be too few justifying texts, today the field's integrity is perhaps even more challenged by the vertigo of too many possibilities" (Lye 2007, 3). Reservations about unrestrained proliferation of the field's discourses also lurk in the background of Donald Geollnicht's important 2015 appraisal of the profession, in which he ponders: "Each expansion of the concept of Asian American identity also speaks to the limitations of the concept ... , pointing up the currently excluded or yet to be included" (Geollnicht 2015, 266).

If the skepticism voiced by these scholars does point to the existence in the field of another center of opinions antithetical to those of categorical affirmation, responses to the questions raised by the second group of scholars are either too general or too ambiguous. For example, Koshy believes that lacking a truly developed theoretical vision of the field's political commitment in the post-*Aiiieeeee!* era is the most important cause for its disciplinary crisis (Koshy 1996, 316). Christopher Lee, in a rebuttal to Koshy, evokes a vaguely defined notion of referentiality proposed by Paul de Man, one of the most ahistorical deconstructivist theorists of the 1970s, to explain away the field's conflicting impulses and multiplying directionality (Lee 2010, 29–31).[1] Based on the surveys and discussions in this book, I suggest that Asian American literary studies appear bursting at its seams as an academic discipline, not because it suffers from a short supply in postmodern or poststructuralist theory, but as a result of its having been thoroughly transformed by such theory in its own image, especially through scholars' unsuspecting adherence to the anti-representational agendas core to post-humanist ideologies. What is little recognized is that proponents of such theory rarely shy away from talking about referentiality, only that, from their point of view, literary referent—a textual substitute for social reality—always takes precedence over what is outside the text and hence the sole venue through which materiality can gain its shape, meaning, and veracity. From this perspective, the various anti-essentialist hypotheses advanced by Asian American critics since the early 1990s may not be reliable guides to either evaluating the field's past or mapping its present or future. By the same token, Asian American creative writing—given its third world origins, its possession of asynchronous structures of feeling, its inherent heterology, and its ongoing belatedness relative to Western modernity—seems at best partially open to the logic, vision, and procedures of semiology or deconstruction.

Generalized critique of essentialism, because of its overemphasis on the desirability of irresolvable tensions, can maintain the coherence of its project only by homogenizing other differences into its preferred sets of distinctions. Within this conceptual space, all arguments are reducible to a vaguely defined battle between essentialism and difference, hence leaving little room for the cultivation of innovative ideas or serious consideration of the limits of using symbolic approaches to resolve structural contradictions. This is the context in which several drastic moves made by Asian American theorists since the mid-1990s seem to have contributed more or less directly to the disciplinary crisis identified by Wong, Koshy, Lye, and Geollnitcht. A case in point is Laura Kang's call for dismantling the existing disciplinary boundaries of Asian American studies in her 2002 monograph *Compositional Subject*, and her recommendation for reinstituting in their place an alternative system of episteme made up of "multiply delineated specificity" and "shifting terms" of "emergence and legibility" (Kang 2002, 18, 21). Reimagined in this way, the disciplinary practice of Asian American literary studies starts to gain features of a random discourse that is capable of shifting freely beyond all requisite order, received protocol, and conventionally understood accountability. Mark Chiang reacts to the disciplinary alterity Kang proposes by pointing out that "the principal intellectual purpose of a discipline is to define legitimate objects and methods of study" and to offer a level of "normative or objective criteria" as an "external point of reference," so that disciplinary work can be meaningfully envisioned and executed. Yet, in her determined drive to reject Asian American knowledge production seen as a minoritarian version of US capitalism, Kang not only overlooks these pragmatic aspects of disciplinary work, but also conflates "disciplinary struggles with political struggles." During this process, Chiang further notices, the crucial question of academic "evaluation" never arises, an omission that leads him to speculate:

If prioritizing difference is meant to free Asian Americans from restrictive limits of identity and subjectivity, it threatens to dissolve the actual differences among Asian Americans, since it forestalls empirical investigation in favor of an axiomatic theoretical presumption and thus does not offer any basis for the comparison and evaluation of differences. In this way, difference itself is produced as the locus of indeterminacy, since there is no way to know what particular differences might exist. (Chiang 2009, 119–20)

Chiang's intervention in Kang's poststructuralist revisioning of the disciplinary function of Asian American literature is a necessary move, while it also points to a related problematic in need of similar scrutiny. What I refer here to is the blurring of a categorical distinction basic to the field's operation and maintenance since the 1980s: namely, that between "Asian American" and "Asian Americanist." The former term is generally understood as a marker for one's ethnic, social, or political affiliation or identity, without necessarily connoting this person's commitment to advancing the well-being of Asian American studies as an academic discipline. The latter signals unequivocally one's dedication to Asian American studies as an institutional practice, regardless of the areas of her/his expertise in the field. Yet, under the dominance of a cultural studies approach to literature in the United States since the mid-1990s—an approach that privileges meta-criticism for its potential for commenting on the function of art-making in larger settings—the swing of the pendulum has shifted decidedly toward the former term. In this process, the committed Asian Americanist becomes displaced due to the ascendency of a new identity politics: that of the post-1965 immigrant subject, whose mission, as Lisa Lowe states, is primarily concerned with promoting an ideology of "disidentification" from all Asian American traditions (Lowe 1996, 103–4). This is the context in which Kandice Chuh's espousal of a subjectless Asian American studies discourse may be seen as an ironic reenactment of the demise of "Asian Americanist" as an institutional signifier, a subject position that she catachrestically reoccupies (through the title of her 2003 monograph *Imagine Otherwise: On Asian Americanist Critique*), from which she goes on to dismantle the field as its insider. Such a dramatic redesignation of the meaning and function of "Asian Americanist" through the trick of deconstruction seems to show, more than anything else, how far Asian American literary studies has traveled down the path of becoming an identity-driven field, one reconfigured to reflect the multiple needs of an Asian American self that is ideologically estranged from institutional memory, collective ethos, and disciplinarily based expertise traditionally represented by this category.

Unburdened by a realistic sense of its goals and limitations, Asian American literary studies thus find its discourse often drawn into a plethora of polarized ideas, such as that between cultural nationalist repression of difference and free associations in diasporic or intersectional space; that between the dogma of ethnic identity quest and untrammeled post-racial or agentless play; or that between the pretension or futility of looking for signs of resistance in literature and an unapologetic retreat to reading literature as an exercise of self-reflections. These irreconcilable positions, though often presented as false by those who construct them, are in fact necessary elements of a poststructuralist imaginary of heterogeneity, which favors, as Chuh puts it, a condition of "collaborative antagonisms" created to keep "contingency, irresolution, and nonequivalence in the foreground." The logic behind Chuh's characterization of what she considers an ideal condition for Asian American literary studies is of explicit Derridean bent, that is, meaning should be made "fatally unstable" (Chuh 2001, 4, 8, 28) so that it could defy the cognitive certainty of the rational and unitary subject presumably mass-produced by the established disciplinary apparatuses that sustain the Asian American literary profession.

Commenting on the contradictions of contemporary Asian American identity politics in the broader context of American culture and society, E. San Juan observes in 1991:

> Perhaps more than other peoples of color, Asian Americans find themselves trapped in a classic postmodern predicament: essentialized by the official pluralism as formerly the "Yellow Peril" and now the "Superminority," they nevertheless seek to reaffirm their complex internal differences in projects of hybrid and syncretic genealogy. Objectified by state-ordained juridical exclusions (Chinese, Japanese, and Filipinos share this historically unique commonality), they pursue particularistic agendas for economic and cultural autonomy. Given these antinomic forces at work, can Asian American writers collectively pursue a "molecular micropolitics" of marginality? … Given the crisis of the postmodern politics of identity, can we legitimately propose an oppositional "emergency" strategy of writing whose historic agency is still on trial, or, as it were, reprieved? (San Juan 1991, 543)

San Juan implies that such Asian American "'molecular micropolitics' of marginality," though pursued in the name of social equity or cultural hybridity, always has in its operating mechanism an exclusive underside. That is, to evoke a perspective developed by Gregory Jay on the problematic of postmodern cultural politics of difference generally, "groups appear less and less willing to engage in real dialogue because they do not see themselves as belonging to a greater whole. So much energy has been spent dismantling former ideals of unity and community—exposing their flaws, treacheries, and injustices—that we are left with little time or passion for imagining positive alternatives that could connect us" (Jay 1997, 53).

It is ironic to observe that what began as a necessary critique of essentialism—that is, an overemphasis on the explanatory power of the national, the scientific, the empirical, and the holistic—has metamorphosized in the course of such critique into a systematic disarticulation and wholesale abandonment of all the founding premises and historical groundings that support and legitimize the practice of Asian American literary studies as a minoritarian intellectual formation. And critics insist on the relevance of their arguments in such an ethical tone and with such sweeping generalizations that the recommendations they offer tend to create more theoretical and practical problems than the projects they dismantle. It should be emphasized in this regard that the Asian American critique of binary opposition as a prime symptom of essentialism may also become a way to undermine dialectical methods, which are key to historicism and cultural materialism. As shown in the preceding surveys of this study, such methods not only mark the heyday of a movement-inspired Asian American cultural renaissance in the 1960s and the 1970s—which consciously bridged the gap between theory and practice, academia and community, and artistic symbol and social reality—but also strongly inform the rigorous guidelines of Russian Formalism in the realm of high theory. The latter is well-known for its positive attitude toward the contradictory performances between two basic functions of literature, the cognitive and the sublimational, as textual features that can be redeployed to legitimize subaltern struggles, voices, and aspirations.

My evaluation of Asian American anti-essentialist critique in the concluding pages of this study resonates with the concerns raised in my rehistoricization of the *Aiiieeeee!* moment in the introductory chapter. In taking these positions, I am fully aware that the waning of dialectical methods in Western humanistic and social science discourses may be an irreversible trend in the twenty-first century. I also believe that the agendas of Asian American literary studies will be continually shaped by what Katu Katrak refers to as "a general climate of a peculiarly North American (U.S. and Canada) multiculturalism" (Katrak 1996, 122), which, given the nature of its ongoing formations, will always be replete with race and gender conflicts, curricular or canon wars, immigration debates, identity politics, and the frequent resurgence of conservative or neoliberal ideologies in national and international politics. This means that the disciplinary crisis in the field would remain and the tension between or among the various binary arguments would only become more severe in the years ahead. Under the circumstances, Asian American literary scholars are faced with the formidable task of rearticulating the purpose, mission, and limits of the field beyond visions informed by ungrounded epistemology or abstract idealism, which works to stimulate, rather than undermine, America's consumerist desire to appropriate Asian American heterogeneity and difference.

This is where a caution advised by R. Radhakrishnan is worthy of serious attention, especially by those interested in developing theoretical paradigms. He states:

Minority intellectuals have to take the knowledge game very seriously and simultaneously sniff at it with rigorous suspicion. ... Rather than be seduced by the avant-gardism of metropolitan epistemologies, they need to develop criteria to differentiate between empowering and alienating knowledges, between knowledges that one can call one's own through the exercise of collective agency and those that call for the sacrifice of subaltern agency in the name of metropolitan success and acceptability. (Radhakrishnan 2001, 255)

In the spirit of Radhakrishnan's cogent advice, I would like to urge Asian American literary scholars to be wary of the cynical underpinnings of Pierre Bourdieu's reductive claim that all humanistic studies are futile and that everything we do smacks of self-interest. For even if there is an element of truth in what he says, following through his argument would play right into the hands of those who have long wished to eliminate the precarious institutional perch we now occupy under US capitalism. On the other hand, Asian American critics may also want to venture beyond the discursive routines of post-humanist theory in which they are trained to reify and dare to contemplate the possibility, against Foucault's analytic of finitude,[2] that history can progress in a non-teleological fashion, that agency can be joyful and collective rather than self-absorbed and duplicitous, and that literary representation can reflect upon tangible worldly situations that are complex and contradictory, but not that tricky or infinitely elusive as a ground for engagement.

NOTES

Introduction

1   The statements made here are premised on what I find to be a representational inequity (or a tendency to privilege certain critical tastes over others) in recent Asian American literary criticism, as well as a resultant citational hierarchy in place, which I avoid reconstituting in this study. Notably, the marginalized opinions tend to be those explicitly concerned with socioeconomic issues, class relations, cultural nationalism, or historical-materialist methods. The undervaluation of these research interests in recent Asian American literary studies will be contextualized in Chapter 1, with a perspective on the implications of such a methodological skewing for the directionality of the field. More at stake here is the practical need of this book's readers, who would appreciate a fuller account of the range of Asian American intellectual investments and heterogeneity, regardless of individual scholars' academic preferences or political alignments (including that of my own as historicized formalism). An important task of this study therefore is to recognize and include underreported intellectual contributions in the field as a necessary part of the ongoing Asian American conversations.

2   Mark Chiang interprets the result of *Aiiieeeee!*'s intervention very differently, asserting that its publication sets in motion a process of Asian American capital accumulation through its attempt to place literary art over political mobilization; see Mark Chiang, *The Cultural Capital of Asian American Studies* (New York: New York University Press, 2009), 19–20. The question of symbolic capital will be addressed in Chapter 6.

3   Stephen Sumida, who has presided over the building of Asian American literary studies since the early 1980s, detects this tendency in a 1989 review of the field, stating that the "words" of Asian American creative expression "ought to receive a critical hearing and reading that cannot otherwise be readily assumed ... [and that it is] imperative that we convey our thoughts to listeners who do not expect to hear only the already stated, proven, and familiar." See Stephen Sumida, "Asian American Literature in the 1980s," in *Frontiers of Asian American Studies: Writing, Research, and Commentary,* eds. Gail M. Nomura et al. (Pullman: Washington State University Press, 1989), 151–2.

4   See Chapter 7 for a survey of such periodizing practices in the field since the early 1990s.

5   According to Paul Smith, the subject formation in a peripheral discourse begins with the "ideological demand" voiced by a "cerned subject"—a subject aware of its self-interest and willing to act upon such awareness in an assertive

and somewhat coherent fashion. Yet, because this subject can make its presence known only in relation to a multiplicity of other subjects in a shared epistemological zone, its enunciated self-knowledge would remain partial and tentative, thus anticipating the awakening to consciousness of other subjects-to-be, as well as the voicing of other subjective demands. These latent subjective positionalities, in his view, will be similarly local, relational, and in need of ideological supplementations in shifting contexts; see Paul Smith, *Discerning the Subject* (Minneapolis: University of Minnesota Press, 1988), 100–2, 107–9.

Chapter 1

1   This white woman figure, a stock character in Chin's literary imaginary, was first introduced in a 1976 letter that Chin wrote to Michael Kirby, editor of *Drama Review*, in which he complained about Asian Americans' treatment in the United States as if they were the offspring of a white "whoremother." See Dorothy Ritsuko McDonald, "Introduction," in *The Chickencoop Chinaman and The Year of the Dragon* (Seattle: University of Washington Press, 1981), xxvii. Chin's construction of female gender in these terms, though aimed to critique white America for being responsible for Asians' alienation and abjection in the country of their birth, clearly reflects his reliance on the ethos and language of the late 1960s counterculture, which were imbued with anti-women bias and sexism.

2   Sui Sin Far studies often go hand in hand with those of her younger sister Winnifred Eaton, a Chinese Canadian writer under the Japanese penname "Onoto Watanna." For book-length analyses of the Eaton sisters' literary careers and their contributions to the emergence of an Asian (North) American literary sensibility, see, for example, Annette White-Parks, *Sui Sin Far/Edith Maude Eaton: A Literary Biography* (Urbana-Champaign: University of Illinois Press, 1995); Dominika Ferens, *Edith Eaton and Winnifred Eaton: Chinatown Missions and Japanese Romances* (Urbana-Champaign: University of Illinois Press, 2002); Zhiming Pan, *Romance as Strategy: A Study of Winnifred Eaton's Novels* (Beijing: Foreign Language Teaching and Research Press, 2008); and Mary Chapman, *Becoming Sui Sin Far: Early Fiction, Journalism, and Travel Writing by Edith Maude Eaton* (Montreal, QC: McGill-Queen's University Press, 2016).

3   Noteworthy in this context is that Jonathan Culler, the foremost American proponent of deconstructive theory, rationalizes the ethical premise of its methods by consciously appropriating the politics of feminism. This tendency, according to Robert Scholes, becomes programmatic in Culler's 1982 monograph, *On Deconstruction: Theory and Criticism after Structuralism* (Ithaca, NY: Cornell University Press, 1982), in which he includes a section under the title "Reading as a Woman" (43–63). See also Robert Scholes, *Protocols of Reading* (New Haven, CT: Yale University Press, 1989), 95.

4   The eclipse of discussions of the socioeconomic dimension of race relations in American ethnic literary studies during this period also reflects the influence of Werner Sollors's monograph *Beyond Ethnicity: Consent and Descent in American Culture* (New York: Oxford University Press, 1986). In this study, Sollors designates race as but one aspect of the discursive formation of ethnicity, a revisionist move that drew criticism from scholars both within and outside the field. See, for example, Alan Wald, "Theorizing Cultural Difference: A Critique of the 'Ethnicity School.'" *MELUS* 14, no. 2 (1987): 21–5; Shirley Geok-lin Lim, "The Ambivalent Asian American Literature on the Cusp," in *Reading the Literatures of Asian America*, eds. Shirley Geok-lin Lim and Amy Ling (Philadelphia, PA: Temple University Press, 1992), 24–5; Sau-ling C. Wong, *Reading Asian American Literature: From Necessity to Extravagance* (Princeton, NJ: Princeton University Press, 1993), 4; Bonnie TuSmith, *All My Relatives: Community in Contemporary Ethnic American Literatures* (Ann Arbor: University of Michigan Press, 1993), 2–3, 12–13; and Donald Goellnicht, "Blurring Boundaries: Asian American Literature as Theory," in *An Interethnic Companion to Asian American Literature*, ed. King-Kok Cheung (New York: Cambridge University Press, 1997), 338–9.

5   Critics interpret Lye's concept of "Asiatic racial form" rather differently: Eric Hayot sees it as an illustration of Lye's "power imaginary" about the workings of the world market; Stephen Yao considers it a manifestation of the "ideological functioning" of cultural imperialism; Joseph Jeon finds it more a symbol of Asian American "racial objectification"; and Christopher Lee recognizes its potential for uncovering the "unseen" forces of "social abstraction" in hegemonic cultural productions. See Eric Hayot, "The Asian Turns," *PMLA* 124, no. 3 (2009): 908; Stephen Yao, *Foreign Accents: Chinese American Verse from Exclusion to Postethnicity* (New York: Oxford University Press, 2010), 30; Joseph Jonghyun Jeon, *Racial Things, Racial Forms: Objecthood in Avant-Garde Asian American Poetry* (Iowa City: University of Iowa Press, 2012), xviii; and Christopher Lee, "Asian American Literature and the Resistances of Theory," *MFS: Modern Fiction Studies* 56, no. 1 (2010): 24–5. Lye's concept of "racial form" will be revisited in the surveys of chapter 2.

Chapter 2

1   Kingston introduces the concept of "claiming America" during a 1980 interview for her newly published non-fiction *China Men*. She states: "What I am doing in this new book is claiming America. ... That seems to be the common strain that runs through all the characters. In story after story Chinese American people are claiming America, who goes all the way from one character saying that a Chinese explorer found this place before Leif Ericsson did to another one buying a house here. Buying a house is a way of saying that America—and not China—is his country." See Timothy Pfaff, "Talking to Mrs. Kingston."

Notes

New York Times Book Review, 18 June (1980), 1. Kingston's remarks were made in the context of her growing frustrations with mainstream reviewers' tendency to misread the Chinese literary or cultural allusions in her 1976 feminist work *The Woman Warrior*, as well as with the criticism voiced by members of the ethnic community for the book's alleged misrepresentation of Asian immigrant males in ways that reinforce the orientalism in the American popular imagination; see Maxine Hong Kingston, "Cultural Mis-Readings by American Reviewers," in *Asian and Western Writers in Dialogue: New Cultural Identities*, ed. Guy Amirthanayagam (London: Macmillan, 1982), 55–65. Elaine Kim considers Kingston's use of "claiming America" to characterize the Chinese male figures described in *China Men* an indication of the latter's preference for resolving the controversies over *The Woman Warrior* with "pacifism," an interpretation that sets precedence for discussing this issue in the field throughout the 1980s and much of the 1990s; see Elaine Kim, *Asian American Literature: An Introduction to the Writings and Their Social Contexts* (Philadelphia, PA: Temple University Press, 1982), 212–13. For a contrasting evaluation of *China Men* in terms of its more sophisticated feminist critique (compared with what Kingston does in *The Woman Warrior*) of the cultural nationalism espoused by the editors of *Aiiieeeee!*, see Jinqi Ling, *Narrating Nationalisms: Ideology and Form in Asian American Literature* (New York: Oxford University Press, 1998), 110–38.

2   As a prominent cultural theorist on the left, Hall's post-national and post-ethnic moves led Terry Eagleton to castigate him for "being inside and outside Marxism simultaneously," as well as for his ultimate alignment, since the mid-1990s, with the non-Marxist camp; see Terry Eagleton, *After Theory* (New York: Basic Books, 2003), 40.

3   The issue of mixed-race identity has generated a relatively small body of sustained analyses in the field. For representative scholarship on the topic, see, for example, Carol Roh Spaulding, "Two Blue-Eyed Asian Maidens: Mixed Race in the Works of Edith Eaton/Sui Sin Far and Winnifred Eaton/Onoto Watanna," in *Re/collecting Early Asian America: Essays in Cultural History*, eds. Josephine Lee et al. (Philadelphia, PA: Temple University Press, 2002), 340–54; Emma Jinhua Teng, "The Eaton Sisters and the Figure of the Eurasian," in *The Cambridge History of Asian American Literature*, eds. Rajini Srikanth and Min Hyoung Song (New York: Cambridge University Press, 2015), 88–104; and Cathy Schlund-Vials and Cynthia Wu, "Rethinking Embodiment and Hybridity: Mixed Race, Adoptee, and Disabled Subjectivities," in *The Cambridge Guide to Asian American Literature*, eds. Crystal Parikh and Daniel Y. Kim (New York: Cambridge University Press, 2015), 197–211.

4   See also Steven Salaita, "Arab American Literature," in *The Routledge Companion to Asian American and Pacific Islander Literature*, ed. Rachel C. Lee (New York: Routledge, 2014), 202–12; and Rajini Srikanth, "'The War on Terror': Post-9/11 South Asian and Arab American Literature," in *The Cambridge Companion to Asian American Literature*, eds. Crystal Parikh and Daniel Y. Kim (New York: Cambridge University Press, 2015), 73–85.

Chapter 3

1   For additional accounts of Japanese American literary activities in the internment camps, see Charles Crow, "A *MELUS* Interview: Hisaye Yamamoto," *MELUS* 14, no. 1 (1987): 73–84; Helen Jaskoski, "A *MELUS* Interview: Mitsuye Yamada" *MELUS* 15, no. 1 (1988): 97–108; Stan Yogi, "Japanese American Literature," in *An Interethnic Companion to Asian American Literature*, ed. King-Kok Cheung (New York: Cambridge University Press, 1997), 128–32; King-Kok Cheung, "Hisaye Yamamoto and Wakako Yamauchi," in *Words Matter: Conversations with Asian American Writers*, ed. King-Kok Cheung (Honolulu: University of Hawaii Press, 2000b), 343–82; and Miryam Leitner-Rudolph, *Janice Mirikitani and Her Work* (Braumüller, Austria: Universitäts-Verlagsbunchhandlung, 2001), 2–4.

2   This anthology contains a short introductory essay (by Oscar Penaranda, Serafin Syquia, and Samuel Tagatac) on Filipino American literature. Among the writers introduced are Jose Garcia Villa, Alfred A. Robles, N. V. M. Gonzales, and Bienvenido Santos; see Kai-yu Hsu and Helen Palubinskas, eds., *Asian-American Authors* (Boston, MA: Houghton Mifflin, 1972), 126–75.

3   An essential linguistic component of Filipino American literature is *Tagalog*, a local dialect in Manila that, according to Denise Cruz, is marked by its distinct class and gendered accents in a language hierarchy that fetishizes English, the last colonial language in the Philippines; see Denise Cruz, *Transpacific Femininities: The Making of the Modern Filipina* (Durham, NC: Duke University Press, 2012), 54–5, 59. This aspect of Filipino American literature is further illustrated in Timothy Yu's analysis of the poems written by Barbara Jane Reyes, a San Francisco-based Filipina writer. He observes: "The colonial history that structures daily encounters on the street of San Francisco is embedded in language itself," a "bilingual space of Spanish and English" with *Tagalog* being a key element in "this mix, represented through the precolonial *Baybayin* script." Yu argues: "Reyes's inclusion of *Baybayin* both alludes to this appropriation and disrupts it, thematizing the white, male explorer's desire for the 'foreign' while refusing to translate the *Tagalog* script, making it a site of resistance to the monolingual Anglophone reader." See Timothy Yu, "Asian American Poetry in the First Decade of 2000s," *Comparative Literature* 52, no. 4 (2011): 832–3.

4   In her recent monograph *Chinese American Literature without Borders: Gender, Genre, and Form* (New York: Palgrave Macmillan, 2016), King-Kok Cheung demonstrates the complex workings of cross-cultural translation and negotiation by weaving together a range of Chinese, diasporic Chinese, and Chinese American writings in English across their overlapping but distinct contexts of production and reception.

5   For example, Josephine Nock-Hee Park provides a close analysis of the duality and self-contradiction of David Hsin-Fu Wand (the critic)/David Rafael Wang (the poet), the editor of *Asian-American Heritage: An Anthology of Prose and Poetry* (New York: Washington Square Press, 1974). Similarly, Hua Hsu focuses on the inconsistent aspects of H. T. Tsiang's career, which is better known for

its affiliation with the cultural leftism of the 1930s; see Park, *Apparitions of Asia: Modernist Form and Asian American Poetics* (New York: Oxford University Press. 2008), 91–7; and Hsu, *A Floating Chinaman: Fantasy and Failure across the Pacific* (Cambridge, MA: Harvard University Press, 2016), 8–19.

Chapter 4

1   For comprehensive recent studies of Yamashita's spatial imagination and novelistic art, see, for example, Jing Ling, *Across Medians: History and Figuration in Karen Tei Yamashita's Transnational Novels* (Stanford: Stanford University Press, 2012); and A. Robert Lee, ed., *Karen Tei Yamashita: Fictions of Magic and Memory* (Honolulu: University of Hawaii Press, 2018).

2   Chuh and Shimakawa's 2001 coedited volume was preceded by a 2000 special issue of *Jouvert* guest-edited by Viet Thanh Nguyen and Tina Chen, who advocate for using the postcolonial concept of migrancy to replace a race-based Asian American identity politics. Nguyen and Chen's positions will be discussed in Chapter 7.

3   For a recent perspective on the assumptions and practices of diverse cultural nationalisms in the Asian Pacific region, see Denise Cruz and Erin Suzuki, "America's Empire and Asia-Pacific: Constructing Hawaii and the Philippines," in *The Cambridge Companion to Asian America Literature*, eds. Crystal Parikh and Daniel Y. Kim (New York: Cambridge University Press, 2015), 20–6.

4   Spivak details her concept of "strategic use of essentialism," in *Outside in the Teaching Machine* (New York: Routledge, 1993), 1–23.

5   In his review of this film, Eng states that "coming out for Asian gays involves many irreconcilable choices between aligning oneself with a predominantly white gay community often tainted by overt racism or an ethnic community often marked by cultural homophobia." He then suggests, "if nothing else, *The Wedding Banquet* illustrates in exacting detail the inevitable compromises that a tortuous, pathological, and unnatural system of compulsory Heterosexuality demands from us all." See David Eng, "*The Wedding Banquet*: You're Not Invited and Some Other Ancillary Thoughts," *Artspiral* 7 (1993).

6   The survey here may serve to recontextualize the role of biculturalism in transnational Asian American literary studies. That is, while this unique interpretive tool has been enabling to both the formative phase and subsequent growth of the field, its redeployment under the post-Fordist conditions of ongoing Asian migration and border-crossing seems to have produced paradoxical results. On the one hand, its comparative ethos is revitalized to a level of greater relevance to transnational studies; on the other, its emphasis on cultural comparability has done more to affirm the efficacy of a general Goethean poetics of cultural plurality fashioned out of the nineteenth century than to critique the problematic of the nation-state—be it US-centrism or Asia-centrism—the main reason for the field's transnational shift in the first place.

7 Yun further develops the arguments made in this article in her monograph *The Coolie Speaks: Chinese Indenture Laborers and African Slaves of Cuba* (Philadelphia, PA: Temple University Press, 2008).

Chapter 5

1 For criticisms of Wong's 1945 autobiography in these terms, see, for example, Frank Chin et al., "Introduction: Fifty Years of Our Whole Voice," in *Aiiieeeee! An Anthology of Asian American Writers*, eds. Frank Chin et al. (Washington, DC: Howard University Press, 1974), xxiv–xxx; Elaine Kim, *Asian American Literature* (1982), 70–2; Karen Su, "Jade Snow Wong's Badge of Distinction in the 1990s," *Critical Mass: A Journal of Asian American Cultural Criticism* 2, no. 1 (1994); and Shirley Lim, "The Tradition of Chinese American Women's Life Stories: Thematics of Race and Gender in Jade Snow Wong's *Fifth Chinese Daughter* and Maxine Hong Kingston's *The Woman Warrior*," in *American Women's Autobiography, Fea(s)ts of Memory*, ed. Margo Cully (Madison: University of Wisconsin Press, 1992), 252–67.

2 For a comprehensive review of the ethnic community's debates over the publication and reception of *The Woman Warrior*, see Deborah Woo, "Maxine Hong Kingston: The Ethic Writer and the Burden of Dual Authenticity," *Amerasia Journal* 16, no. 1 (1990).

3 See Leslie Bow, *Betrayal and Other Acts of Subversion* (Princeton, NJ: Princeton University Press, 2001), 115–36; and Viet Thanh Nguyen, *Race and Resistance: Literature and Politics in Asian America* (New York: Oxford University Press, 2002), 107–24.

4 For contrasting assessments of the meaning and significance of Hwang's *M. Butterfly*, Mukherjee's *Jasmine*, and Tan's *Joy Luck Club*, see, for example, Dorinne Kondo, "*M. Butterfly*: Orientalism, Gender, and a Critique of Essentialist Identity," *Cultural Critique* 16 (1990); Colleen Lye, "*M. Butterfly* and the Rhetoric of Antiessentialism: Minority Discourse in an International Frame," in *The Ethnic Cannon: Histories, Institutions, and Interventions*, ed. David Palumbo-Liu (Minneapolis: University of Minnesota Press, 1995), 260–89; Sandra Ponzanesi, "Bharati Mukherjee's *Jasmine*: The Exuberance of Imagination, Feminist Struggle and Multicultural Negotiation," in *Studies of Indian Writing in English*, eds. Rajeshwar Mittapalli and Pier Paolo Piciucco (New Delhi: Atlantic Publishers and Distributors, 2001), 77–107; E. San Juan, Jr., *Hegemonies and Strategies of Transgression: Essays on Cultural Studies and Comparative Literature* (New York: State University of New York Press, 1995), 179–80; Frank Chin, "Come All Ye Asian American Writers of the Real and the Fake," in *The Big Aiiieeeee! An Anthology of Chinese American and Japanese American Literature*, eds. Jeffrey Paul Chan et al. (New York: Meridian, 1991), 2–3; and Sau-ling Wong, "'Sugar Sisterhood': Situating the Amy Tan Phenomenon," in *The Ethnic Canon: Histories, Institutions, and Interventions*,

ed. David Palumbo-Liu (Minneapolis: University of Minnesota Press, 1995), 174–209.

5   For different assessments of the nature and function of literary resistance, see, for example, the positions taken by Patricia E. Chu in "The Trials of the Ethnic Novel: Susan Choi's *American Woman* and the Post-Affirmative Action Era," *American Literary History* 23, no. 3 (2011): 531; Yoonmee Chang, *Writing the Ghetto: Class, Authorship, and the Asian American Ethnic Enclave* (New Brunswick, NJ: Rutgers University Press, 2010), 75; and Rachel Lee, *The Exquisite Corpse of Asian America: Biopolitics, Biosociality, and Posthuman Ecologies* (New York: New York University Press, 2014b), 23–4.

Chapter 6

1   Pierre Bourdieu, *Distinction: A Social Critique of the Judgement of Taste*, trans. Richard Nice (Cambridge, MA: Harvard University Press, [1979] 1984), 257–371.

2   Additional titles of book-length studies of literary form in the field include, among others, Rocío Davis and Sämi Ludwig, eds., *Asian American Literature in the International Context: Readings on Fiction, Poetry, Performance* (Hamburg: Lit Verlag, 2002); Xiaojing Zhou and Samina Najmi, eds., *Form and Transformation in Asian American Literature* (Seattle: University of Washington Press, 2005); Elda Tsou, *Unique Tropes: Form, Race, and Asian American Literature* (Philadelphia, PA: Temple University Press, 2015); and Audrey Wu Clark, *The Asian American Avant-Garde: Universalist Aspirations in Modernist Literature and Art* (Philadelphia, PA: Temple University Press, 2015).

3   "Socially symbolic" and "formally motivated" are interrelated concepts that I use rather liberally in the surveys and discussions throughout this book. Readers familiar with Fredric Jameson's works should know that these lexicons are basic to his argument that "history is not a text," but "it is inaccessible to us except in textual forms," and to his urging critics to identify rhetorical figures as substitutes for history through socially symbolic interpretation of texts. See Fredric Jameson, *The Political Unconscious: Narrative as a Socially Symbolic Act* (Ithaca, NY: Cornell University Press, 1981), 35.

Chapter 7

1   Wong further develops this aspect of Cheung and Yogi's annotated bibliography in her own monograph *Reading Asian American Literature*, in which she presents the field as possessing a thematically coherent and "internally meaningful literary tradition" marked by its "mutual allusion, qualification,

complication, and transmutation" as an Asian American textual coalition (1993), 11.

2 Thu-Huong Nguyên-Vo complicates the meaning of "mourning" by shifting the grounds of its discussion from those focused on the paradox of Asian assimilation to those concerning Vietnamese American memory work, asking: "How shall we remember rather than just appropriate the dead for our own agendas, precluding what the dead can tell us? ... Whom among the dead shall we mourn? How do we retrieve our histories containing events that had passed, with the dead, into accomplished fates? Finally, how shall we speak to those who survived, who now remember various histories among us?" Based on these questions, she argues: "In mourning all the dead, we must respect their radical alterity not entirely knowable to us. We must patiently interpret what will remain the indeterminacy of various histories. ... In talking to the dead as they speak in us, we open up spaces in ourselves to speak to the living amongst us who may tell our various histories rather than the single one that has become us. Only then can we invite in the living as the living, who may be different from us, with histories different from our retold tale." See Nguyên-Vo, "Forking Paths: How Shall We Mourn the Dead?" *Amerasia Journal* 31, no. 2 (2005): 172.

3 Other book-length studies that explore post-identity concerns include Tina Chen's *Double Agency: Acts of Impersonation in Asian American Literature and Culture* (Stanford: Stanford University Press, 2005); Crystal Parikh's *An Ethics of Betrayal: The Politics of Otherness in Emergent U.S. Literatures and Culture* (New York: Fordham University Press, 2009); Christopher Lee's *The Semblance of Identity: Aesthetic Mediation in Asian American Literature* (Stanford: Stanford University Press, 2012); and Long Le-Khac's *Giving Form to an Asian and Latinx America* (Stanford: Stanford University Press, 2020).

Chapter 8

1 Rachel Lee makes a similar point about the Asian American body by problematizing the tendency in the field to approach race as nothing but a discursive construction overdetermined by diverse power relations, to the neglect of its biological nuance and complexity as an "ontological" or "phenomenological" entity; see Rachel C. Lee, *The Exquisite Corpse of Asian America: Biopolitics, Biosociality, and Posthuman Ecologies* (New York: New York University Press, 2014), 9–11.

2 The legal consequences of the nineteenth-century American nativist fear of racial mixing highlighted by Schlund-Vials and Wu are among the issues analyzed by Susan Koshy in terms of how "a biopolitics of the population," "technologies of sex," or policies for containing the "reproduction of Asian immigrant communities" were actively pursued through the anti-miscegenation laws instituted at the various state levels in the United States from 1897 to 1969;

Notes

see Susan Koshy, *Sexual Naturalization: Asian Americans and Miscegenation* (Stanford: Stanford University Press. 2004), 1–2.

Conclusion

1   For a critical analysis of de Man's ahistorical hermeneutics and its influence on poststructuralist translation theory, see E. San Juan, Jr., *Hegemonies and Strategies of Transgression: Essays on Cultural Studies and Comparative Literature* (New York: State University of New York Press, 1995), 17–33.

2   The phrase "analytic of finitude" is a section title in chapter 9 ("Man and His Doubles") of Foucault's philosophical study, *The Order of Things: An Archeology of the Human Sciences*, Editions Gallimard (New York: Random House, Inc. [1966] 1970), 312–17. This concept is central to Foucault's early explorations of what he sees as a general condition of human entrapment between the limits of being and those of knowing, as well as a related paradox between the solidity of finitude, on the one hand, and a tantalizing but unrealizable promise of hope, on the other. Commenting on the pessimistic nature of Foucault's discourse theory as a whole, Hayden White points out that, in his linguistically based critique of Western capitalist modernity, Foucault typically undertakes to expose "the dark underside of every discursive formation": His analyses always "begin in paradox and end in negative apocalypse, their middles are heavy with what Foucault calls 'positivity.'" See Hayden White, *The Content of the Form: Narrative Discourse and Historical Representation* (Baltimore, MD: Johns Hopkins University Press, 1987), 107, 113.

BIBLIOGRAPHY

Alquizola, Marilyn C. 1991. "Subversion or Affirmation: The Text and Subtext of *America Is in the Heart*." In *Asian Americans: Comparative and Global Perspectives*, edited by Shirley Hune, Russell Endo, Stephen H. Sumida, and Russell C. Leong, 199–209. Pullman: Washington State University Press.

Asian Women United California. Ed. 1989. *Making Waves: An Anthology of Writings by and about Asian American Women*. Boston, MA: Beacon Press.

Attridge, Derek. 1994. "Literary Form and the Demands of Politics: Otherness in J. M. Coetzee's *The Age of Iron*." In *Aesthetics and Ideology*, edited by George Levine, 243–63. New Brunswick, NJ: Rutgers University Press.

Bahng, Aimee. 2017. *Migrant Futures: Decolonizing Speculation in Financial Times*. Durham, NC: Duke University Press.

Bakhtin, Mikhail M., and Medvedev, Pavel N. [1928] 1978. *The Formal Method in Literary Scholarship: A Critical Introduction to Sociological Poetics*, translated by Albert J. Wehrle. Baltimore, MD: John Hopkins University.

Bao, Quang, and Yanagihara, Hanya. Eds. 2000. *Take Out: Queer Writing from Asian Pacific America*. New York: Asian American Writers Workshop.

Barrett, Michèle. 1988. "The Place of Aesthetics in Marxist Criticism." In *Marxism and the Interpretation of Culture*, edited by Cary Nelson and Lawrence Grossberg, 697–713. Urbana-Champaign: University of Illinois Press.

Bascara, Victor. 2006. *Model-Minority Imperialism*. Minneapolis: University of Minnesota Press.

Bascara, Victor. 2015. "Looking Backward, from 2019 to 1882." In *Techno-Orientalism: Imagining Asia in Speculative Fiction, History, and Media*, edited by David S. Roh, Betsy Huang, and Greta Niu, 52–63. New Brunswick, NJ: Rutgers University Press.

Beaumont, Alexander. 2015. *Contemporary British Fiction and the Cultural Politics of Disenchantment*. London: Palgrave Macmillan.

Beevi, Mariam. 1997. "The Passing of Literary Traditions: The Figure of the Woman from Vietnamese Nationalism to Vietnamese American Transnationalism." *Amerasia Journal* 23, no. 2: 27–53.

Bennett, Tony. 1993. "Texts in History: The Determinations of Readings and Their Texts." In *Poststructuralism and the Question of History*, edited by Derek Attridge, Geoff Bennington, and Robert Young, 63–81. New York: Cambridge University Press.

Berman, Russell A. 1989. *Modern Culture and Critical Theory: Art, Politics, and the Legacy of the Frankfurt School*. Madison: University of Wisconsin Press.

Blinde, Patricia Lin. 1980. "The Icicle in the Desert: Perspective and Form in the Works of Two Chinese-American Writers." *MELUS* 6, no. 3: 51–71.

Bolaki, Stella. 2009. "'It Translated Well': The Promise and the Perils of Translation in Maxine Hong Kingston's *The Woman Warrior*." *MELUS* 34, no. 4: 39–60.

Bonacich, Edna. 1995. "The Site of Class." In *Privileging Positions: The Sites of Asian American Studies*, edited by Gary Y. Okihiro, Marilyn Alquizola, Dorothy Fujita Rony, and Wong K. Scott, 67–81. Pullman: Washington State University Press.

Bourdieu, Pierre. [1979] 1984. *Distinction: A Social Critique of the Judgement of Taste*, translated by Richard Nice. Cambridge, MA: Harvard University Press.

Bové, Paul A. 1995. "Preface: Literary Postmodernism." In *Early Postmodernism: Foundational Essays*, edited by Paul Bové, 1–16. Durham, NC: Duke University Press.

Bow, Leslie. 2001. *Betrayal and Other Acts of Subversion: Feminism, Sexual Politics, Asian American Women's Literature*. Princeton, NJ: Princeton University Press.

Bow, Leslie. 2002. "Beyond Rangoon: An Interview with Wendy Law-Yone." *MELUS* 27, no. 4: 183–200.

Bow, Leslie. 2010. *"Partly Colored": Asian Americans and Racial Anomaly in the Segregated South*. New York: New York University Press.

Bulosan, Carlos. [1943] 1973. *America Is in the Heart*. Seattle: University of Washington Press.

Bürger, Peter. 1984. *Theory of the Avant-Garde*, translated by Michael Shaw. Minneapolis: University of Minnesota Press.

Burns, Lucy Mae San Pablo. 2013. *Puro Arte: Filipinos on the Stage of Empire*. New York: New York University Press.

Burns, Lucy Mae San Pablo. 2015. "The Art of the Asian American Movement's Social Protest Performance." In *The Cambridge History of Asian American Literature*, edited by Rajini Srikanth and Min Hyoung Song, 237–53. New York: Cambridge University Press.

Cabusao, Jeffrey Arellano. 2011. "Decolonizing Knowledges: Asian American Studies, Carlos Bulosan, and Insurgent Filipino Diasporic Imagination." *Kritika Kultura* 16: 122–44.

Cabusao, Jeffrey Arellano. 2014. "Forum Kritika: Reflections on Carlos Bulosan and Becoming Filipino." *Kritika Kultura* 23: 129–53.

Camacho, Keith L. 2011. "Transoceanic Flows: Pacific Islander Interventions across the American Empire." *Amerasia Journal* 37, no. 3: ix–xxxiv.

Campomanes, Oscar V. 1992. "Filipinos in the United States and Their Literature of Exile." In *Reading the Literatures of Asian America*, edited by Shirley Geok-lin Lim and Amy Ling, 49–78. Philadelphia, PA: Temple University Press.

Campomanes, Oscar V., and Gernes, Todd S. 1988. "Two Letters from America: Carlos Bulosan and the Act of Writing." *MELUS* 15, no. 3: 15–46.

Carby, Hazel V. 1987. *Reconstructing Womanhood: The Emergence of the Afro-American Woman Novelist*. New York: Oxford University Press.

Cha, Theresa Hak Kyung. [1982] 1995. *Dictée*. Berkeley, CA: Third Woman Press.

Chang, Juliana. 1996. "Reading Asian-American Poetry." *MELUS* 21, no. 0: 81–98.

Chang, Juliana. 2007. "Interpreting Asian American Identity and Subjectivity." *MFS: Modern Fiction Studies* 53, no. 4: 867–75.

Chang, Yoonmee. 2010. *Writing the Ghetto: Class, Authorship, and the Asian American Ethnic Enclave*. New Brunswick, NJ: Rutgers University Press.

Chapman, Mary Megan. 2016. *Becoming Sui Sin Far: Early Fiction, Journalism, and Travel Writing by Edith Maude Eaton*. Montreal: McGill-Queen's University Press.

Chen, Kuan-Hsing. 2013. "Missile Internationalism." In *Sinophone Studies: A Critical Reader*, edited by Shu-Mei Shih, Chien-hsin Tsai, and Brian Bernards, 172–85. New York: Columbia University Press.

Chen, Tina Y. 2005. *Double Agency: Acts of Impersonation in Asian American Literature and Culture*. Stanford: Stanford University Press.

Chen, Tina Y. 2011. "Emergent Cartographies and the Directions of Asian American Literary Studies." *American Literary History* 23, no. 4: 885–98.

Cheng, Anne Anlin. 2000. *The Melancholy of Race: Psychoanalysis, Assimilation, and Hidden Grief*. New York: Oxford University Press.

Cheng, Anne Anlin. 2014. "Modernism." In *The Routledge Companion to Asian American and Pacific Islander Literature*, edited by Rachel Lee, 315–28. New York: Routledge.

Cheung, Floyd. 2003. "Introduction." In *And China Has Hands*, by H. T. Tsiang, 7–15. New York: Ironweed Press.

Cheung, Floyd. 2005. "Early Chinese American Autobiography: Reconsidering the Works of Yan Phou Lee and Yung Wing." In *Recovered Legacies: Authority and Identity in Early American Literature*, edited by Keith Lawrence and Floyd Cheung, 24–39. Philadelphia, PA: Temple University Press.

Cheung, King-Kok. 1988. "'Don't Tell': Imposed Silences in *The Color Purple* and *The Woman Warrior*." *PMLA* 103, no. 2: 162–74.

Cheung, King-Kok. 1989. "The Woman Warrior versus the Chinaman Pacific: Must a Chinese American Critic Choose between Feminism and Heroism?" In *Conflicts in Feminism*, edited by Marianne Hirsch and Evelyn Fox Keller, 234–51. New York: Routledge.

Cheung, King-Kok. 1993. *Articulate Silences: Hisaye Yamamoto, Maxine Hong Kingston, Joy Kogawa*. Ithaca, NY: Cornell University Press.

Cheung, King-Kok. 1997. "Re-Viewing Asian American Literary Studies." In *An Interethnic Companion to Asian American Literature*, edited by King-Kok Cheung, 1–36. New York: Cambridge University Press.

Cheung, King-Kok. 2000a. "Art, Spirituality, and the Ethic of Care: Alternative Masculinities in Chinese American Literature." In *Masculinity Studies and Feminist Theory: New Directions*, edited by Judith Kegan Gardiner, 261–89. New York: Columbia University Press.

Cheung, King-Kok. 2000b. "Hisaye Yamamoto and Wakako Yamauchi." In *Words Matter: Conversations with Asian American Writers*, edited by King-Kok Cheung, 343–82. Honolulu: University of Hawaii Press.

Cheung, King-Kok. 2016. *Chinese American Literature without Borders: Gender, Genre, and Form*. New York: Palgrave Macmillan.

Cheung, King-Kok, and Yogi, Stan. Eds. 1988. *Asian American Literature: Annotated Bibliography*. New York: Modern Language Association of America.

Chiang, Mark. 2002. "Coming Out into the Global System: Postmodern Patriarchies and Transnational Sexualities in *The Wedding Banquet*." In

Screening Asian Americans, edited by Peter X. Feng, 273–92. New Brunswick, NJ: Rutgers University Press.

Chiang, Mark. 2008. "Capitalizing Form: The Globalization of the Literary Field: A Response to David Palumbo-Liu." *American Literary History* 20, no. 4: 838–44.

Chiang, Mark. 2009. *The Cultural Capital of Asian American Studies*. New York: New York University Press.

Chin, Frank. [1976] 1979. "Afterword" to *No-No Boy*, by John Okada, 253–60. Seattle: University of Washington Press.

Chin, Frank. [1974] 1981. *The Chickencoop Chinaman and The Year of the Dragon*. Seattle: University of Washington Press.

Chin, Frank. [1976] 1988. "Eat and Run Midnight People." In *The Chinaman Pacific & Frisco R. R. Co.*, by Frank Chin, 8–23. Minneapolis, MN: Coffee House Press.

Chin, Frank. 1991. "Come All Ye Asian American Writers of the Real and the Fake." In *The Big Aiiieeeee! An Anthology of Chinese American and Japanese American Literature*, edited by Jeffrey Paul Chan, Frank Chin, Lawson Fusao Inada, and Shawn Wong, 1–92. New York: Meridian.

Chin, Frank, Chan, Jeffrey Paul, Inada, Lawson Fusao, and Wong, Sean. 1974. "Introduction: Fifty Years of Our Whole Voice." In *Aiiieeeee! An Anthology of Asian American Writers*, edited by Frank Chin, Jeffrey Paul Chan, Lawson Fusao Inada, and Sean Wong, vii–xlviii. Washington, DC: Howard University Press.

Cho, Eric. Ed. 1978. *Talk Story: An Anthology of Hawaii's Local Writers*. Honolulu: Frank Stewart.

Chon, Sharon Ro. 2018. "Narrating the Visual: Seeing Race in Asian American Literature." PhD dissertation. Los Angeles: University of California.

Choy, Catherine Ceniza, and Choy, Gregory Paul. 2003. "Transformative Terrains: Korean Adoptees and the Social Constructions of an American Childhood." In *The American Child: A Cultural Studies Reader*, edited by Caroline Field Levander and Carole J. Singley, 262–79. New Brunswick, NJ: Rutgers University Press.

Chu, Louis. [1961] 1979. *Eat a Bowl of Tea*. Seattle: University of Washington Press.

Chu, Patricia E. 2011. "The Trials of the Ethnic Novel: Susan Choi's *American Woman* and the Post-Affirmative Action Era." *American Literary History* 23, no. 3: 529–54.

Chu, Patricia P. 2000. *Assimilating Asians: Gendered Strategies of Authorship in Asian America*. Durham, NC: Duke University Press.

Chu, Patricia P. 2001. "The Woman Warrior: Memoirs of a Girlhood among Ghosts, by Maxine Hong Kingston." In *A Resource Guide to Asian American Literature*, edited by Sau-ling C. Wong and Stephen H. Sumida, 86–96. New York: Modern Language Association of America.

Chu, Seo-Young. 2010. *Do Metaphors Dream of Literal Sleep? A Science-Fictional Theory of Representation*. Cambridge, MA: Harvard University Press.

Chua, Cheng Lok. 1982. "Golden Mountain: Chinese Version of the American Dream in Lin Yutang, Louis Chu, and Maxine Hong Kingston." *Ethnic Group* 4, no. 1/2: 33–59.

Chuang Hua. [1968] 1986. *Crossings*. Boston, MA: Northeastern University Press.

Chuh, Kandice. 2001. "Imaginary Borders." In *Orientations: Mapping Studies in the Asian Diaspora*, edited by Kandice Chuh and Karen Shimakawa, 277–95. Durham, NC: Duke University Press.

Chuh, Kandice. 2003. *Imagine Otherwise: On Asian Americanist Critique*. Durham, NC: Duke University Press.

Chuh, Kandice, and Shimakawa, Karen. 2001. "Introduction: Mapping Studies in the Asian Diaspora." In *Orientations: Mapping Studies in the Asian Diaspora*, edited by Kandice Chuh and Karen Shimakawa, 1–21. Durham, NC: Duke University Press.

Chun, Wendy Hui Kyong. 2012. "Race and/as Technology or How to Do Things Race." In *Race After the Internet*, edited by Lisa Nakamura and Peter Chow-White, 38–60. New York: Routledge.

Chung, Cristy, Alison Kim, and Lemeshewsky A. Kaweah. Eds. 1987. *Between the Lines: An Anthology by Pacific/Asian Lesbians of Santa Cruz*. California: Dancing Bird Press.

Clark, Audrey Wu. 2015. *The Asian American Avant-garde: Universalist Aspirations in Modernist Literature and Art*. Philadelphia, PA: Temple University Press.

Crow, Charles L. 1987. "A *MELUS* Interview: Hisaye Yamamoto." *MELUS* 14, no. 1: 73–84.

Cruz, Denise. 2012. *Transpacific Femininities: The Making of the Modern Filipina*. Durham, NC: Duke University Press.

Cruz, Denise. 2013. " 'Love Is Not a Bowl of Quinces': Food, Desire, and the Queer Asian Body in Monique Truong's *The Book of Salt*." In *A Food Studies Reader*, edited by Robert J-Song Ku, Martin F. Manalansan IV, and Anita Mannur, 354–70. New York: New York University Press.

Cruz, Denise, and Suzuki, Erin. 2015. "America's Empire and Asia-Pacific: Constructing Hawaii and the Philippines." In *The Cambridge Companion to Asian America Literature*, edited by Crystal Parikh and Daniel Y. Kim, 16–28. New York: Cambridge University Press.

Culler, Jonathan. 1982. *On Deconstruction: Theory and Criticism after Structuralism*. Ithaca, NY: Cornell University Press.

Dao-Shan, Anh Thang, and Pelaud, Isabelle Thuy. 2015. "The American War in Vietnam and Its Diaspora." In *The Cambridge History of Asian American Literature*, edited by Rajini Srikanth and Min Hyoung Song, 469–83. New York: Cambridge University Press.

Davis, Rocío G. 2000. Review of *The Americas of Asian American Literature: Gendered Fictions of Nation and Transnation*, by Rachel C. Lee. (Princeton, NJ: Princeton University Press, 1999). *MFS: Modern Fiction Studies* 46, no. 4: 1043–4.

Davis, Rocío G. 2006. "Begin Here: A Critical Introduction to the Asian American Childhood." In *Transnational Asian American Literature: Sites and Transits*, edited by Shirley Geok-lin Lim, John Blair Gamber, Stephen Hong Sohn, and Gina Valentino, 161–80. Philadelphia, PA: Temple University Press.

Davis, Rocío G., and Lee, Sue-Im. Eds. 2005. *Literary Gestures: The Aesthetic in Asian American Writing*. Philadelphia, PA: Temple University Press.

Bibliography

Davis, Rocío G., and Ludwig, Sämi. 2002. "Introduction: Asian American Literature in the International Context." In *Asian American Literature in the International Context: Readings on Fiction, Poetry, Performance*, edited by Rocío G. Davis and Sämi Ludwig, 8–18. Hamburg: Lit Verlag.

Day, Iyko. 2007. "Lost in Translation: Uncovering Canada in Asian America." *Amerasia Journal* 33, no. 2: 67–86.

Day, Iyko. 2016. *Alien Capital: Asian Racialization and the Logic of Settler Colonial Capitalism.* Durham, NC: Duke University Press.

Denning, Michael. 1997. *The Cultural Front: The Laboring of American Culture in the Twentieth Century.* New York: Verso.

Derrida, Jacques. [1967] 1976. *Of Grammatology*, translated by Gayatri Chakravorty Spivak. Baltimore, MD: Johns Hopkins University Press.

Dirlik, Arif. 1994. "The Postcolonial Aura: Third World Criticism in the Age of Global Capitalism." *Critical Inquiry* 20: 328–56.

Dirlik, Arif. 2003. "Locating Asian American Studies Today: Origins, Identities, and Crises." *Amerasia Journal* 29, no. 2: 167–9.

Dirlik, Arif. 2007. "Contemporary Challenges to Marxism: Postmodernism, Postcolonialism, Globalization." *Amerasia Journal* 33, no. 3: 1–17.

Du, Nguyen. 1983. *The Tale of Kieu*, a bilingual edition, translated by Huynh Sanh Thong. New Haven, CT: Yale University Press.

Eagleton, Terry. 1983. *Literary Theory: An Introduction.* Minneapolis: University of Minnesota Press.

Eagleton, Terry. 1990. *The Ideology and the Aesthetics.* Cambridge, MA: Blackwell.

Eagleton, Terry. 2003. *After Theory.* New York: Basic Books.

Elliot, Mathew. 2009. "Sins of Omission: Hisaye Yamamoto's Vision of History." *MELUS* 34, no. 1: 47–68.

Eng, David L. 1993. "*The Wedding Banquet*: You're Not Invited and Some Other Ancillary Thoughts." *Artspiral* 7: 8–10.

Eng, David L. 2001. *Racial Castration: Managing Masculinity in Asian America.* Durham, NC: Duke University Press.

Eng, David L. 2008. "The End(s) of Race." *PMLA* 123, no. 5: 1479–93.

Eng, David L., and Han, Shinhee. 2003. "A Dialogue on Racial Melancholia." In *Loss: The Politics of Mourning*, edited by David L. Eng and David Kazanjian, 343–71. Berkeley: University of California Press.

Eng, David L., and Hom, Alice Y. Eds. 1998. *Q & A: Queer in Asian America.* Philadelphia, PA: Temple University Press.

Espiritu, Augusto. 1998. "The 'Pre-History' of an 'Asian American' Writer: N. V. M. Gonzales's Allegory of Decolonization." *Amerasia Journal* 24, no. 3: 126–41.

Espiritu, Yen Lê. 1992. *Asian American Panethnicity: Bridging Institutions and Identities.* Philadelphia, PA: Temple University Press.

Espiritu, Yen Lê. 2005. "Asian American Studies and Ethnic Studies: About Kin Disciplines." *Amerasia Journal* 29, no. 2: 195–209.

Esty, Jed, and Lye, Colleen. 2012. "Peripheral Realism Now." *Modern Language Quarterly* 73, no. 3: 269–88.

Feng, Peter X. 2000. "Asian Americans and the Modern Imaginary." *American Quarterly* 52, no. 4: 756–63.

Feng, Peter X. 2002. "Introduction." In *Screening Asian Americans*, edited by Peter X. Feng, 1–18. New Brunswick, NJ: Rutgers University Press.

Feng, Pin-chia. 1998. The *Female Bildungsroman by Toni Morrison and Maxine Hong Kingston: A Postmodern Reading*. New York: Peter Lang.

Feng, Pin-chia. 2014. "East Asian Approaches to Asian American Literary Studies." In *The Routledge Companion to Asian American and Pacific Islander Literature*, edited by Rachel C. Lee, 257–67. New York: Routledge.

Fenkl, Heinz Insu. 1997. *Memories of My Ghost Brother*. New York: Blume.

Ferens, Dominika. 2002. *Edith Eaton and Winnifred Eaton: Chinatown Missions and Japanese Romances*. Urbana-Champaign: University of Illinois Press.

Fickle, Tara. 2019. *The Race Card: From Gaming Technologies to Model Minorities*. New York: New York University Press.

Foucault, Michel. [1966] 1970. *The Order of Things: An Archeology of the Human Sciences*, by Editions Gallimard. New York: Random House, Inc.

Fujikane, Candace. 1994. "Between Nationalisms: Hawaii's Local Nation and Its Troubled Racial Paradise." *Critical Mass: A Journal of Asian American Cultural Criticism* 1, no. 2: 23–57.

Fujitani, T., White, Geoffrey M., and Yoneyama, Lisa. 2001. "Introduction." In *Perilous Memories: The Asia-Pacific War(s)*, edited by T. Fujitani, Geoffrey M. White, and Lisa Yoneyama, 1–29. Durham, NC: Duke University Press.

Fung, Richard. 1996. "Looking for My Penis: The Eroticized Asian in Gay Video Porn." In *Asian American Sexualities: Dimensions of the Gay and Lesbian Experience*, edited by Russell Leong, 181–98. New York: Routledge.

Gardner, Eileen, and Musto, Ronald D. 2015. *The Digital Humanities: A Primer for Students and Scholars*. New York: Cambridge University Press.

Gates, Jr., Henry Louis. 1986. "Editor's Introduction: Writing 'Race' and the Difference It Makes." In *Race, Writing, and Difference*, edited by Henry Louis Gates, Jr., 1–20. Chicago: University of Chicago Press.

Gilroy, Paul. 1992. "Cultural Studies and Ethnic Absolutism." In *Cultural Studies*, edited by Lawrence Grossberg, Cary Nelson, and Paula Treichler, 187–98. London: Routledge.

Goellnicht, Donald C. 1992. "Tang Ao in America: Male Subject Positions in *China Men*." In *Reading the Literatures of Asian America*, edited by Shirley Geok-lin Lim and Amy Ling, 191–212. Philadelphia, PA: Temple University Press.

Goellnicht, Donald C. 1997. "Blurring Boundaries: Asian American Literature as Theory." In *An Interethnic Companion to Asian American Literature*, edited by King-Kok Cheung, 338–75. New York: Cambridge University Press.

Goellnicht, Donald C. 2000. "A Long Labor: The Protracted Birth of Asian Canadian Literature." *Essays on Canadian Writing Journal* 72: 1–41.

Goellnicht, Donald C. 2015. "Inventing Identity: The Manifestos of Pioneering Asian American Literary Anthologies." In *The Cambridge History of Asian American Literature*, edited by Rajini Srikanth and Min Hyoung Song, 254–70. New York: Cambridge University Press.

Gong, Stephen. 2002. "A History in Progress: Asian American Media Arts Centers, 1970–1990." In *Screening Asian Americans*, edited by Peter X. Feng, 101–10. New Brunswick, NJ: Rutgers University Press.

Grice, Helena. 2002. "Mending the Sk(e)in of Memory: Trauma, Narrative, and the Recovery of Identity in Patricia Chao, Aimee Liu and Joy Kogawa." In *Asian American Literature in the International Context: Readings on Fiction, Poetry, Performance*, edited by Rocío G. Davis and Sämi Ludwig, 81–95. Hamburg: Lit Verlag.

Grice, Helena. 2004. "Artistic Creativity, Form, and Fictional Experimentation in Filipina American Fiction." *MELUS* 29, no. 1: 181–98.

Grice, Helena. 2014. "European Asian American Literary Studies." In *The Routledge Companion to Asian American and Pacific Islander Literature*, edited by Rachel C. Lee, 279–89. New York: Routledge.

Grice, Helena, and Parikh, Crystal. 2014. "Feminisms and Queer Interventions into Asian America." In *The Routledge Companion to Asian American and Pacific Islander Literature*, edited by Rachel C. Lee, 169–82. New York: Routledge.

Grotjohn, Robert. 2003. "Remapping Internment: A Postcolonial Reading of Mitsuye Yamada, Lawson Fusao Inada, and Janice Mirikitani." *Western American Literature* 38, no. 3: 246–69.

Hagedorn, Jessica Tarahata. 1993. "Introduction." In *Charlie Chan Is Dead: An Anthology of Contemporary Asian American Fiction*, edited by Jessica Tarahata Hagedorn, xxi–xxx. New York: Penguin.

Hagedorn, Jessica Tarahata. 1999. "The Exile Within/The Question of Identity" (with a Postscript/Interview by Karin Aguilar-San Juan). In *The State of Asian America: Activism and Resistance in the 1990s*, edited by Karin Aguilar-San Juan, 173–82. Boston, MA: South End Press.

Hall, Stuart. 1980. "Race, Articulation and Societies structured in Dominance." In *Sociological Theories: Race and Colonialism*, edited by UNESCO, 305–45. Paris: UNESCO.

Hall, Stuart. 1985. "Signification, Representation, Ideology: Althusser and the Post-Structuralist Debates." *Critical Studies in Mass Communication* 2, no. 2: 91–114.

Hall, Stuart. 1995. "New Ethnicities." In *The Post-Colonial Studies Reader*, edited by Hellen Tiffin, Bill Ashcroft, Gareth Griffiths, and Helen Tiffin, 223–7. London: Routledge.

Hamalian, Leo, and Chang, Diana. 1995. "A *MELUS* Interview: Diana Chang." *MELUS* 20, no. 4: 29–43.

Harvey, David. 2005. *The New Imperialism*. New York: Oxford University Press.

Hattori, Tomo. 1999. "Model Minority Discourse and Asian American Jouis-Sense." *Differences: A Journal of Feminist Studies* 11, no. 2: 228–47.

Hayot, Eric. 2009. "The Asian Turns." *PMLA* 124, no. 3: 906–17.

Hayot, Eric. 2014. "Coolie." In *The Routledge Companion to Asian American and Pacific Islander Literature*, edited by Rachel C. Lee, 81–90. New York: Routledge.

Hayslip, Le Ly (with Jay Wurts). 1989. *When Heaven and Earth Changed Places: A Vietnamese Woman's Journey from War to Peace*. New York: Doubleday.

Hegeman, Susan. 2012. *The Cultural Return*. Berkley: University of California Press.

Hill, Raquel. 2003. "'Guilt Passed on Our Bones': Generational Trauma in Three Poems by Janice Mirikitani." *Pacific and American Studies* 3: 147–61.

Hillenbrand, Margaret. 2013. "Letters of Penance: Writing America in Chinese and the Location of Chinese American Literature." *MELUS* 38, no. 3: 44–66.

Hirabayashi, Lane Ryo. Ed. 1998. *Teaching Asian America: Diversity and the Problem of Community.* New York: Rowan & Littlefield.

Hirabayashi, Lane Ryo. 2002. "Reconsidering Transculturation and Power." *Amerasia Journal* 28, no. 2: ix–xxii.

Ho, Jennifer Anne. 2005. *Consumption and Identity in Asian American Coming-of-Age Novel.* New York: Routledge.

Ho, Jennifer Anne. 2013. "Acting Asian American, Eating Asian American: The Politics of Race and Food in Don Lee's *Wrack and Ruin*." In *A Food Studies Reader*, edited by Robert J-Song Ku, Martin F. Manalansan IV, and Anita Mannur, 303–22. New York: New York University Press.

Ho, Tamara C. 2014. "Burmese American Literature." In *The Routledge Companion to Asian American and Pacific Islander Literature*, edited by Rachel C. Lee, 244–56. New York: Routledge.

Ho, Wendy. 1991. "Mother/Daughter Writing and the Politics of Race and Sex in Maxine Hong Kingston's *The Woman Warrior*." In *Asian Americans: Comparative and Global Perspectives*, edited by Shirley Hune, Amy Ling, Stephen S. Fujita, and Hyung Chan Kim, 225–37. Pullman: Washington State University Press.

Ho, Wendy. 1999. *In Her Mother's House: The Politics of Asian American Mother-Daughter Writing.* Walnut Creek, CA: Altamira Press.

Hom, Marlon K. 1982. "Chinatown Literature during the Last Ten Years (1939–1949) By *Wenquan*." *Amerasia Journal* 9, no. 1: 75–100.

Hong, Grace Kyungwon. 2006. *The Ruptures of American Capital: Women of Color Feminism and the Culture of Immigrant Labor.* Minneapolis: University of Minnesota Press.

Hong, Grace Kyungwon. 2015. *Death Beyond Disavowal: The Impossible Politics of Difference.* Minneapolis: University of Minnesota Press.

Hongo, Garrett K. 1982. *Yellow Light.* Middletown, CT: Wesleyan University Press.

Hongo, Garrett K. 1993. "Introduction." In *The Open Boat: Poems from Asian America*, edited by Garrett K. Hongo, xvi–xlii. New York: Doubleday.

Hongo, Garrett K. 1994. "Asian American Literature: Questions of Identity" (The Academy of American Poets Symposium, UCLA Asian American Studies Center, April 23, 1992). *Amerasia Journal* 20, no. 3: 1–8.

hooks, bell. 1992. "Representing Whiteness in the Black Imagination." In *Cultural Studies*, edited by Lawrence Grossberg, Cary Nelson, and Paula Treichler, 338–46. New York: Routledge.

Houston, Velina Hasu. Ed. 1990. *The Politics of Life: Four Plays by Asian American Women.* Philadelphia, PA: Temple University Press.

Hsu, Hua. 2016. *A Floating Chinaman: Fantasy and Failure across the Pacific.* Cambridge, MA: Harvard University Press.

Hsu, Kai-yu, and Palubinska, Helen. 1972. "Introduction." In *Asian-American Authors*, edited by Kai-yu Hsu and Helen Palubiaska, 1–6. Boston, MA: Houghton Mifflin.

Hsu, Ruth Y. 2006. "The Cartography of Justice and Truthful Refractions in Karen Tei Yamashita's *Tropic of Orange*." In *Transnational Asian American*

Literature: Sites and Transits, edited by Shirley Geok-lin Lim, John Blair Gamber, Stephen Hong Sohn, and Gina Valentino, 75–99. Philadelphia, PA: Temple University Press.

Hsu, Ruth Y. 2018. "Karen Tei Yamashita's *Tropic of Orange* and Chaos Theory." In *Karen Tei Yamashita: Fictions of Magic and Memory*, edited by A. Robert Lee, 105–22. Honolulu: University of Hawaii Press.

Huang, Betsy. 2010. *Contesting Genres in Contemporary Asian American Fiction.* New York: Palgrave Macmillan.

Huang, Yunte. 2008. *Transpacific Imaginations: History, Literature, Counterpoetics.* New York: Cambridge University Press.

Huang, Yunte. 2009. "Angel Island and the Poetics of Error." In *Poetry and Cultural Studies: A Reader*, edited by Maria Damon and Ira Livingston, 301–9. Urbana-Champaign: University of Illinois Press.

Hu-Dehart, Evelyn. 1989. "Latin America in Asia-Pacific Perspective." In *What Is in a Rim? Critical Perspectives on the Pacific Region Idea*, edited by Arif Dirlik, 251–81. New York: Rowan & Littlefield.

Hu-Dehart, Evelyn. 1999. "Women, Work, and Globalization in Late 20th Century Capitalism." *Working Papers Series*, Department of Comparative American Cultures, 1–24. Pullman: Washington State University.

Huh, Jinny. 2015. "Racial Speculations: (Bio)technology, Battlestar Galactica, and a Mixed-Race Imagining." In *Techno-Orientalism: Imagining Asia in Speculative Fiction, History, and Media*, edited by David S. Roh, Betsy Huang, and Greta Niu, 101–12. New Brunswick, NJ: Rutgers University Press.

Hutnyk, John. [1999] 2000. "Hybridity Saves? Authenticity and/or the Critique Appropriation." *Amerasia Journal* 25, no. 3: 39–58.

Hwang, David Henry. 1986. *M. Butterfly.* New York: Plume.

Inada, Lawson Fusao. 1992. *Legends from Camp.* Minneapolis, MN: Coffee House Press.

Izumi, Masumi. 2016. "Teaching Asian American Studies in Japan: Challenges and Possibilities." In *Trans-Pacific Japanese American Studies: Conversations on Race and Racialization*, edited by Yasuko Takezawa and Gary Y. Okihiro, 315–41. Honolulu: University of Hawaii Press.

Jameson, Fredric. 1972. *The Prison-House of Language: A Critical Account of Structuralism and Russian Formalism.* Princeton, NJ: Princeton University Press.

Jameson, Fredric. 1979. *Fables of Aggression: Wyndham Lewis, the Modernist as Fascist.* Berkeley: University of California Press.

Jameson, Fredric. 1981. *Schlund-Vials: Narrative as a Socially Symbolic Act.* Ithaca, NY: Cornell University Press.

Jameson, Fredric. 1991. *Postmodernism or, the Cultural Logic of Late Capitalism.* Durham, NC: Duke University Press.

Janette, Michele. 2003. "Vietnamese American Literature in English, 1963–1994." *Amerasia Journal* 29, no. 1: 267–86.

Jaskoski, Helen. 1988. "A *MELUS* Interview: Matsuye Yamada." *MELUS* 15, no. 1: 97–108.

Jay, Gregory S. 1997. *American Literature and the Culture Wars.* Ithaca, NY: Cornell University Press.

Jay, Martin. 1993. *Force Field: Between Intellectual, Historical, and Cultural Critique.* New York: Routledge.

Jeon, Joseph Jonghyun. 2012. *Racial Things, Racial Forms: Objecthood in Avant-Garde Asian American Poetry.* Iowa City: University of Iowa Press.

Jerng, Mark C. 2010. *Claiming Others: Transracial Adoption and National Belonging.* Minneapolis: University of Minnesota Press.

Jerng, Mark C. 2014. "Adoptee." In *The Routledge Companion to Asian American and Pacific Islander Literature*, edited by Rachel C. Lee, 21–32. New York: Routledge.

Jin, Wen. 2006. "Transnational Criticism and Asian Immigrant Literature in the U.S.: Reading Yan Geling's *Fusang* and Its English Translation." *Contemporary Literature* 47, no. 4: 570–600.

Jung, Moon-Ho. 2006. *Coolies and Cane: Race, Labor, and Sugar in the Age of Emancipation.* Baltimore, MD: Johns Hopkins University Press.

Kang, Laura Hyun Yi. 1995. "The 'Liberatory Voice' of Theresa Hak Kyung Cha's *Dictée.*" In *Writing Self, Writing Nation*, edited by Elaine H. Kim and Norma Alarcón, 73–99. Berkeley, CA: Third Woman Press.

Kang, Laura Hyun Yi. 2002. *Compositional Subjects: Enfiguring Asian/Asian American Women.* Durham, NC: Duke University Press.

Kang, Younghill. [1937] 1997. *East Goes West: The Making of an Oriental Yankee.* New York: Kaya Production.

Katrak, Ketu H. 1996. "South Asian American Writers: Geography and Memory." *Amerasia Journal* 22, no. 3: 121–38.

Keith, Joseph. 2015. "Comparative Race Studies and Interracialism." In *The Cambridge Companion to Asian America Literature*, edited by Crystal Parikh and Daniel Y. Kim, 183–97. New York: Cambridge University Press.

Keller, Nora Okja. 1997. *Comfort Woman.* New York: Penguin.

Keller, Nora Okja. 2002. *Fox Girl.* New York: Viking.

Kim, Claire Jean. 1999. "The Racial Triangulation of Asian Americans." *Politics and Society* 27, no. 1: 105–38.

Kim, Daniel Y. 2005. *Writing Manhood in Black and Yellow: Ralph Ellison, Frank Chin, and the Literary Identity.* Stanford: Stanford University Press.

Kim, Elaine H. 1982. *Asian American Literature: An Introduction to the Writings and Their Social Contexts.* Philadelphia, PA: Temple University Press.

Kim, Elaine H. 1990a. "Defining Asian American Realities through Literature." In *The Nature and Context of Minority Discourse*, edited by Abdul R. Jan Mohamed and David Lloyd, 146–70. New York: Oxford University Press.

Kim, Elaine H. 1990b. " 'Such Opposite Creatures': Men and Women in Asian American Literature." *Michigan Quarterly* 9, no. 1: 68–93.

Kim, Elaine H. 1992. "Foreword." In *Reading the Literatures of Asian America*, edited by Shirley Geok-lin Lim and Amy Ling, xi–xvii. Philadelphia, PA: Temple University Press.

Kim, Elaine H. 1994. "Room for a View from a Marginal Sight: Texts, Contexts, and Asian American Studies." *Critical Mass: A Journal of Asian American Cultural Criticism* 1, no. 2: 3–22.

Bibliography

Kim, Elaine H. 1995. "Beyond Railroads and Internment: Comments on the Past, Present, and Future of Asian American Studies." In *Privileging Positions: The Sites of Asian American Studies*, edited by Gary Y. Okihiro, Marilyn Alquizola, Dorothy Fujita Rony, and Wong K. Scott, 11–19. Pullman: Washington State University Press.

Kim, Heidi Kathleen. 2013. "Incarceration, Cafeteria Style: The Politics of the Mess Hall in Japanese American Incarceration." In *A Food Studies Reader*, edited by Robert J-Song Ku, Martin F. Manalansan IV, and Anita Mannur, 125–46. New York: New York University Press.

Kim, Heidi Kathleen. 2016. *Invisible Subjects: Asian America in Postwar Literature*. New York: Oxford University Press.

Kim, Jodi. 2010. *Ends of Empire: Asian American Critique and Cold War*. New York: Oxford University Press.

Kim, Jodi. 2014. "Militarization." In *The Routledge Companion to Asian American and Pacific Islander Literature*, edited by Rachel C. Lee, 154–66. New York: Routledge.

Kim, Ronyoung. 1987. *Clay Walls*. Sag Harbor, NY: Permanent Press.

Kingston, Maxine Hong. 1976. *The Woman Warrior: Memoirs of a Girlhood among Ghosts*. New York: Alfred A. Knopf.

Kingston, Maxine Hong. 1980. *China Men*. New York: Alfred A. Knopf.

Kingston, Maxine Hong. 1982. "Cultural Mis-Readings by American Reviewers." In *Asian and Western Writers in Dialogue: New Cultural Identities*, edited by Guy Amirthanayagam, 55–65. London: Macmillan.

Kondo, Dorinne K. 1990. "*M. Butterfly*: Orientalism, Gender, and a Critique of Essentialist Identity." *Cultural Critique* 16: 5–29.

Kondo, Dorinne K. 1995. "Poststructuralist Theory as Political Necessity." *Amerasia Journal* 21, no. 1/2: 95–100.

Koshy, Susan. 1996. "The Fiction of Asian American Literature." *Yale Journal of Criticism* 9, no. 2: 315–46.

Koshy, Susan. 2000. Review of *Imagining the Nation: Asian American Literature and Cultural Consent*, by David Leiwei Li (Stanford: Stanford University Press, 1998). *Journal of Asian American Studies* 3, no. 1: 115–18.

Koshy, Susan. 2004. *Sexual Naturalization: Asian Americans and Miscegenation*. Stanford: Stanford University Press.

Koshy, Susan. 2008. "Once More, with Feeling: Reflections on Racial Formation." *PMLA* 123, no. 5: 1549–65.

Koshy, Susan. 2011. "The Rise of the Asian American Novel." In *Cambridge History of the American Novel*, edited by Leonard Cassuto, Claire Virginia Eby, and Benjamin Reiss, 1046–63. New York: Cambridge University Press.

Krieger, Murray. 1993. *The Ideological Imperative: Representation and Resistance in Recent American Theory*. Taipei, Taiwan: The Institute of European and American Studies Academia Sinica.

Ku, Robert Ji-Song. 2013. "Gannenshoyu or First-Year Soy Sauce? Kikkoman Soy Sauce and the Corporate Forgetting of the Early Japanese American Consumer." In *A Food Studies Reader*, edited by Robert J-Song Ku, Martin F. Manalansan IV, and Anita Mannur, 208–27. New York: New York University Press.

Kukkè, Surabhi, and Shah, Svati. [1999] 2000. "Reflections on Queer South Asian Progressive Activism in the U.S." *Amerasia Journal* 25, no. 3: 129–37.

Kurashige, Lon. 2016. "Asian American History across the Pacific." In *Trans-Pacific Japanese American Studies: Conversations on Race and Racialization*, edited by Yasuko Takezawa and Gary Y. Okihiro, 378–84. Honolulu: University of Hawaii Press.

LaCapra, Dominick. 1989. *Soundings in Critical Theory*. Ithaca, NY: Cornell University Press.

Laclau, Ernesto, and Mouffe, Chantal. 1985. *Hegemony and Socialist Strategy: Toward a Radical Democratic Practice*. London: Verso.

Lacsamana, Anne E. 1998. "Academic Imperialism and the Limits of Postmodernist Discourse: An Examination of Nicole Constable's *Maid to Order in Hong Kong: Stories of Filipina Workers*." *Amerasia Journal* 24, no. 3: 37–42.

Lai, Him, Mark, Lim, Jenny, and Yung, Judy. 1980. "Introduction." In *Island: Poetry and History of Chinese Immigrants on Angel Island, 1910–1940*, edited by Him Mark Lai, Genny Lim, and Judy Yung, 8–29. San Francisco: HOCDOI (History of Chinese Detained on Island).

Lai, Wally Look. 1989. "Chinese Indentured Labor: Migration to the British West Indies in the Nineteenth Century." *Amerasia Journal* 15, no. 2: 117–38.

Lawrence, Keith, and Cheung, Floyd. 2005. "Introduction." In *Recovered Legacies: Authority and Identity in Early Asian American Literature*, edited by Keith Lawrence and Floyd Cheung, 1–23. Philadelphia, PA: Temple University Press.

Law-Yone, Wendy. 1987. *The Coffin Tree*. New York: Alfred A. Knopf.

Lay, Sody. 2001. "The Cambodian Tragedy: Its Writers and Representations." *Amerasia Journal* 27, no. 2: 171–82.

Le-Khac, Long. 2020. *Giving Form to an Asian and Latinx America*. Stanford: Stanford University Press.

Lee, A. Robert. 2008. *Multicultural American Literature: Comparative Black, Native, Latino/a, and Asian American Fictions*. Jackson: University Press of Mississippi.

Lee, A. Robert. Ed. 2018. *Karen Tei Yamashita: Fictions of Magic and Memory*. Honolulu: University of Hawaii Press.

Lee, Chang-Rae. 1995. *Native Speaker*. New York: Penguin Putnam.

Lee, Christopher. 2007. "The Lateness of Asian Canadian Studies." *Amerasia Journal* 33, no. 2: 1–17.

Lee, Christopher. 2010. "Asian American Literature and the Resistances of Theory." *MFS: Modern Fiction Studies* 56, no. 1: 19–39.

Lee, Christopher. 2012. *The Semblance of Identity: Aesthetic Mediation in Asian American Literature*. Stanford: Stanford University Press.

Lee, Christopher. 2015. "The Writing of Translation." In *The Cambridge Companion to Asian America Literature*, edited by Crystal Parikh and Daniel Y. Kim, 129–41. New York: Cambridge University Press.

Lee, Erika. 2007. "Hemispheric Orientalism and the 1907 Pacific Coast Race Riots." *Amerasia Journal* 33, no. 2: 19–47.

Lee, James Hyung-Jin. 2004. *Urban Triage: Race and Fictions of Multiculturalism*. Minneapolis: University of Minnesota Press.

Bibliography

Lee, James Hyung-Jin. 2006. "Warfare, Asian American Literature, and Commitment." *Amerasia Journal* 32, no. 3: 79–87.

Lee, James Hyung-Jin. 2008. "The Transitivity of Race and the Challenge of the Imagination." *PMLA* 1550–6.

Lee, James Hyung-Jin. 2014. "Pathography/Illness Narratives." In *The Routledge Companion to Asian American and Pacific Islander Literature*, edited by Rachel C. Lee, 451–60. New York: Routledge.

Lee, Josephine D. 1997. *Performing Asian America: Race and Ethnicity on the Contemporary Stage*. Philadelphia, PA: Temple University Press.

Lee, Julia H. 2005. "The Capitalist and Imperialist Critique in H. T. Tsiang's *And China Has Hands*." In *Recovered Legacies: Authority and Identity in Early Asian American Literature*, edited by Keith Lawrence and Floyd Cheung, 80–97. Philadelphia, PA: Temple University Press.

Lee, Julia H. 2011. *Interracial Encounters: Reciprocal Representations in African American and Asian American Literatures, 1896–1937*. New York: New York University Press.

Lee, Kun Jong. 2008a. "Heinz Insu Fenkl's *Memories of My Ghost Brother*: An American Rewriting of Rudyard Kipling's *Kim*." *Journal of American Studies* 42, no. 2: 317–40.

Lee, Kun Jong. 2008b. "Korean Language American Literary Studies: An Overview." *Amerasia Journal* 34, no. 2: 14–35.

Lee, Rachel C. 1999. *The Americas of Asian American Literature: Gendered Fictions of Nation and Transnation*. Princeton, NJ: Princeton University Press.

Lee, Rachel C. 2014a. "Biopolitics." In *The Routledge Companion to Asian American and Pacific Islander Literature*, edited by Rachel C. Lee, 68–80. New York: Routledge.

Lee, Rachel C. 2014b. *The Exquisite Corpse of Asian America: Biopolitics, Biosociality, and Posthuman Ecologies*. New York: New York University Press.

Lee, Robert G. 1995. "Introduction." In *Dear Miye: Letters Home from Japan, 1939–1946* (by Mary Kimoto Tomita), edited by Robert G. Lee, 1–22. Stanford: Stanford University Press.

Lee, Robert G. 1999. *Orientals: Asian Americans in Popular Culture*. Philadelphia, PA: Temple University Press.

Lee, Sue-Im. 2007. "'We Are Not the World': Global Village, Universalism, and Karen Tei Yamashita's *Tropic of Orange*." *MFS: Modern Fiction Studies* 52, no. 3: 501–27.

Lee, Yoon Sun. 2013. *Modern Minority: Asian American Literature and Everyday Life*. New York: Oxford University Press.

Lee, Young-Oak. 2003. "Nora Okja Keller and the Silenced Woman: An Interview." *MELUS* 28, no. 4: 145–65.

Leitner-Rudolph, Miryam. 2001. *Janice Mirikitani and Her Work*. Braumüller, Austria: Universitäts-Verlagsbunchhandlung.

Leong, Russell C. Ed. 1996. *Asian American Sexualities: Dimensions of the Gay and Lesbian Experience*. New York: Routledge.

Leong, Russell C. 2011. "Poetry within Earshot: Noes on an Asian American Generation 1968–1978." *Amerasia Journal* 37, no. 1: 1–29.

Lew, Walter K. 2001. "Crafts, Transplants, Translation: The Americanizing of Younghill Kang." In *Modernism, Inc.: Body, Memory, Capital*, edited by Jani Scandura, 171–90. New York: New York University Press.

Li, David Leiwei. 1990. "*China Men*: Maxine Hong Kingston and the American Canon." *American Literary History* 2, no. 3: 482–502.

Li, David Leiwei. 1998. *Imagining the Nation: Asian American Literature and Cultural Consent*. Stanford: Stanford University Press.

Li, David Leiwei. 2003. "The State and Subject of Asian American Criticism: Psychoanalysis, Transnational Discourse, and Democratic Ideals." *American Literary History* 15, no. 3: 603–24.

Li, David Leiwei. 2010. "Can Asian American Studies Abandon 'Nation?'" In *Navigating Islands and Continents: Conversations and Contestations in and around the Pacific*, edited by Cynthia G. Franklin, Ruth Hsu, and Suzanne Kosanke, 101–16. Honolulu: University of Hawaii Press.

Li, David Leiwei. 2012. "(In Lieu of an) Introduction: The Asian American Subject between Liberalism and Neoliberalism." In *Asian American Literature*, edited by David Leiwei Li, volume 1 Literary History: Criticism and Theory, 1–29. London: Routledge.

Libretti, Tim. 1996. Review of *The Ethnic Canon: Histories, Institutions, and Interventions*, edited by David Palumbo-Liu. (Minneapolis: University of Minnesota Press, 1995). *Amerasia Journal* 22, no. 3: 157–60.

Libretti, Tim. 1999. "Leaping over the Color Line: Postethnic Ideology and the Evasion of Racial Oppression." *Working Paper Series*, Department of Comparative American Cultures. Pullman: Washington State University, 1–20.

Lim, Shirley Geok-lin. 1987. "Reconstructing Asian-American Poetry: A Case for Ethnopoetics." *MELUS* 14, no. 2: 51–63.

Lim, Shirley Geok-lin. Ed. 1991. *Approaches to Teaching Kingston's The Woman Warrior*. New York: Modern Language Association of America.

Lim, Shirley Geok-lin. 1992a. "The Ambivalent Asian American Literature on the Cusp." In *Reading the Literatures of Asian America*, edited by Shirley Geok-lin Lim and Amy Ling, 13–32. Philadelphia, PA: Temple University Press.

Lim, Shirley Geok-lin. 1992b. "The Tradition of Chinese American Women's Life Stories: Thematics of Race and Gender in Jade Snow Wong's *Fifth Chinese Daughter* and Maxine Hong Kingston's *The Woman Warrior*." In *American Women's Autobiography, Fea(s)ts of Memory*, edited by Margo Cully, 252–67. Madison: University of Wisconsin Press.

Lim, Shirley Geok-lin. 1993a. "Assaying the Gold: Or, Contesting the Ground of Asian American Literature." *New Literary History* 24, no. 1: 147–69.

Lim, Shirley Geok-lin. 1993b. "Feminist and Ethnic Literary Theories in Asian American Literature." *Feminist Studies* 19, no. 3: 571–95.

Lim, Shirley Geok-lin. 1997. "Immigration and Diaspora." In *An Interethnic Companion to Asian American Literature*, edited by King-Kok Cheung, 289–311. New York: Cambridge University Press.

Lim, Shirley Geok-lin, and Ling, Amy. 1992. "Introduction." In *Reading the Literatures of Asian America*, edited by Shirley Geok-lin Lim and Amy Ling, 3–9. Philadelphia, PA: Temple University Press.

Bibliography

Lim, Shirley Geok-lin, and Tsutakawa, Mayumi. Eds. 1989. *The Forbidden Stitch: An Asian American Women's Anthology*. Corvallis, OR: Calyx.

Lim, Shirley Geok-lin, Gamber, John Blair, Hong Sohn, Stephen, and Valentino, Gina. 2006. "Introduction." In *Transnational Asian American Literature: Sites and Transits*, edited by Shirley Geok-lin Lim, John Blair Gamber, Stephen Hong Sohn, and Gina Valentino, 1–26. Philadelphia, PA: Temple University Press.

Lim, Walter S. H. 2004. "Under Eastern Eyes: Ghosts and Cultural Haunting in Maxine Hong Kingston's *The Woman Warrior* and *China Men*." In *Crossing Oceans: Reconfiguring American Literary Studies in the Pacific Rim*, edited by Noelle Brada-Williams and Karen Chow, 155–63. Hong Kong: Hong Kong University Press.

Lim, Walter S. H. 2008. "Some Musings on Cultural Responses to Asian American Literature in Singapore." *Amerasia Journal* 34, no. 2: 137–44.

Lim-Hing, Sharon. Ed. 1994. *The Very Inside: An Anthology of Writing by Asian and Pacific Islander Lesbian and Bisexual Women*. Toronto: Sister Vision Press.

Ling, Amy. 1981. "A Perspective on Chinamerican Literature." *MELUS* 8, no. 2: 76–81.

Ling, Amy. 1990. *Between Worlds: Women Writers of Chinese Ancestry*. New York: Pergamon.

Ling, Amy. 2002. "Cultural Cross-Dressing in *Mona in the Promised Land*." In *Asian American Literature in the International Context: Readings on Fiction, Poetry, Performance*, edited by Rocío G. Davis and Sämi Ludwig, 227–36. Hamburg: Lit Verlag.

Ling, Jinqi. 1998. *Narrating Nationalisms: Ideology and Form in Asian American Literature*. New York: Oxford University Press.

Ling, Jinqi. 2006. "Forging a North-South Perspective: Nikkei Migration in Karen Tei Yamashita's Novels." *Amerasia Journal* 32, no. 2: 1–22.

Ling, Jinqi. 2012. *Across Meridians: History and Figuration in Karen Tei Yamashita's Transnational Novels*. Stanford: Stanford University Press.

Ling, Jinqi. 2014. "Speculative Fiction." In *The Routledge Companion to Asian American and Pacific Islander Literature*, edited by Rachel C. Lee, 497–508. New York: Routledge.

Ling, Jinqi. 2015. "Asian American Short Fiction and the Contingencies of Form, 1930s to 1960s." In *The Cambridge History of Asian American Literature*, edited by Rajini Srikanth and Min Hyoung Song, 187–218. New York: Cambridge University Press.

Lionnet, François, and Shih, Shu-mei. 2005. "Introduction: Thinking through the Minor, Transnationally." In *Minor Transnationalism*, edited by François Lionnet and Shu-mei Shih, 1–23. Durham, NC: Duke University Press.

Liu, Warren. 2015. "Queer Excavations: Technology, Temporality, and Race." In *Techno-Orientalism: Imagining Asia in Speculative Fiction, History, and Media*, edited by David S. Roh, Betsy Huang, and Greta Niu, 64–75. New Brunswick, NJ: Rutgers University Press.

Lo, Karl K. 1984. "The Chinese Vernacular Presses in North America 1900–1950: Their Role in Social Cohesion." *The Annals of the Chinese Historical Society of the Pacific West*, 170–8.

Lowe, Lisa. 1991. "Heterogeneity, Hybridity, Multiplicity: Marking Asian American Differences." *Diaspora* 1, no. 1: 34–5.

Lowe, Lisa. 1995a. "Canon, Institutionalization, Identity: Contradictions for Asian American Studies." In *The Ethnic Canon: Histories, Institutions, and Interventions*, edited by David Palumbo-Liu, 48–68. Minneapolis: University of Minnesota Press.

Lowe, Lisa. 1995b. "On Contemporary Asian American Projects." *Amerasia Journal* 21, no. 1/2: 41–52.

Lowe, Lisa. 1995c. "Unfaithful to the Original: The Subject of *Dictée*." In *Writing Self, Writing Nation*, edited by Elaine H. Kim and Norma Alarcón, 35–72. Berkeley, CA: Third Woman Press.

Lowe, Lisa. 1996. *Immigrant Acts: On Asian American Cultural Politics*. Durham, NC: Duke University Press.

Lowe, Lisa. 1998a. "The International within the National: American Studies and Asian American Critique." *Cultural Critique* 40: 29–47.

Lowe, Lisa. 1998b. "The Power of Culture." *Journal of Asian American Studies* 1, no. 1: 5–29.

Lowe, Lisa. 2001. "Epistemological Shifts: National Ontology and the New Asian Immigrant." In *Orientations: Mapping Studies in the Asian Diaspora*, edited by Kandice Chuh and Karen Shimakawa, 267–76. Durham, NC: Duke University Press.

Luangphinith, Seri. 2015. "Beyond Solitary Confinement: Rethinking the Sociological Context of Local Literature in Hawaii." In *The Cambridge History of Asian American Literature*, edited by Rajini Srikanth and Min Hyoung Song, 389–405. New York: Cambridge University Press.

Lye, Colleen. 1995a. "*M. Butterfly* and the Rhetoric of Antiessentialism: Minority Discourse in an International Frame." In *The Ethnic Cannon: Histories, Institutions, and Interventions*, edited by David Palumbo-Liu, 260–89. Minneapolis: University of Minnesota Press.

Lye, Colleen. 1995b. "Toward an Asian (American) Cultural Studies: Postmodernism and the 'Peril of Yellow Capital and Labor.'" In *Privileging Positions: The Sites of Asian American Studies*, edited by Gary Y. Okihiro, Marilyn Alquizola, Dorothy Fujita Rony, and Wong K. Scott, 47–56. Pullman: Washington State University Press.

Lye, Colleen. 2005. *America's Asia: Racial Form and American Literature, 1893–1945*. Princeton, NJ: Princeton University Press.

Lye, Colleen. 2007. "Introduction: In Dialogue with Asian American Studies." *Representation* 99, no. 1: 1–12.

Lye, Colleen. 2008a. "The Afro-Asian Analogy." *PMLA* 123, no. 5: 1732–6.

Lye, Colleen. 2008b. "Form and History in Asian American Studies." *American Literary History* 20, no. 3: 548–55.

Lye, Colleen. 2014. "The Asian American 1960s." In *The Routledge Companion to Asian American and Pacific Islander Literature*, edited by Rachel C. Lee, 213–23. New York: Routledge.

Ma, Sheng-Mei. 2000. *The Deathly Embrace: Orientalism and Asian American Identity*. Minneapolis: University of Minnesota Press.

Bibliography

Maeda, Daryl J. 2009. *Chains of Babylon: The Rise of Asian America.* Minneapolis: University of Minnesota Press.

Mannur, Anita. 2010. *Culinary Fictions: Food in South Asian Diasporic Culture.* Philadelphia, PA: Temple University Press.

Mannur, Anita. 2013. "Perfection on Plate: Readings in the South Asian Transnational Queer Kitchen." In *A Food Studies Reader,* edited by Robert J-Song Ku, Martin F. Manalansan IV, and Anita Mattur, 393–408. New York: New York University Press.

Mannur, Anita, and Isaac, Allan Punzalan. 2015. "Heterogeneity to Multiplicity: Building Asian American Critique." In *The Cambridge History of Asian American Literature,* edited by Rajini Srikanth and Min Hyoung Song, 324–38. New York: Cambridge University Press.

Maxey, Ruth, and Alexander, Meena. 2006. "Interview: Meena Alexander." *MELUS* 31, no. 2: 21–39.

McDonald, Dorothy Ritsuko. 1981. "Introduction." In *The Chickencoop Chinaman and The Year of the Dragon,* ix–xxix. Seattle: University of Washington Press.

McGowan, John P. 1991. *Postmodernism and Its Critics.* Ithaca, NY: Cornell University Press.

Mirikitani, Janice. 1978. *Awake in the River.* Madison, WI: Isthmus.

Mori, Toshio. [1949] 1985. *Yokohama, California.* Seattle: University of Washington Press.

Moy, James S. 1993. *Marginal Sights: Staging the Chinese in America.* Iowa City: University of Iowa Press.

Mukherjee, Bharati. 1989. *Jasmine.* New York: Fawcett Crest.

Murayama, Milton. (1959) 1975. *All I Asking for Is My Body.* San Francisco: Supa Press.

Mullen, Bill V. 2004. *Afro-Orientalism.* Minneapolis: University of Minnesota Press.

Nadal, Paul J. 2021. "Cold War Remittance Economy: US Creative Writing and the Importation of New Criticism into the Philippines." *American Quarterly* 73, no. 3: 557–95.

Nadkarni, Asha. 2015. "The South Asian American Challenge." In *The Cambridge History of Asian American Literature,* edited by Rajini Srikanth and Min Hyoung Song, 355–70. New York: Cambridge University Press.

Najita, Susan Y. 2006. *Decolonizing Cultures in the Pacific: Reading History and Trauma in Contemporary Fiction.* New York: Routledge.

Najita, Susan Y. 2014. "Oceania." In *The Routledge Companion to Asian American and Pacific Islander Literature,* edited by Rachel C. Lee, 167–74. New York: Routledge.

Nakamura, Lisa. 2008. *Digitizing race: Visual Cultures of the Internet.* Minneapolis: University of Minnesota Press.

Nakamura, Lisa, and Chow-White, Peter. 2012. "Introduction—Race and Digital Technology: Code, the Color Line, and the Information Society." In *Race After the Internet,* edited by Lisa Nakamura and Peter Chow-White, 1–18. New York: Routledge.

Nakamura, Rika. 2016. "Reorienting Asian American Studies in Asia and the Pacific." In *Trans-Pacific Japanese American Studies: Conversations on Race and Racialization*, edited by Yasuko Takezawa and Gary Y. Okihiro, 288–312. Honolulu: University of Hawaii Press.

Newfield, Christopher. 2008. "Can American Studies Do Economics?" *American Quarterly* 60, no. 4: 1125–33.

Ng, Konrad. 2015. "Asian American New Media as Literature for the Digital Age." In *The Cambridge History of Asian American Literature*, edited by Rajini Srikanth and Min Hyoung Song, 551–66. New York: Cambridge University Press.

Nguyen, Phoung. [2004] 2005. Review of *Race and Resistance: Literature and Politics in Asian America*, by Viet Thanh Nguyen. (New York: Oxford University Press, 2002). *Amerasia Journal* 30, no. 3: 107–10.

Nguyen, Viet Thanh. 1998. Review of *An Interethnic Companion to Asian American Literature*, edited by King-Kok Cheung. (New York: Cambridge University Press, 1997). *Amerasia Journal* 24, no. 3: 236–9.

Nguyen, Viet Thanh. 2000. "The Remasculinization of Chinese America: Race, Violence, and the Novel." *American Literary History* 12, no. 1/2: 130–57.

Nguyen, Viet Thanh. 2002. *Race and Resistance: Literature and Politics in Asian America*. New York: Oxford University Press.

Nguyen, Viet Thanh. 2008. "At Home with Race." *PMLA* 123, no. 5: 1557–63.

Nguyen, Viet Thanh. 2013. "Just Memory: War and the Ethics of Remembrance." *American Literary History* 25, no. 1: 144–63.

Nguyen, Viet Thanh, and Chen, Tina. 2000. "Editor's Introduction." *Jouvert* 4, no. 1: 1–7.

Nguyên-Vo, Thu-Huong. 2005. "Forking Paths: How Shall We Mourn the Dead?" *Amerasia Journal* 31, no. 2: 157–75.

Ninh, Erin Khuê. 2011. *Ingratitude: The Debt-Bound Daughter in Asian American Literature*. New York: New York University Press.

Ninh, Erin Khuê. 2015. "Model Minority Narratives and the Asian American Family." In *The Cambridge Companion to Asian American Literature*, edited by Crystal Parikh and Daniel Y. Kim, 114–27. New York: Cambridge University Press.

Okada, John. [1957] 1976. *No-No Boy*. Seattle: University of Washington Press.

Omi, Michael, and Howard Winant. [1986] 1994. *Racial Formation in the United States: From the 1960s to the 1990s*. New York: Routledge.

Omi, Michael, and Howard Winant. 2008. "Once More, with Feeling: Reflections on Racial Formation." *PMLA* 123, no. 5: 1565–71.

Ong, Aihwa. 1999. *Flexible Citizenship: The Cultural Logics of Transnationality*. Durham, NC: Duke University Press.

Otano, Alicia. 2004. *Breaking the Past: Child Perspective in Asian American Bildungsroman*. Münster: Lit Verlag.

Owaki, Michiko. 2001. "'Her Body Speaks': The Body, Sexuality, and Identity in the Work of Janice Mirikitani." *AALA Journal* 7, no. 7: 43–58.

Padoonpatt, Mark. 2013. "'Oriental Cookery': Devouring Asian and Pacific Cuisine during the Cold War." In *A Food Studies Reader*, edited by Robert J-Song Ku, Martin F. Manalansan IV, and Anita Mannur, 186–207. New York: New York University Press.

Pak, Gary. 1998. *Ricepaper Airplane*. Honolulu: University of Hawaii Press.

Palumbo-Liu, David. 1995a. "The Ethnic as 'Post-': *Reading the Literatures of Asian America*." *American Literary History* 7, no. 1: 161–8.

Palumbo-Liu, David. 1995b. "Introduction." In *The Ethnic Canon: Histories, Institutions, and Interventions*, edited by David Palumbo-Liu, 1–30. Minneapolis: University of Minnesota Press.

Palumbo-Liu, David. 1995c. "Theory and the Subject of Asian American Studies." *Amerasia Journal* 21, no. 1/2: 55–65.

Palumbo-Liu, David. 1999. *Asian/American: Historical Crossings of a Racial Frontier*. Stanford: Stanford University Press.

Palumbo-Liu, David. 2008. "The Occupation of Form: (Re)theorizing Literary History." *American Literary History* 20, no. 4: 814–35.

Pan, Zhiming. 2008. *Romance as Strategy: A Study of Winnifred Eaton's Novels*. Beijing: Foreign Language Teaching and Research Press.

Pao, Angela Chia-yi. 2010. *No Safe Spaces: Recasting Race, Ethnicity, and Nationality in American Theatre*. Ann Arbor: University of Michigan Press.

Parikh, Crystal. 2002. " 'The Most Outrageous Masquerade': Queering Asian American Masculinity." *MFS: Modern Fiction Studies* 48, no. 4: 858–98.

Parikh, Crystal. 2009. *An Ethics of Betrayal: The Politics of Otherness in Emergent U.S. Literatures and Culture*. New York: Fordham University Press.

Park, Hyungji. 2015. "Toward a Definition of Diaspora Literature." In *The Cambridge Companion to Asian America Literature*, edited by Crystal Parikh and Daniel Y. Kim, 155–66. New York: Cambridge University Press.

Park, Josephine Nock-Hee. 2006. " 'Composed of Many Lengths of Bone': Myung Mi Kim's *Reimagination of Image and Epic*." In *Transnational Asian American Literature: Sites and Transits*, edited by Shirley Geok-lin Lim, John Blair Gamber, Stephen Hong Sohn, and Gina Valentino, 235–56. Philadelphia, PA: Temple University Press.

Park, Josephine Nock-Hee. 2008. *Apparitions of Asia: Modernist Form and Asian American Poetics*. New York: Oxford University Press.

Pecora, Vincent P. 1992. "What Was Deconstruction?" *Contention* 1, no. 3: 59–79.

Pecora, Vincent P. 1995. "Culture Wars and the Profession of Literature." In *After Political Correctness: The Humanities and Society in the 1990s*, edited by Christopher Newfield and Ronald Strickland, 199–211. Boulder, CO: Westview Press.

Pfaff, Timothy. 1980. "Talking to Mrs. Kingston." *New York Times Book Review*, 18 June 1: 25–7.

Ponzanesi, Sandra. 2001. "Bharati Mukherjee's *Jasmine*: The Exuberance of Imagination, Feminist Struggle and Multicultural Negotiation." In *Studies of Indian Writing in English*, edited by Rajeshwar Mittapalli and Pier Paolo Piciucco, 77–107. New Delhi: Atlantic.

Prashad, Vijay. 2001. *Everybody Was Fung Fu Fighting: Afro-Asian Connection and Myth of Cultural Purity*. Boston, MA: Beacon.

Quayum, Mohammed A., and Lim, Shirley Geok-lin. 2003. "Shirley Geok-lin Lim: An Interview." *MELUS* 28, no. 4: 83–100.

Quintana, Alvina E. 2002. "Performing Tricksters: Karen Tei Yamashita and Guillermo Gómez-Peña." *Amerasia Journal* 28, no. 2: 217–25.

Radhakrishnan, R. 2001. "Conceptual Identities, Academic Agencies." In *Orientations: Mapping Studies in the Asian Diaspora*, edited by Kandice Chuh and Karen Shimakawa, 249–63. Durham, NC: Duke University Press.

Rankin, Jo. Ed. 1997. *Seeds from a Silent Tree: An Anthology by Korean Adoptees*. Glendale, CA: Pandal Press.

Ratti, Rakesh. Ed. 1993. *Lotus of Another Color: An Unfolding of the South Asian Gay and Lesbian Experience*. Boston, MA: Alyson.

Reed, T. V. Ed. 2021. *The Bloomsbury Introduction to Postmodern Realist Fiction: Resisting Master Narratives*. London: Bloomsbury Academic.

Rodrigues, Darlene. 2000a. "Al Robles." In *Words Matter: Conversations with Asian American Writers*, edited by King-Kok Cheung, 154–72. Honolulu: University of Hawaii Press.

Rodrigues, Darlene. 2000b. "Imagining Ourselves: Reflections on the Controversy over Lois-Ann Yamanaka's *Blu's Hanging*." *Amerasia Journal* 26, no. 2: 195–207.

Rody, Caroline. 2004. "The Transnational Imagination: Karen Tei Yamashita's *Tropic of Orange*." In *Asian North American Identities Beyond Hyphen*, edited by Eleanor Ty and Donald C. Goellnicht, 130–48. Bloomington: Indiana University Press.

Roh, David S., Huang, Betsy, and Niu, Greta. 2015. "Technological Orientalism: And Introduction." In *Techno-Orientalism: Imagining Asia in Speculative Fiction, History, and Media*, edited by David S. Roh, Betsy Huang, and Greta Niu, 1–19. New Brunswick, NJ: Rutgers University Press.

Rustomji-Kerns, Roshni. 2002. "Mirrha-Catarina de San Juan." *Amerasia Journal* 28, no. 2: 29–36.

Said, Edward W. 1983. *World, Text, and Context*. Cambridge, MA: Harvard University Press.

Said, Edward W. 2004. *Humanism and Democratic Criticism*. New York: Columbia University Press.

Salaita, Steven. 2014. "Arab American Literature." In *The Routledge Companion to Asian American and Pacific Islander Literature*, edited by Rachel C. Lee, 202–12. New York: Routledge.

San Juan, Jr., E. 1972. *Carlos Bulosan and the Imagination of Class Struggle*. Quezon City: University of the Philippines Press.

San Juan, Jr., E. 1991. "Beyond Identity Politics: The Predicament of the Asian American Writer in Late Capitalism." *American Literary History* 3, no. 3: 542–65.

San Juan, Jr., E. 1992. *Racial Formations/Critical Transformations: Articulations of Power in Ethnic and Racial Studies in the United States*. Atlantic Highlands, NJ: Humanities Press International.

San Juan, Jr., E. 1995. *Hegemonies and Strategies of Transgression: Essays on Cultural Studies and Comparative Literature*. New York: State University of New York Press.

San Juan, Jr., E. [1995] 1996. "From National Allegory to the Performance of the Joyful Subject: Reconstituting Philip Vera Cruz's Life." *Amerasia Journal* 21, no. 34: 137–53.

Bibliography

San Juan, Jr., E. 1996. *The Philippine Temptation: Dialectics of Philippines–U.S. Literary Relations*. Philadelphia, PA: Temple University Press.

San Juan, Jr., E. 1998. *Beyond Postcolonial Theory*. New York: St. Martin's Press.

San Juan, Jr., E. 2003. "Challenging the Theory and Practice of Contemporary American Studies." *Review of Education, Pedagogy, and Cultural Studies*, no. 25: 303–33.

San Juan, Jr., E. 2006. "Edward Said's Affiliations: Secular Humanism and Marxism." *Atlantic Studies* 3, no. 1: 43–61.

San Juan, Jr., E. 2009. "The Contemporary Predicament of Asian American Studies: Toward a Racial Critique." *DANYAG: Journal of Humanities and Social Sciences* 14, no. 2: 79–90.

Santa Ana, Jeffrey J. 2004. "Affect-Identity: The Emotions of Assimilation, Multiraciality, and Asian American Subjectivity." In *Asian North American Identities beyond the Hyphen*, edited by Eleanor Ty and Donald C. Goellnicht, 15–42. Bloomington: Indiana University Press.

Sartre, Jean-Paul. 1988. *"What Is Literature?" and Other Essays*, translated by Steven Ungar. Cambridge, MA: Harvard University Press.

Schein, Louisa, and Thoj, Va-Megn. 2008. "Violence, Hmong American Visibility, and the Precariousness of Asian Race." *PMLA* 123, no. 5: 1752–6.

Schlund-Vials, Cathy J. 2012. *War, Genocide, and Justice: Cambodian American Memory Work*. Minneapolis: University of Minnesota Press.

Schlund-Vials, Cathy J. 2015. "Refugee Aesthetics: Cambodia, Laos, and the Hmong." In *The Cambridge History of Asian American Literature*, edited by Rajini Srikanth and Min Hyoung Song, 484–500. New York: Cambridge University Press.

Schlund-Vials, Cathy J., and Wu, Cynthia. 2015. "Rethinking Embodiment and Hybridity: Mixed Race, Adoptee, and Disabled Subjectivities." In *The Cambridge Guide to Asian American Literature*, edited by Crystal Parikh and Daniel Y. Kim, 197–211. New York: Cambridge University Press.

Scholes, Robert. 1989. *Protocols of Reading*. New Haven, CT: Yale University Press.

Schueller, Malini Johar. 1989. "Questioning Race and Gender Definitions: Dialogic Subversions in *The Woman Warrior*." *Criticism* 31, no. 4: 421–37.

Schueller, Malini Johar. 2004. "Claiming Postcolonial America: The Hybrid Asian-American Performances of Tseng Kwong Chi." In *Asian American Identities beyond the Hyphen*, edited by Eleanor Ty and Donald C. Goellnicht, 170–85. Bloomington: Indiana University Press.

Sharpe, Jenny. 1995. "Is the United States Postcolonial?: Transnationalism, Immigration, and Race." *Diaspora* 4, no. 2: 181–99.

Shigematsu, Setsu, and Camacho, Keith L. 2010. "Introduction: Militarized Currents, Decolonizing Futures." In *Militarized Currents: Toward a Decolonized Future in Asia and the Pacific*, edited by Setsu Shigematsu and Keith L. Camacho, xv–xlviii. Minneapolis: University of Minnesota Press.

Shih, David. 2005. "The Self and Generic Convention: Winnifred Eaton's *Me, A Book of Remembrance*." In *Recovered Legacies: Authority and Identity in Early Asian Literature*, edited by Keith Lawrence and Floyd Cheung, 41–59. Philadelphia, PA: Temple University Press.

Shih, Shu-mei. 2014. "Sinophone American Literature." In *The Routledge Companion to Asian American and Pacific Islander Literature*, edited by Rachel C. Lee, 329–38. New York: Routledge.

Shimakawa, Karen. 2001. "(Re)viewing an Asian American Diaspora: Multiculturalism, Interculturalism, and the Northwest Asian American Theatre." In *Orientations: Mapping Studies in the Asian Diaspora*, edited by Kandice Chuh and Karen Shimakawa, 41–56. Durham, NC: Duke University Press.

Shimakawa, Karen. 2002. *National Abjection: The Asian American Body Onstage*. Durham, NC: Duke University Press.

Simpson, Caroline Chung. 2002. *An Absent Presence: Japanese Americans in Postwar American Culture, 1945–1960*. Durham, NC: Duke University Press.

Slowik, Marcin. 2000. "Beyond Lot's Wife: The Immigrant Poems of Marilyn Chin, Garrett Hongo, Li-Young Lee, and David Mura." *MELUS* 25, no. 3/4: 221–42.

Smith, Paul. 1988. *Discerning the Subject*. Minneapolis: University of Minnesota Press.

So, Christine. 1989. " 'Hold the Chow Mein, Gimme Soca': Creolization of the Chinese in Guyana, Trinidad and Jamaica." *Amerasia Journal* 15, no. 2: 3–25.

So, Christine. 2007. *Economic Citizens: A Narrative of Asian American Visibility*. Philadelphia, PA: Temple University Press.

So, Richard Jean. 2016. *Transpacific Community: America, China, and the Rise and Fall of a Cultural Network*. Chicago: University of Chicago Press.

Sohn, Stephen Hong. 2006. " 'Valuing' Transnational Queerness: Politicized Bodies and Commodified Desires in Asian American Literature." In *Transnational Asian American Literature: Sites and Transits*, edited by Shirley Geok-lin Lim, John Blair Gamber, Stephen Hong Sohn, and Gina Valentino, 100–22. Philadelphia, PA: Temple University Press.

Sohn, Stephen Hong. 2014. *Racial Asymmetries: Asian American Fictional Worlds*. New York: New York University Press.

Sohn, Stephen H., Lai, Paul, and Goellnicht, Donald C. 2010. "Introduction: Theorizing Asian American Fiction." *MFS: Modern Fiction Studies* 56, no. 1: 1–18.

Solberg, S. E. 1988. "The Literature of Korean America." *The Seattle Review* (Spring/Summer): 19–32.

Sollors, Werner. 1986. *Beyond Ethnicity: Consent and Descent in American Culture*. New York: Oxford University Press.

Sone, Monica. 1953. *Nisei Daughter*. Boston, MA: Little, Brown.

Song, Cathy. 1983. *Picture Bride*. New Haven, CT: Yale University Press.

Song, Min Hyoung. 2005. *Strange Future: Pessimism and the 1992 Los Angeles Riots*. Durham, NC: Duke University Press.

Song, Min Hyoung. 2013. *The Children of 1965: On Writing, and Not Writing, as an Asian American*. Durham, NC: Duke University Press.

Song, Min Hyoung. 2015. "Asian American Literature within and beyond the Immigrant Narrative." In *The Cambridge Companion to Asian America Literature*, edited by Crystal Parikh and Daniel Y. Kim, 3–15. New York: Cambridge University Press.

Bibliography

Spaulding, Carol Roh. 2002. "Two Blue-Eyed Asian Maidens: Mixed Race in the Works of Edith Eaton/Sui Sin Far and Winnifred Eaton/Onoto Watanna." In *Re/collecting Early Asian America: Essays in Cultural History*, edited by Josephine D. Lee, Imogene Lim, and Yuko Matsukawa, 340–54. Philadelphia, PA: Temple University Press.

Spivak, Gayatri Chakravorty. 1993. *Outside in the Teaching Machine.* New York: Routledge.

Srikanth, Rajini. 2004. *The World Next Door: South Asian American Literature and the Idea of Home.* Philadelphia, PA: Temple University Press.

Srikanth, Rajini. 2015. " 'The War on Terror': Post-9/11 South Asian and Arab American Literature." In *The Cambridge Companion to Asian American Literature*, edited by Crystal Parikh and Daniel Y. Kim, 73–85. New York: Cambridge University Press.

Stefans, Brian Kim. 1994. Review of *Excerpts From: ΔIKTH DIKTE* 딕테/딕티 *for DICTEE* (1982), by Walter K. Lew. (Seoul, Korea: Yeuleum Publishing Company, 1991). *Amerasia Journal* 20, no. 2: 124–7.

Stefans, Brian Kim. 2002. "Remote Parsee: An Alternative Grammar of Asian North American Poetry." In *Telling It Slant: Avant-Garde Poetics of the 1990s*, edited by Mark Wallace and Steven Marks, 43–75. Tuscaloosa: University of Alabama Press.

Stefans, Brian Kim. 2014. "New Media." In *The Routledge Companion to Asian American and Pacific Islander Literature*, edited by Rachel C. Lee, 439–50. New York: Routledge.

Stierle, Karheinz. 1980. "The Reading of Fictional Text." In *The Reader in the Text: Essay on Audience*, edited by Susan Suleiman and Inge Crosman, 83–105. Princeton, NJ: Princeton University Press.

Su, Karen. 1994. "Jade Snow Wong's Badge of Distinction in the 1990s." *Critical Mass: A Journal of Asian American Cultural Criticism* 2, no. 1: 3–52.

Sumida, Stephen H. 1984. Review of *Asian American Literature: An Introduction to the Writings and Their Social Contexts*, by Elaine H. Kim. (Philadelphia, PA: Temple University Press, 1982). *Amerasia Journal* 11, no. 1: 105–9.

Sumida, Stephen H. 1986. "First Generations in Asian American Literature: As Viewed in Some Second Generation Works." In *Asian American and Pacific American Education*, edited by Nobuya Tsuchida, 64–70. Minneapolis, MN: Asian/Pacific American Learning Center.

Sumida, Stephen H. 1989. "Asian American Literature in the 1980s." In *Frontiers of Asian American Studies: Writing, Research, and Commentary*, edited by Gail M. Nomura, Russell Endo, Stephen H. Sumida, and Russell C. Leong, 151–8. Pullman: Washington State University Press.

Sumida, Stephen H. 1991. *And the View from the Shore: Literary Traditions of Hawaii.* Seattle: University of Washington Press.

Sumida, Stephen H. 1992. "Sense of Place, History, and the Concept of the 'Local' in Hawaii's Asian/Pacific Literatures." In *Reading the Literatures of Asian America*, edited by Shirley Geok-lin Lim and Amy Ling, 215–37. Philadelphia, PA: Temple University Press.

Sumida, Stephen H. 1998. "East of California: Points of Origin in Asian American Studies." *JAAS* 1, no. 1: 83–100.

Sumida, Stephen H. 2008. "*No-No Boy* and the Twisted Logic of Internment." *AALA Journal* 13: 33–49.

Sumida, Stephen H., and Wong, Sau-ling C. 2001. "Introduction." In *A Resource Guide to Asian American Literature*, edited by Sau-ling C. Wong and Stephen H. Sumida, 1–9. New York: Modern Language Associate of America.

Suzuki, Erin. 2014. "Transpacific." In *The Routledge Companion to Asian American and Pacific Islander Literature*, edited by Rachel C. Lee, 352–64. New York: Routledge.

Takagi, Dana Y. 1996. "Maiden Voyage: Excursion into Sexuality and Identity Politics in Asian America." In *Asian American Sexualities: Dimensions of the Gay and Lesbian Experience*, edited by Russell Leong, 21–35. New York: Routledge.

Takezawa, Yasuko. 2016. "Toward More Equal Dialogue." In *Trans-Pacific Japanese American Studies: Conversations on Race and Racialization*, edited by Yasuko Takezawa and Gary Y. Okihiro, 396–400. Honolulu: University of Hawaii Press.

Tan, Amy. 1989. *The Joy Luck Club*. New York: Penguin.

Tang, Amy C. 2016. *Repetition and Race: Asian American Literature after Multiculturalism*. New York: Oxford University Press.

Tchen, John Kuo Wei. 2011. "Foreword." In *Him Mark Lai: Autobiography of a Chinese American*. Los Angeles: UCLA Asian American Studies Center and Chinese Historical Society of America.

Teng, Emma Jinhua. 2015. "The Eaton Sisters and the Figure of the Eurasian." In *The Cambridge History of Asian American Literature*, edited by Rajini Srikanth and Min Hyoung Song, 88–104. New York: Cambridge University Press.

Thananopavarn, Susan. 2018. *LatinAsian Cartographies: History, Writing, and National Imaginary*. New Brunswick, NJ: Rutgers University Press.

The Women of South Asian Descent Collective. Ed. 1993. *Our Feet Walk the Sky: Women of the South Asian Diaspora*. San Francisco: Aunt Lute Books.

Thoma, Pamela S. 2013. *Asian American Women's Popular Literature: Feminizing Genres and Neoliberal Belonging*. Philadelphia, PA: Temple University Press.

Ting, Jennifer P. 1998. "The Power of Sexuality." *Journal of Asian American Studies* 1, no. 1: 65–82.

Todorov, Tzvetan. [1986] 1987. *Literature and Its Theorists: A Personal View of Twentieth-Century Criticism*, translated by Catherine Porter. Ithaca, NY: Cornell University Press.

Tolentino, Cynthia. 2014. "Equatorial Archipelagos." In *The Routledge Companion to Asian American and Pacific Islander Literature*, edited by Rachel C. Lee, 268–78. New York: Routledge.

Truong, Monique Thuy-D-Dung. 1993. "The Emergence of Voices: Vietnamese American Literature 1975–1990." *Amerasia Journal* 19, no. 3: 27–50.

Truong, Monique Thuy D-Dung. 1997. "Vietnamese American Literature." In *An interethnic Companion to Asian American Literature*, edited by King-Kok Cheung, 219–46. New York: Cambridge University Press.

Truong, Monique Thuy D-Dung. 2003. *A Book of Salt*. New York: Mariner Books.

Tsiang, Hsi Tseng. 1937. *And China Has Hands*. New York: Robert Speller.

Tsou, Elda E. 2015. *Unique Tropes: Form, Race, and Asian American Literature*. Philadelphia, PA: Temple University Press.

TuSmith, Bonnie. 1993. *All My Relatives: Community in Contemporary Ethnic American Literatures*. Ann Arbor: University of Michigan Press.

Ty, Eleanor. 2004. *The Politics of the Visible in Asian North American Narratives*. Toronto: University of Toronto Press.

Ty, Eleanor. 2015. "Contemporary Filipino American Writers and the Legacy of Imperialism." In *The Cambridge History of Asian American Literature*, edited by Rajini Srikanth and Min Hyoung Song, 371–86. New York: Cambridge University Press.

Uba, George. 1992. "Versions of Identity in Post Activist Asian American Poetry." In *Reading the Literatures of Asian America*, edited by Shirley Geok-lin Lim and Amy Ling, 33–48. Philadelphia, PA: Temple University Press.

Uba, George. 2001. "Coordinates of Asian American Poetry: A Survey of the History and a Guide to Teaching." In *A Resource Guide to Asian American Literature*, edited by Sau-ling C. Wong and Stephen H. Sumida, 309–31. New York: Modern Language Associate of America.

Unali, Lina, and Connery, Christopher Leigh. Eds. 1998. *Talk-Story in Chinatown and Away: Essays on Chinese American Literature and on US–China Relations*. Rome: Sun Moon Lake.

Ungar, Steven. 1988. "Introduction" to *"What Is Literature?" and Other Essays* by Jean-Paul Sartre, translated by Steven Ungar, 3–20. Cambridge, MA: Harvard University Press.

Uno, Roberta. Ed. 1993. *Unbroken Thread: An Anthology of Plays by Asian American Women*. Boston: University of Massachusetts Press.

Võ, Linda Trinh. 2003. "Vietnamese American Trajectories: Dimensions of Diaspora." *Amerasia Journal* 29, no. 2: ix–xviii.

Wald, Alan M. 1981. "The Culture of 'Internal Colonialism': A Marxist Perspective." *MELUS* 8, no. 3: 18–27.

Wald, Alan M. 1987. "Theorizing Cultural Difference: A Critique of the 'Ethnicity School.'" *MELUS* 14, no. 2: 21–33.

Wald, Alan M. 1996. "Introduction to H. T. Tsiang." In *Into the Fire: Asian American Prose*, edited by Sylvia Watanabe and Carlo Bruchac, 341–4. Greenfield Center, NY: Greenfield Review Press.

Wallace, Molly. 2001. "Tropics of Globalization: Reading the New North America." *Symploke* 9, nos. 1–2: 145–60.

Wand, David Hsin-Fu. Ed. 1974. *Asian-American Heritage: An Anthology of Prose and Poetry*. New York: Washington Square Press.

Wang, Dorothy J. 2002. "Undercover Asian: John Yau and the Politics of Ethnic Self-Identification." In *Asian American Literature in the International Context: Readings on Fiction, Poetry, Performance*, edited by Rocío G. Davis and Sämi Ludwig, 135–55. Hamburg: Lit Verlag.

Wang, Dorothy J. 2014. *Thinking Its Presence: Form, Race, and Racial Subjectivity in Contemporary Asian American Poetry*. Stanford: Stanford University Press.

Wang, Dorothy J. 2015. "Asian American Poetry and Politics of Form." In *The Cambridge History of Asian American Literature*, edited by Rajini Srikanth and Min Hyoung Song, 437–53. New York: Cambridge University Press.

Watanabe, Sylvia, and Bruchac, Carol. Eds. 1990. *Home to Stay: Asian American Women's Fiction*. Greenfield Center, NY: Greenfield Review Press.

Weisner, Ken, and Chin, Marilyn. 2012. "Interview with Marilyn Chin." *MELUS 73*, no. 3: 215–26.

White, Hayden. 1987. *The Content of the Form: Narrative Discourse and Historical Representation*. Baltimore, MD: Johns Hopkins University Press.

White-Parks, Annette. 1995. *Sui Sin Far/Edith Maude Eaton: A Literary Biography*. Urbana-Champaign: University of Illinois Press.

Williams, Raymond. 1977. *Marxism and Literature*. New York: Oxford University Press.

Wong, Cynthia F. 1999. "Anonymity and Self-Laceration in Early Twentieth Century Chinese Immigrant Writing." *MELUS* 24, no. 4: 3–18.

Wong, Edlie L. 2014. "In a Future Tense: Immigration Law, Counterfactual Histories, and Chinese Invasion Fiction." *American Literary History* 26, no. 3: 511–35.

Wong, Jade Snow. [1945] (1950). *Fifth Chinese Daughter*. New York: Harper & Row.

Wong, Sau-ling C. 1988. "Tales of Postwar Chinatown: Short Stories of *The Bud*, 1947–1948." *Amerasia Journal* 14, no. 2: 61–79.

Wong, Sau-ling C. 1991a. "Immigrant Autobiography: Some Questions of Definition and Approach." In *American Autobiography: Retrospect and Prospect*, edited by Paul John Eakin, 143–70. Madison: University of Wisconsin Press.

Wong, Sau-ling C. 1991b. "The Politics and Poetics of Folksong Reading: Literary Portrayals of Life under Exclusion." In *Entry Denied: Exclusion and the Chinese Communities in America, 1882–1943*, edited by Sucheng Chan, 246–67. Philadelphia, PA: Temple University Press.

Wong, Sau-ling C. 1992. "Ethnicizing Gender: An Exploration of Sexuality as a Sign in Chinese Immigrant Literature." In *Reading the Literatures of Asian America*, edited by Shirley Geok-lin Lim and Amy Ling, 111–29. Philadelphia, PA: Temple University Press.

Wong, Sau-ling C. 1993. *Reading Asian American Literature: From Necessity to Extravagance*. Princeton, NJ: Princeton University Press.

Wong, Sau-ling C. 1995a. "Denationalization Reconsidered: Asian American Cultural Criticism at a Theoretical Crossroads." *Amerasia Journal* 21, no. 1/2: 1–27.

Wong, Sau-ling C. 1995b. " 'Sugar Sisterhood': Situating the Amy Tan Phenomenon." In *The Ethnic Canon: Histories, Institutions, and Interventions*, edited by David Palumbo-Liu, 174–209. Minneapolis: University of Minnesota Press.

Wong, Sau-ling C. Ed. 1999. *Maxine Hong Kingston's Woman Warrior: A Case Book*. New York: Oxford University Press.

Wong, Sau-ling C. 2001. "Navigating Asian American Panethnic Literary Anthologies." In *A Resource Guide to Asian American Literature*, edited by

Sau-ling C. Wong and Stephen H. Sumida, 235–51. New York: Modern Language Association of America.

Wong, Sau-ling C. 2004. "When Asian American Literature Leaves 'Home': On Internationalizing Asian American Studies." In *Crossing Oceans: Reconfiguring Literary Studies in the Pacific*, edited by Noelle Brada-Williams and Karen Chow, 29–40. Hong Kong: Hong Kong University Press.

Wong, Shelley S. 1995. "Unnaming the Same: Theresa Hak Kyung Cha's *Dictee*." In *Writing Self, Writing Nation*, edited by Elaine H. Kim and Norma Alarcón, 103–40. Berkeley, CA: Third Woman Press.

Wong, Shelley S. 2001. "Sizing Up Asian American Poetry." In *A Resource Guide to Asian American Literature*, edited by Sau-ling Cynthia Wong and Stephen H. Sumida, 285–307. New York: Modern Language Association of America.

Wong, Shelley S. 2015. "'I Seek Out Poems Now Incomplete': Writing from the Angel Island Immigration Station." In *The Cambridge History of Asian American Literature*, edited by Rajini Srikanth and Min Hyoung Song, 71–87. New York: Cambridge University Press.

Woo, Deborah. 1990. "Maxine Hong Kingston: The Ethic Writer and the Burden of Dual Authenticity." *Amerasia Journal* 16, no. 1: 173–200.

Wu, William F. 1982. *The Yellow Peril: Chinese Americans in American Fiction, 1850–1940*. Hamden, CT: Archon Books.

Xu, Wenying. 2008. *Eating Identities: Reading Food in Asian American Literature*. Honolulu: University of Hawaii Press.

Yamada, Mitsuye. 1976. *Camp Notes and Other Writings*. New York: Atheneum.

Yamamoto, Hisaye. 1988. *Seventeen Syllables and Other Stories*. Latham, NY: Kitchen Table.

Yamamoto, Traise. 1999. *Masking Selves, Making Subjects: Japanese American Women, Identity, and the Body*. Berkeley: University of California Press.

Yamamoto, Traise. 2015. "Coded Critiques: Japanese American Incarceration Literature." In *The Cambridge History of Asian American Literature*, edited by Rajini Srikanth and Min Hyoung Song, 171–86. New York: Cambridge University Press.

Yamanaka, Lois Ann. 1998. *Blu's Hanging*. New York: Harper Perennial.

Yamashita, Karen Tei. 1997. *Tropic of Orange*. Minneapolis, MN: Coffee House Press.

Yamashita, Karen Tei. 2010. *I-Hotel*. Minneapolis, MN: Coffee House Press.

Yang, Caroline. 2010. "Indispensable Labor: The Worker as a Category of Critique in *China Men*." *MFS: Modern Fiction Studies* 56, no. 1: 63–89.

Yang, Kao Lalia. 2008. *The Latehomecomer: A Hmong Family Memoir*. Minneapolis, MN: Coffee House.

Yao, Stephen G. 2010. *Foreign Accents: Chinese American Verse from Exclusion to Postethnicity*. New York: Oxford University Press.

Yin, Kathleen Loh Swee, and Paulson, Kristoffer F. 1982. "The Divided Voice of Chinese American Narration: Jade Snow Wong's *Fifth Chinese Daughter*." *MELUS* 9, no. 1: 53–9.

Yin, Xiao-Huang. 2000. *Chinese American Literature since the 1850s*. Urbana-Champaign: University of Illinois Press.

Yogi, Stan. 1996. "Yearning for the Past: The Dynamics of Memory in Sansei Internment Poetry." In *Memory and Cultural Politics: New Approaches to American Ethnic Literatures*, edited by Amritjit Singh, Joseph T. Skerrett, and Robert E. Hogan, 245–65. Boston, MA: Northeastern University Press.

Yogi, Stan. 1997. "Japanese American Literature." In *An Interethnic Companion to Asian American Literature*, edited by King-Kok Cheung, 125–55. New York: Cambridge University Press.

Yoneyama, Lisa. 2005. "On the Unredressability of U.S. War Crimes: Vietnam and Japan." *Amerasia Journal* 31, no. 2: 140–4.

Yu, Timothy. 2004. "'The Hand of a Chinese Matter': José Garcia Villa and the Modernist Orientalism." *MELUS* 29, no. 1: 41–59.

Yu, Timothy. 2009. *Race and the Avant-Garde: Experimental and Asian American Poetry since 1965*. Stanford: Stanford University Press.

Yu, Timothy. 2011. "Asian American Poetry in the First Decade of 2000s." *Comparative Literature* 52, no. 4: 818–51.

Yun, Lisa. 2002. "Under the Hatches: American Coolie Ships and Nineteenth-Century Narratives of the Pacific Passage." *Amerasia Journal* 28, no. 2: 38–61.

Yun, Lisa. 2008. *The Coolie Speaks: Chinese Indentured Laborers and African Slaves of Cuba*. Philadelphia, PA: Temple University Press.

Zheng, Da. 2010. *Chiang Yee: The Silent Traveler from the East—A Cultural Biography*. New Brunswick, NJ: Rutgers University Press.

Zhou, Xiaojing. 2005. "Introduction: Critical Theories and Methodologies in Asian American Literary Studies." In *Form and Transformation in Asian American Literature*, edited by Xiaojing Zhou and Samina Najmi, 3–29. Seattle: University of Washington Press.

Zhou, Xiaojing. 2006. *The Ethics and Poetics of Alterity in Asian American Poetry*. Iowa City: University of Iowa Press.

Zhou, Xiaojing. 2014. *Cities of Others: Reimagining Urban Spaces in Asian American Literature*. Seattle: University of Washington Press.

Zhou, Xiaojing, and Najmi, Samina. Ed. 2005. *Form and Transformation in Asian American Literature*. Seattle: University of Washington Press.

INDEX

Index

Index

Index